SUL ROSS
at Texas A&M

For Mike Gilbert '06
Gig 'em
Richard Oilman, Jr. '73

Number 132
Centennial Series of the Association of Former Students,
Texas A&M University

SUL ROSS
at Texas A&M

John A. Adams Jr. '73

Foreword by

John Sharp '72

TEXAS A&M UNIVERSITY PRESS
COLLEGE STATION

This paper meets the requirements of ANSI/NISO Z39.48–1992
(Permanence of Paper).
Binding materials have been chosen for durability.
Manufactured in the United States of America

LIBRARY OF CONGRESS CATALOGING-IN-PUBLICATION DATA

Library of Congress Control Number: 2021034223

ISBN: 978-1-62349-938-9 (cloth)
ISBN: 978-1-62349-939-6 (ebook)

*In memory
of Henry C. Dethloff*

Contents

Foreword

John Sharp '72

Chancellor, The Texas A&M University System

Texas A&M University is among the most unique universities in the United States. While known for its excellence in teaching, research, and extension, the aspect that defines the image of the institution is its rich traditions and loyal alumni. The source of this loyalty dates from the fledgling days, starting in the mid-1870s. After a decade of change and struggle, what was then known as the "Agricultural and Mechanical College of Texas" was placed under the leadership of Lawrence Sullivan Ross. "Sul," as he was known to all Texans, arrived at A&M after a distinguished career as a Texas Ranger, military leader, sheriff, and statesman—most notably, governor of Texas from 1886 to 1891.

While much has been chronicled about his early history, little has been noted of Sul Ross's tenure as president at A&M during the last decade of his life. This presentation by John A. Adams, Jr. '73, a noted author of numerous volumes on aspects of Aggie lore, will help readers understand the impact and role Sul Ross had in shaping the future of Texas A&M.

Sul Ross was unquestionably one of the best-known Texans of the late 1800s. Following his governorship, he could have pursued other elective office or a role in commercial business, but instead he chose A&M. Given his high stature and respect among Texans, it was said that parents across the state sent their sons, not to the A&M College, but instead "to Sul Ross."

It is often difficult to explain to campus visitors about the role and heritage of the Corps of Cadets and the unique traditions and events at the university. To do so requires an understanding of the environment and esprit de corps instilled by Sul to place the institution on a path of growth and marked contribution by its faculty, staff, and former students to the economy and growth of Texas. In this setting during the 1890s, many of the most honored traditions in Aggieland had their roots: Muster, collegiate football, the Aggie ring, corps trips, and the birth of the Fightin' Texas Aggie Band, to name but a few.

Beyond his efforts to set the college on a positive course, Ross was very focused on the enhancement of the level of education, research, and extension services provided by the college. Sul revised the admissions requirements, expanded the library, broadened the curriculum to attract new faculty, improved the campus facilities, and set the stage for a state-wide agricultural extension network. Furthermore, he encouraged and sponsored faculty research and membership in academic conferences and programs: a first at A&M. His focus on excellence is reflected in the institution's graduates during and after his tenure, known as the "Sul Ross Boys," and their successes in all walks of careers in commercial, military, educational, and governmental endeavors.

One of his most important legacies was his continued support and defense of higher education across the state. As the chief administrator of the Prairie View Normal College, he stood firm, both as governor and president of A&M, for its continued growth and expansion at a time when many politically motivated groups opposed any educational assistance for African American Texans in the state.

The multifaceted institution Ross envisioned is today one of the most diverse universities in the nation. Thus, the author combines the story of the formative years of the A&M College with Ross's broader impact on higher education excellence, selfless service, and equal rights for all Texans.

What is surely a fact is that Texas A&M University would have been killed in its infancy, were it not for Sul Ross.

Acknowledgments

This project began over fifty years ago. Thus I thank my commanding officer of Squadron One in 1969–70, Frank Montalbano, who in early September 1969 sent me to Cushing Archives to find out more about Sul Ross—beyond just the inscription on the statue—and report back. I journeyed down the stairs into the musty basement where the early archives of the school were located and was greeted by archivist Charles R. Schultz. He opened an old rusty file cabinet that had initially been set up by the university's first archivist, Dr. Brooks Cofer, in the early 1950s, and handed me a clippings file labeled "Sul Ross." The rest is history.

I am deeply indebted to numerous people throughout Texas for their timely assistance and encouragement in the preparation of this book. The project began many years ago with a few letters written by Sul Ross from the A&M College of Texas in the 1890s. I especially thank professors Drs. Henry Dethloff, Allan Ashcraft, and Larry Hill for their guidance, professional expertise, and continued encouragement. As I began the quest to locate more letters and material on this critical era in the history of Texas A&M, I was assisted by archivist and librarians at Baylor University, the Briscoe Center at the University of Texas, the Alamo in San Antonio, the National Archives in Washington and Maryland, and Cushing Memorial Archives at Texas A&M. I greatly appreciate the ongoing assistance and patience of David Chapman, Robin Hutchison, Anton duPlessis, and Leslie Winters. I extend a significant thanks to Bill Page, who for decades has been a tremendous sounding board and source of leads for critical documents and references, in addition to providing timely comments on sections of the book.

Special thanks are extended to Ray Bowen, Jerry Cooper, Tom Parsons, Joe Ashy, Sue Owen, Buck Henderson, Rachel Paul, C. C. Taylor, and David Chapman, who reviewed portions of the manuscript and provided excellent suggestions and critical corrections. Many, many friends and colleagues have extended their comments and support, all of which are appreciated: Carl Walker, John Keck, Tom Autrey, Bill Bambrick, Mike Casey, David Perez, Malon Southerland, Don Johnson, Tom Darling, James Woodall, Joe Utay, and A. J. "Niley" Smith.

I further would like to thank the staff at the Texas A&M University Press. Most of my books have been published by Texas A&M University Press, since *We Are the Aggies* in 1979. Their patience, advice, creative touch, and professionalism are second to none. Many thanks to Jay Dew, Shannon Davies, Thom Lemmons, Gayla Christiansen, Mary Ann Jacob, Kristie Lee, Pat Clabaugh, Katie Duelm, Dianna Sells, Kyle Littlefield, Christine Brown, Kathryn Lloyd, Mike Martin, and Nicole duPlessis.

And, most importantly, as always, my beloved wife Sherry has endured my quest to complete this book and a dozen other projects. Without her encouragement and support, this would not have been possible.

SUL ROSS
at Texas A&M

Introduction

The cool, wet, gloomy February day was all that greeted Sul Ross and his family as they stepped off the train onto the wooden platform at the "College" depot. The train ride from Austin following the inauguration of Ross's successor did not shed any light on the former governor's next and last adventure. There was no band, no saber arch by an honor guard, or welcoming speeches—only an open carriage ride through the main campus entrance at "Westgate." Driving along the cinder path from the railroad station toward Old Main—in 1891, the largest building between Houston and Dallas—Ross could not help but notice the treeless landscape and remoteness of his new home. As a product of frontier Texas and a hero in the eyes of many of its settlers, it was fitting that he entered the bleak A&M campus from the west.

For some five decades, I searched for and accumulated the letters of Governor Lawrence Sullivan Ross, as well as documents pertaining to the decade of the 1890s when he served as president of the Agricultural & Mechanical College of Texas. A legend in his own time, "Sul" Ross, as he was known by Texans statewide, in August 1890 accepted the invitation of the board of directors of the A&M College to assume the presidency upon the completion of his gubernatorial term in January 1891. The fledgling college, as well as the state of Texas, was in a turbulent time of transition in the era following Radical Reconstruction—the last of the old guards of frontier Texans and the veterans of the Confederate Lost Cause gave way to the approaching turn of the century, fueled by more progressive viewpoints on the recovery of agriculture, education reform, the development of abundant resources, railroad expansion and regulation, and the growth and attraction of new industry to Texas, in what some termed the rise of the New South.

The A&M College, the first institution of public higher education in Texas, struggled to gain both credibility and stability in its formative years. The Morrill Land Grant Act of 1862, with its federal mandate to establish public institutions of higher education in each state, was not embraced by Texas until the early 1870s. Following legislative approval and consideration of some half-dozen sites across the central part of the state, an open tract of land six miles south of the small farming town of Bryan, Texas, adjacent to the Houston and Texas Central Railroad that linked Houston with Dallas, was selected for the new A&M campus. The raw 2,614-acre patch of mesquite and post oak chosen for the college was as rough as its new faculty and the cadets. A formal dedication of the Agricultural and Mechanical College was held on October 4, 1876, presided over by Gov. Richard Coke and a small group of onlookers. The legislative action came with few instructions on how the college was to be structured, other than that it was to offer a broad curriculum in the "agricultural and mechanical arts," along with provisions to provide training in "military tactics." The words of Governor Coke's dedication speech to the students would be carved into the marble of the building named in his honor in 1957: "Let your watchword be DUTY, and know no other talisman of success than LABOR. Let HONOR be your guiding star in your dealings with your superiors, your fellows, with all. Be as true to a trust reposed as the needle to the pole, stand by the right even to the sacrifice of life, and learn that death is preferable to dishonor."

Sul Ross, who in formal settings was addressed either as "general" or "governor," was not at the dedication, yet in time, he would preside over legislative actions and observe the growing pains of the A&M College. Following his service as a brigadier general in the Confederacy and his petition to the federal government for reinstatement, he returned to his farm in McLennan County near Waco in 1865. His father, Shapley Prince Ross, one of Texas's earliest pioneers, was himself deeply influential in settling the region, known far and wide among pioneering newcomers looking for a new start in Texas. As Texas A&M archivist, David Chapman, noted: "It was a time of graft, corruption, carpetbaggers and Radical Republican rule. When combined with the trials and tribulations of frontier Texas, it made for interesting times." Sul worked with his father and, given the wave of crime across the region, was encouraged to serve as county sheriff. The post–Civil War period in Texas was characterized by the struggle of returning veterans, sharecroppers, and tenant farmers in dismal living conditions, as well as a high degree of lawlessness as the economy of the state struggled to recover. Hundreds were destitute and prone to criminal activity to survive. Serving as a sheriff in East Texas during the tumultuous post-Reconstruction era, Ross used his influence to curb banditry and reactive vigilante movements, seeking to quell the unrest and restore order.

The last quarter of the nineteenth century in Texas was firmly in the hands of the conservative-agricultural wing of the Democratic Party, which took statewide power from the Republicans after 1875. The transition back to local and state control following federal occupation was hallmarked by the election of Sul Ross's boyhood friend from Virginia, the popular Richard Coke, as governor. Coke was the prime leader of the rising clamor to recast the state's new constitution, post-Reconstruction. Following the approval of the new sitting legislature, Ross was among the ninety delegates, three from each of the thirty state senatorial districts, to answer the call to gather in Austin in late 1875. Other stalwarts of the era attending the Constitutional Convention included distinguished Texans John H. Reagan and Rangers John S. "Rip" Ford and Thomas Lewis Nugent.

Dominated by the farmer-bloc delegates, the Texas constitution of 1876 reflected what has been described as the Jeffersonian view of limited government, free enterprise, and frugal fiscal policy and budgets. Concern expressed by rising farm organizations such as the Grange or the Patrons of Husbandry regarding big government, the rise of industry, and the coming of the railroad produced provisions to monitor and regulate corporations and new bank charters, as well as strict adherence to a state debt ceiling of $200,000. Power was vested in the legislative body, as the new constitution allowed the limited powers of the governor to veto laws, allowing for a two-thirds legislative override. The governor's term of office was reduced from four to two years, and in the spirit of austerity, the chief executive's salary was lowered to $4,000 annually. Texas voters approved the new constitution by a two-to-one margin. Observers of the constitutional proceedings and ultraconservative outcome registered their blistering assessment in the *Houston Daily Telegraph*: "The harness is so small, the straps drawn so tight, the check rein pulled up to the last buckle hole, and the load to draw so heavy that the legislative horse will be galled from collar to crupper in the attempt to work, and the State wagon will go creaking along the highway of progress, in the rear of the procession."

This new direction of the Texas state government in the late 1870s would have a significant impact on the course of the growth and development of education at all levels in general and at Texas A&M in particular. At the level of secondary education, the state legislature determined a stipend for each county for teaching and facilities. The legislature held the purse strings, and the governor controlled appointments to the respective boards of directors. Furthermore, in 1876, the new Texas constitution established what came to be known as the Permanent School Fund, with revenue generated from public land to foster public schools. In time, with the discovery of oil after 1900 on state lands, investments in education would prove vital to the future funding and expansion of Texas higher education.

An important element of this study is its narrative exposition of the politics, factors, mores, culture, and dynamics of the era of the late 1880s through 1890s—presented for educational purposes in a way that neither condones nor justifies any past (or subsequently current) inherent inequalities in Texas society. While some of the social or political norms presented herein are far removed from those of any current, future, or former periods in Texas, one calls to mind the words of southern historian William C. Davis, who notes: "The Confederates were men and women of their era; we can only judge them legitimately in that context. Otherwise, we could reject virtually all human history on one currently acceptable ground or another." This approach does not in any way excuse or seek to sensationalize abhorrent events such as lynchings; systematic disenfranchisement of African Americans, women, the economically disadvantaged, Mexican immigrants and persons of Mexican origin who were living in Texas long before its independence or statehood, and Native Americans; or inequities in education, land policy, and economic opportunities. Discrimination was an ever-present reality in the state of Texas during the period when Governor Ross served as the president of Texas A&M. To understand the governor's impact on both the state and the university is to understand the context of the era in which he lived. This book attempts to see the bigger picture of history so that we might learn and grow from it, exploring the life of an individual who was highly influential and played a pivotal role in Aggieland.

During the last decade before the turn of the twentieth century, Texas was still a raw, emerging, post-Reconstruction frontier environment dominated by open land and fence wars, subsistence farmers, ranching, distrust of railroad expansion, drought, economic shortages and a lack of currency, and a dispersed but growing rural population. Much has changed. One example of a glaring anomaly and point of confusion regarding the late-nineteenth-century era in Texas is related to the political-party labels and emerging factions in the state during the post–Radical Reconstruction period. The then Democratic and Republican parties did not represent or reflect the views held by these parties today. The Republican Party, by fiat and mandate of the Reconstruction fabric imposed by the federal government and supported by African Americans and many whites in Texas, dominated postwar politics and elected offices both in Texas and across the South. Their reign was uncompromising and non-inclusive to local white citizens as well as returning Confederate veterans—who were, by law, forbidden from holding office. With the end of the Reconstruction and the call for a new Texas Constitutional Convention in Austin, the political tables turned. The Republican Party of Lincoln in Texas was composed of a small number of white, northern carpetbaggers and a majority of African Americans, both rural and urban. The radical Texas administration of Gov. Edmund Davis was upended and expelled by a conservative party led by Richard Coke. The new Texas constitution of 1876 was indeed drafted and ratified as one of the most conservative documents in the state's history—a complete repudiation of the mismanagement of the Davis administration. For the first dozen years after the adoption of the 1876 constitution, conservative Democrats took near-total control of the Texas government, from local to statewide offices. However, by 1890, a new rising political element composed of followers of the Grange and Farmers' Alliance emerged to demand more control, which aided the rise of the progressive movement both within and beyond the Texas Democratic party.

While this work is about the decade-long presidency of Lawrence S. Ross at the A&M College in the 1890s, the full story cannot be understood without an overview of the political, social, and economic dynamics of the last quarter of the nineteenth century. In addition to these factors, emerging global agricultural-market dynamics shaped Ross's every move, along with his fellow Texans who endeavored to transform the state. Ross played a significant role in the rise of progressivism, which ushered in the twentieth century in Texas. The friction that dominated the Texas Democratic Party during this period has often been gauged in light of interparty rivalry and the clash between the old-line planter-landed class of Bourbon Texans and the gradually more-progressive commercial-minded New South entrepreneurs. And in the mix was an environment of political pressure created by newly arriving immigrants, the ongoing struggles faced by African Americans, and the heavy-handed expansion of the railroad across the state.

The narrative of this book is influenced in part by *Gone to Texas: A History of the Lone Star State* (2003) by Randolph B. Campbell. For an overview of the cultural, social, political, and industrial aspects of the South in general and Texas in particular, a broad cross section of sources was consulted, including classic works such as C. Vann Woodward, *Origins of the New South 1877–1913* (1951); John S. Spratt, *The Road to Spindletop: Economic Change in Texas, 1875–1901* (1955); Alwyn Barr, *Reconstruction to Reform: Texas Politics, 1876–1906* (1971), John S. Exell, *The South Since 1865* (1975); Frank Vandiver, *Southwest: South or West* (1990); and Patrick G. Williams, *Beyond Redemption* (2007).

The rapid industrialization of farm equipment, transportation, and production facilities was both a blessing and a curse for Texas farmers. Higher production and more depressed prices caused the rise of middlemen who further undercut profits for farmers and ranchers. As prices plummeted, organizations such as the Grange and Farmers' Alliance developed to assist the plight of the farmer. Increased immigration into Texas created additional pressure for land, jobs, and commercial services. Interestingly, on the one hand, immigration was promoted, specifically by Governor Ross, to attract new settlers; yet in some quarters, this was seen as unwanted competition during a period plagued by poor agricultural markets, tight finances, and general unrest. One benchmark was the price of cotton per pound. In the era from 1880 to 1900, the price fluctuated from $0.066 to $0.100 per pound—an average of $0.07—while the cost of supplies, financing, and transportation rose by 8 to 10 percent. Farmer demand for low-interest loans and more specie—currency—in circulation soon evolved from commercial business concerns to outright popular political demands to provide relief to the agricultural sector.

By the time Lawrence Sullivan Ross departed the governorship and arrived on the A&M campus in February 1891, the statewide population of Texas had increased more than 250 percent since 1860 and numbered 2,235,521 (versus 818,175 in 1870), with more than 90 percent of the population living in rural areas—20 percent African American, 4 percent Hispanic, and less than 1 percent Native American. The fastest-growing segment of the Texas population during the last quarter of the century comprised white immigrants from Southern states and new arrivals from Europe. Only about 340,000 Texans lived in urban areas, and these remote areas were only fledging, underserved concentrations and not fully linked by roads, rail, utilities, and amenities. The largest city in Texas was Dallas, followed by the port town of Galveston. Dallas's growth was directly related to the introduction of railroads, the cotton exchange, and the increased north-bound freight of cattle and lumber. Galveston dominated the Texas Gulf Coast, with a mix of port activity (Houston did not have a functioning seaport until 1900, only a steamboat terminus on Buffalo Bayou) and trans-shipping for export of more than half of all cotton grown in Texas. During the decade of the 1890s, the Port of Galveston ranked third nationally in terms of total export values shipped, lagging only the ports of New York and New Orleans. San Antonio, Waco, Fort Worth, and Austin were still smaller, yet growing communities. There was little or no standardization of health care, school programs, or infrastructure, such as improved roads and seaports. The urban growth in Texas cities was due to the rise of light industry, increased trade, and fresh new immigrants, primarily from Georgia, Tennessee, Mississippi, and Kentucky—lured westward by the promise of cheap land, progress, and freedom. One factor that particularly impacted the transition from the farm-to-market agrarian economy (and, in time, railroad rate disputes, taxation, and land speculation) and urban growth in Texas was the arrival of the often-controversial railroad to connect the state's regions, cities, and seaports.

"I Think I Shall Like It"

A great deal has been written on Sul Ross's experience as a Texas Ranger on the Texas frontier, along with numerous detailed chronicles of his time as the commander of the Ross Brigade in the Confederate army. His two-term, four-year period as governor from 1886 to 1891 has also been detailed in numerous anthologies of the governors of Texas, but there has been no substantial study or analysis of his tenure as president of the A&M College of Texas from February 1891 until his untimely death in office in early January 1898. The impact of Sul Ross on Texas A&M, as well as his lasting contribution to education and industry in the state, have been overshadowed by his Ranger and military exploits—for which he was famous throughout his lifetime. In some aspects, his acceptance of the A&M presidency may have been seen as out of character when he easily could have assumed an additional elective office in Texas, entertained other jobs in the private sector, or retired to his ranch and farm in Waco.

Notwithstanding what could have been, his acceptance of the A&M board's offer to become president forever changed and shaped the formative course and legacy of what the college and future university was to become. There is little doubt that he improved the image and mandate of the college and saved the institution from closure—or at the least from being reduced to a forgotten state farm or what was to become known as a low-key agricultural or "extension" unit. During the last years of his governorship, he was well aware of the lurking forces in Austin and beyond who desired to limit and marginalize the growth and development of the Brazos campus. The stature and gravitas that Ross brought to Texas A&M, in the face of vocal politics and organized civic discourse, would provide a cornerstone and foundation for the college's traditions and image, helping to right the ship of higher education in Texas. Ross laid the foundation for the spirit and ethos of service that would hallmark the contribution of Texas A&M to the state and nation in the decades that followed his leadership.

The following story chronicles Ross's years at Texas A&M, formulated around more than four dozen letters the former governor penned while president, and selected letters, archival documents, and vignettes following his return from the war. Speculation on what Governor Ross would do when he left the governor's office in early 1891 was soon answered statewide by a feature article in the *Galveston Daily News*, the leading newspaper in the state, with the headline "Called to the College." From the time of Ross's appointment by the A&M College board of directors in July 1890 until his arrival on campus in February 1891, his path was rocky and fraught with obstacles (as will be discussed further herein). The Ross family arrived on campus on a cold and wet morning in early February, and even after serving four years as governor, Ross's initial experience at the college was no picnic or revival. Yet, after surveying campus conditions and the challenge before him, in a candid letter to his former chief of staff in Austin, Ross exuded a confident and focused resolve, concluding, "I think I shall like it."

And like it he did. Fortunately, the feeling was mutual, as cadets, former students, patrons, and parents alike from across the state revered the former governor, with many publicly stating that the doubts they had about the fledgling institution were now tempered by the prospect that they were not sending their sons off to college but instead were "sending their sons to Sul Ross." However, this sentiment was far from universal, and Ross faced significant opposition from politicians and organized agricultural organizations of the era who, in spite of the governor's reputation and stature, were quick to attack the college for political ends, financial gain, and their respective personal agendas. Nonetheless, Ross was still able to position the college on a sound footing, discrediting political naysayers and establishing a positive statewide image that ultimately led to new legislative funding for dormitories, equipment, livestock, enhanced utilities, classrooms, and facilities. He helped the college advance beyond its bruised reputation from the late 1880s, prior to his arrival.

During his tenure as governor, Ross was in frequent contact with the A&M board of directors and faculty representatives of the college. He attended a number of June graduation ceremonies at A&M and fostered close relations with a growing number of "ex-cadets"—former students—who established leadership roles in political, agricultural, and commercial circles across the state. In addition to his longtime mentor, Richard Coke (a lifelong family friend from Waco), three of his closest contacts with Texas A&M were board chairman Archibald Johnson Rose of Salado, Bryan lawyer and businessman William R. Cavitt, and his former chief of staff, Major Holmes. Rose was appointed president of the board (chairman) in 1887 by Ross. Cavitt, one of the longest-serving board members, was named to the board in 1883 and served thirteen years.

Rose, an immigrant to Texas from North Carolina in 1857, was the primary reason Ross agreed to come to Texas A&M. A political mentor to a number of state officials, Rose was a part of the organizing group of farmers that formed the Grange of the Patrons of Husbandry in Texas in mid-1873, rising to Grand Master. He later maintained a substantial leadership role in the vocal Farmers' Alliance, which supported change in the 1890s. In addition to his agricultural-reform activities, he was considered one of the foremost crusaders for education in Texas, at all levels. From the time Ross became Texas governor until his death, Rose would serve as an advisor and buffer for Sul between radical elements of the Grange and political hotheads in Austin who punitively attacked both the A&M College of Texas and its (would-be) president.

Perspective

This book will chronicle a brief overview of Sul Ross's life, as well as some of the historical events prior to his arrival in College Station in 1891. As noted previously, much has been written on Ross's life as a Texas Ranger, soldier, and governor, prior to his presidency at the A&M College. For those who are interested in a broader overview of Ross's many exploits, I have included a detailed bibliography with many resources for those interested in his dynamic career in full.

Our focus here will be on the foundational years of the A&M College, set on the stage of a dynamic era of political, economic, and social change in Texas. Texas A&M archivist David Brooks Cofer, who chronicled much of the first tangible evidence on Texas A&M in the early 1950s, noted, "The early history of this college shows a scarcity of records and the investigator must catch the fragments wherever available." Thus, the last chapter in the life of Sul Ross and the focus of this study would be written during the decade of the 1890s on the campus of the A&M College of Texas—today Texas A&M University. This is the story of a heralded frontier pioneer, statesman, educator, and man of action.

Sul Ross was a gritty young teenage Texas Ranger who rose to become a governor and a college president. His influence on the spirit, traditions, lore, and image of Texas A&M continues to inspire to this day and can never be overemphasized nor fully understood or appreciated. A number of official primary documents and public records are available to provide insight into the life, times, and influence of Ross. Some examples of these documents of interest include inaugural addresses, governors' messages, Texas Senate records, A&M College board of directors minutes, and statewide newspaper coverage—all of which are valuable sources for aspiring historians piecing together his life's story. Yet, Ross's private letters are by far the most indispensable window and candid link into his life and times, politics, family concerns, and confidential observations.

The courage, focus on excellence, and the Spirit of Aggieland, personified in the grit and aura of Sul Ross, are alive and well.

Note: In transcribing the personal letters of Sul Ross, I went to great lengths to clarify certain words. Yet some of the text that flowed from the pen of Sul was unidentifiable, even after multiple attempts to discern the true meaning. Thus, in a few spots in the transcriptions, where the text was illegible or missing, I have left a simple line (_____) for future cryptologists to discern. In addition, I added any needed clarification in places using brackets [ ], often for the sake of identifying key persons. Finally, note that there are likely other Sul Ross letters in private collections that have not been included here.

CHAPTER 1

"This Intrepid, Daring Knight"

Your success in protecting the frontier gives me great satisfaction.
I am satisfied that, with the same opportunities, you would rival,
if not excel, the great exploits of McCulloch or Jack Hays . . . the
people [of Texas] will not withhold their praise and reward you.

—Gov. Sam Houston, 1859

Shortly after the war against Mexico for Texas independence, Shapley
Prince Ross and his wife Catherine, weary of the cold winters in Iowa
Territory, moved their family of four children to the Republic of Texas
in 1839. Lured by the promise of cheap land and fertile soil by promotional guidebooks such as David Woodman's *Guide to Texas Emigrants*
and Charles Edward's *Texas and Coahuila*, the Ross family first settled
in the Robertson colony. And within two years, after taking the oath
of allegiance to the Republic of Texas, Shapley secured a 640-acre land
grant near the present-day city of Cameron on the Little River. Together
with a group of other immigrant families, they began to clear the land
and build homes. The challenge of establishing a sustainable homestead
was further complicated by a lack of farm equipment, medical care, and
a shortage of currency. In addition, the group faced frequent raids by
Comanches, opposing the intrusion of the new settlers. Shapley was part
of the committee that selected the permanent seat of Milam County, and
he was a member of Capt. Jack Hays's Ranger company, organized to
resist Indian attacks. The second Ross son, "Little Sul," as he was known
in his youth to differentiate him from his Uncle Sullivan, learned daily
life lessons as his family faced hardships on the open Texas frontier.

Sul, his older brother Peter, and his father had a number of scrapes with hostile Indians in Central Texas, but they avoided serious injury.[1]

Concerned for their safety, Shapley moved the family to Austin in 1845, just as the seat of the Texas government was returned from its brief tenure of residence at Washington-on-the-Brazos. Then a fledgling city of some five hundred inhabitants, Austin was on the edge of the western reaches of the Texas frontier. As Shapley remained in contact with his investments on the Little River and his Ranger duties, the Ross children were able to attend school and witness the dynamics of the reinvigoration of the fledging capital and the new republic now on the verge of accepting statehood in the Union. Following his election as a captain of a volunteer Ranger company tasked to protect settlements on the frontier and combined with Shapley Ross's familiarity with the region and the Indian leaders, residents in Waco Village encouraged him to return with his family to help defend and forge the growing development of the region. In 1849 he was deeded four town lots in the newly platted city and was also given exclusive rights to operate the primitive ferry concession across the Brazos River, as well as ownership of an adjacent eighty acres at the price of one dollar per acre. Shapley Ross built the first home and hotel in Waco in 1850 and became the town's first postmaster. Young Peter and Sul were truly early witnesses to the emergence of Texas.[2]

During the early 1850s, on the front porch of the Ross hotel, The Waco House, along what was known as "Rat Row," young Sul would spend time with a newly arrived lawyer and Virginian, Richard Coke—a big-boned, 250-pound, 6′3″, heavy-bodied, 21-year-old man. Coke's friendship with Ross would last a lifetime. Following graduation from William and Mary College, Coke solicited advice from his uncle, Richard, then a sitting senior US senator from Virginia. The senator invited his nephew to Washington to visit and meet a number of the capital's leaders—among them the big, red-headed, and popular Texas senator Sam Houston. Coke's meeting with "the Raven" would in a small way shape the fate of two pioneering Texans and influence decades of Texas history. In Henderson R. Shuffler's classic 1951 monograph, *Son, Remember*, on the Ross-Coke friendship, it was noted: "Sam Houston was generous by nature, but it is quite likely that he also had the big man's traditional liking for men of his own size and stature. He liked young Coke, and promptly advised him to move to the state of Texas and hang out his shingle in the newly-established Waco Village. Conflicting Spanish and Mexican land grants in that area, a canny Houston pointed out, would furnish the basis for litigation over land titles for generations to come. It would be a truly 'happy hunting ground' for lawyers, he believed." And it was. Coke recalled, "General Houston gave me several letters of introduction, one of them to ex-Lieutenant Governor J. W. 'Smoky' Henderson. I hunted up Gov. Henderson [after arriving in Galveston], who received me with the utmost kindness. I then took the stage to the town of Washington [on the Brazos River], where I bought a pony and saddle, and thus—mounted, with a six-shooter in my belt, I started out and landed in Waco. I hung out my shingle and went to work."[3]

As Richard Coke established his new law practice in Waco, a village of fewer than three hundred people, Sul worked with his family's farm-

Sul Ross in 1859 shortly after graduating from Florence College in Alabama. He worked during the summers for his father, Shapley Ross, at the Brazos Reserve near Graham, Texas. Source: Author's collection

ing and ranch operations and attended the Baylor Preparatory School at Independence. Yet the bulk of Sul's frontier education would come when he assumed additional duties working with his father, by then Indian agent at the Brazos Indian Reserve, located in Young County. The ten-square-mile reservation along the upper Brazos River south of Graham, Texas, was occupied by a mix of friendly members from the Waco, Caddo, Anadarko, Kickapoo, Wichita, Tawakoni, and Tonkawa tribes.[4] While Sul loved the excitement of the raw frontier, horses, and hunting, a formal education was also a distinctive part of Ross family tradition. His older brother, Peter, attended the Mount Vernon Military Academy in Ithaca, New York, from 1853 to 1855, returning to assist at the reserve and enlist in the Texas Rangers. Encouraged by the example of his brother, Sul enrolled in Wesleyan University at Florence, Alabama, in 1856. Decades later, Sul, in "a retrospective mood," recalled: "I rode 750 miles on horseback from Texas to Alabama. I had on a buckskin suit of clothes, my hair hung down on my shoulders and I wore a big six-shooter at my belt. I was so sun-burnt when I got to Florence Ala., that a regular procession followed me, thinking I was an Indian." He obtained a general university education without specialization. The education of Sul and Peter was extraordinary and rare, given the fact that very few Americans attended college at the time and just 1 percent of working-age men graduated. Following the completion of their college studies, the brothers planned to eventually return home and serve as frontier Rangers for the state. The duo returned home each summer between semesters to work at the Brazos Reserve with Indians from a number of tribes. They assisted in the establishment of numerous leadership roles among the Indians to help protect the reserve and pursued Indians who attacked both rival tribes and white settlers moving westward. Sul soon had his first major leadership—and near-fatal—opportunity.[5]

Antelope Hills

In the summer of 1858, nineteen-year-old Sul returned from college to work with his father at the Brazos Reserve and was selected to lead a band of friendly Indian auxiliaries against Comanche raiders in Indian Territory north of the Red River. In his command position of more than one hundred agency warriors, Shapley Ross—whom young Sul idolized and hoped to emulate—gave his approval and insisted on their full allegiance, which was assured by all the tribesmen. Sul assumed the title and role of captain. The expedition northward was under the command of Bvt. Maj. Earl Van Dorn of the Second Cavalry of the US Army. The army had enlisted the help of Ross and the Brazos Reserve Indians to locate a number of Penateka Comanches—including their chief, Buffalo Hump, who was responsible for a string of deadly raids on white settlers and peaceful Indians in Texas. Each time, after the attacks, the Penateka raiders escaped back across the Red River into the rugged Oklahoma Territory, out of reach of the Army or Rangers.[6]

The joint Army-Indian unit headed north in late September across the Red River into the uncharted Oklahoma Territory. Scouts searched for days before they discovered a large band of Comanches camped in a Wichita village on Rush Creek. After a conference between Sul and Van Dorn, it was decided to move at night to catch the raiders by surprise. After a fifteen-hour ride, the men were saddle weary as they caught sight of the village through a thick sunrise fog. Van Dorn quickly divided the troops, ordering Ross to attack the right flank and keep his Indian auxiliaries in place so they would not be mistaken for the enemy. Confusion followed as the attackers drove off the Comanche horses and turned toward the village, where the opposing forces had formed a defensive circle with knives and bows, ready to stand and fight.[7]

At the height of the Battle of Antelope Hills, a large group of Indians broke from the skirmish and ran to escape the camp in an intense firefight. Sul discovered the breach and yelled for a unit of men to join him to cut off the foe. However, only three men turned to follow Ross in his pursuit. After overrunning the foe and thus being cut off from the main body of troops, Ross and his men were quickly surrounded by some two dozen warriors, who attacked with a deadly shower of arrows. Instantly, the army lieutenant to his side was torn from his saddle and killed by what Sul recalled as a deadly shot that gave him a "feeling of horror that took possession of me when I saw the arrow clear up to the feathers into the body and heart of the gallant Lt. Van Camp." A second cavalryman, Private Alexander, was hit and knocked off his horse, dropping his loaded and cocked Springfield carbine to the ground. Only Ross and agency scout Caddo John remained to face the charging Comanches.[8]

Bracing for an attack, Ross turned to fight, and his weapon misfired just as an arrow went into his left shoulder. As he struggled to stay in the saddle and calm his horse, one of the advancing warriors picked up Alexander's Sharps .58 caliber carbine and, looking up at Ross, shot him point-blank. Bleeding profusely from his wounds, he slid stunned from his saddle with his right side partially paralyzed, landing on his six-shooter sidearm, and was unable to pull his weapon out of the holster. As Sul looked up, a warrior who had been a childhood friend—now turned enemy—named Mohee approached him with his scalping knife drawn for the kill. But at the last second, Mohee turned to flee the oncoming cavalry reinforcements, who overtook him and his band, leaving no survivors.[9]

As the battlefield soon became quiet, Ross lapsed into unconscious-ness from the pain and shock of his wounds. Coming to his aid was scout Caddo John, who upon examination, realized that Sul had two massive wounds of four holes from fragments of the .58 caliber ball that, according to Sul Ross in a February 1894 article in the *Galveston Daily News*, "passed through the left arm and side, coming out near the spine." Concerned with the loss of blood, the scout patched the arrow wound to stop the bleeding and used his rifle ramrod with a silk rag to probe and clean the wound. He then added bandages. More than a score of Indian warriors were killed, with many wounded. Much to the irritation of the troops, Chief Buffalo Hump escaped with a large band. Four troopers were killed and twelve were wounded, including both Ross and expedi-tion commander Major Van Dorn.[10]

The fact that Sul was not killed instantly is a miracle. The shock of a rifle shot alone would have killed most men. For five painful days, Caddo John stayed at his side under a post oak on the battlefield. Once he was moved southward, his wounds became infected and the pain intensified as the Indians worked to carry him on a mule-drawn litter over very rough and irregular ground to Fort Belknap. As the fever increased, Ross appealed to his Indian escorts to end his misery, yet none would comply, resorting to carrying him on their shoulders to reduce the jar-ring trek. After more than two weeks of travel, Sul arrived back at the Brazos Reserve, alive but still in critical condition, and as Zachariah Ellis Coombes, the reservation school teacher, recorded in his journal, *The*

An early Texas pioneer, Shapley Prince Ross immigrated to Texas in 1839 and was the founder of the village of Waco, opening a ferry across the Brazos River and establishing the first post office and commercial business. Source: Author's collection

Diary of a Frontiersman 1858–1859, Sul was, "verry [*sic*] much wasted by fatigue and his wound," but still "full of life and fun."[11]

Once Ross's fever broke and the infection waned, the army doctors were amazed and surprised that he had survived. Ross, for the remainder of his life, credited Caddo John with saving his life. Doctors inquired what the scout had used on the silk rag to swab Sul's wounds, and he only replied that it was a secret substance, which in later years was reported to be a homemade liniment of *pouip* or *Yerva del Indio*—a medicine man's "wonder drug." The "Boy Captain" had survived, with Sul conceding in later years that he considered the near-death experience at the Wichita Village "the most creditable incident of all relating to myself."[12]

The encounter with the rogue warriors brought Ross instant fame, as it became statewide news and was reported to the War Department and the US Congress. Major Van Dorn recommended to the Army Chief of Staff Gen. Winfield Scott that Ross be considered for an immediate promotion to captain in the regular US Army. Sul declined the offer.

His gallantry in action as a teenager made him a frontier standout and the subject of many stories. His courage under fire would be recounted regularly throughout his life. In 1859 Gov. Sam Houston recognized Ross's valor and "great exploits," predicting that "the people [of Texas] will praise and reward you."[13]

Sul returned to Waco to rest and recover. He soon returned to Alabama to graduate from Wesleyan in the summer of 1859. Returning home, he adopted a young settler's child, rescued in the Wichita Village, naming her Lizzie Ross in honor of his fiancée, Lizzie Tinsley. After about one year of further recovery from his wounds, Ross enlisted as a lieutenant in a new Ranger company raised in Waco by Capt. J. M. Smith. The raiding activity of Indians had not stopped. Much time was spent chasing them without any results, and Smith's company was disbanded. In September 1860, Gov. Sam Houston authorized Ross to enlist sixty mounted volunteers under his command. The Rangers were dispatched to Fort Belknap in mid-October 1860 to protect the local settlers from a wave of new Indian raids led by Chief Peta Nocona. Under Nocona's leadership, Comanche raiding parties killed dozens of settlers, stole horses, and burned homes. The *Houston Weekly Telegraph* reported details of the murder of several families near Belknap and the death of a driver on the Overland Mail Stage Line—concluding, "the frontier at present is entirely unprotected." To address the threat, the Ross Ranger company was joined by regular army troops from Fort Cooper to pursue the attackers.[14]

Pease River

After weeks of pursuit, the Indian raiders were located in their winter encampment. Ross scouted ahead, and in a blowing dust storm, he gained sight of the tribe camped on the riverbank. Sending his soldiers to circle around the camp to cut off a retreat, Ross and the Rangers attacked headlong into the Comanches. The surprise attack did not lessen the will of the Indians, as much of the fighting was hand-to-hand. The chief, Peta Nocona, broke from the fight and attempted to escape. Following a chase, Ross and his men overtook and killed him. Among the small group that was captured, Ross noted a blue-eyed captive—not of Indian blood. Much to his surprise, he had captured Cynthia Ann Parker, who had been taken captive at nine years old along with her brother John, age six, in the massacre at Fort Parker in 1836 by a band of Comanches and Kiowa—two years before Sul was born. She grew to adulthood as a Comanche, and after years of captivity, she became acculturated to the ways of the tribe, becoming the wife of Peta Nocona and mother to two sons—Quanah and Pecos—and a daughter, Topsannah (Prairie Flower).[15]

Cynthia was thirty-four years old with a two-year-old child. The baby clung to the woman, dressed in ashened buckskins and covered in dried blood and buffalo oil. The 1836 Fort Parker raid, near current-day Groesbeck, is one of the most repeated stories of the frontier era, told in newspapers nationwide and in J. Marvin Hunter's tabloid *Frontier Times*. Fort Parker and a reproduction of the stockade still stand today. The uncle of the recaptured girl, Col. Isaac Parker, was summoned to identify her and take custody. Having forgotten almost all of her mother tongue, Cynthia Ann mumbled a constant mix of Comanche and Spanish as she mourned the loss of her husband and two unaccounted-for sons. She tried to escape back to the frontier numerous times, was sent to various relatives for shelter, and never recovered from the shock of being returned to a civilization she could not and would not embrace. Soon after her small daughter died, the Texas Legislature awarded her a pension of $100 per year. Cynthia Ann was never reunited with her two sons. However, the eldest, Quanah Parker, grew to become one of the last revered Comanche chiefs, who, as one of the last great warriors, worked in his old age to pacify and comfort his people. Cynthia Ann Parker died in 1870 and was buried in the Foster graveyard in Henderson, Texas.[16]

In his later years on the campaign trail, reporters would flock around Ross to ask questions, not about political issues, but about the frontier and old Indian war days. The intrigue of the recapture of Cynthia Ann Parker and the high profile of her son, Quanah, only added to the mystique, in the eyes of many Texans, of Ross's early years on the frontier. In 1880, in correspondence on the eve of his run for the Texas Senate seat with biographer and political supporter Victor Rose, Ross was fully aware of the publicity value of his frontier experience that "would swell my vote greatly." A few politically motivated detractors would claim that he was given too much credit for his actions; yet a majority of Texans roundly revered his grit and image as a champion of the frontier settlers.

Pease Ross, a native Comanche boy who was adopted by the
Ross family and raised in Waco. Source: Texas Collection,
Baylor University

Perception oftentimes shapes reality. Thus this was but the first chapter
in an exciting and challenging life to come for young Sul.[17]

In addition to Cynthia Ann Parker and her child, a Comanche boy
was also captured. He was the only male survivor of the raid, spared
and brought back by the Ranger company. The Ross family named him
"Pease" and raised him as one of their own. Even though he was given
numerous opportunities to return to his people throughout his life, Pease
chose to remain as part of the Ross family and was raised to adulthood
by Sul.

Captain Ross returned from the Pease River campaign with even more
fame. Some have concluded that his frontier and Ranger exploits would
prove to be a "springboard to a dazzling career." For the first time, it

seemed the frontier was a safe place for settlers. Back in Waco, the Ross Ranger company was ordered disbanded by Governor Houston, and much to the surprise of Sul, a second company of Rangers was organized without his knowledge. Apparently, in the transition, Houston had made the offer to another Ranger captain in February 1861 without informing Ross—who immediately resigned his Ranger commission and returned home. To make amends, Houston named Sul to the post of *aide-de-camp* on his personal staff, with the rank of colonel. It is hard to tell if Ross was the victim of too much media stardom and coverage or just bad timing; most likely, in retrospect, he was caught up in political intrigue in Austin, with the rising storm clouds of Confederate rebellion on the horizon.[18]

The question of southern secession and states' rights dominated the newspapers and talk among Texans. The US Census of 1860 for McLennan County notes that Shapley Ross held a few slaves and house servants, primarily for domestic work in his Waco home and hotel, while young Sul Ross owned no slaves. The grizzled old Shapley Ross, while a staunch Democrat, was—like his dear friend Sam Houston—opposed to Texas secession and association with the Confederacy. He urged, instead, that Texas separate from the Union and form its own "Lone Star" nation. After a statewide referendum on March 3, votes tallied 46,126 for secession and 14,697 against—with Houston coldly stating, "Texas is lost." Unlike their father, the young Ross sons answered the call to Southern arms. In early 1861, Peter Ross organized a new military company of volunteers in Waco, with Sul enlisting as a private. Prior to reporting for duty, Sul carried out a secret mission to the Five Civilized Tribes for Gov. Edward Clark, who replaced Houston following his refusal to take an oath of allegiance to the new Confederacy. Ross's mission was to make sure the tribes would not be hostile to the new Confederate army or support the much-hated Union army. With yet another frontier mission complete, his next primary priority was to marry his longtime fiancée, Elizabeth Dorothy "Lizzie" Tinsley, in a whirlwind wedding and honeymoon, on May 28. Within days, responding to "Texians to Arms!" Peter's volunteer unit mustered in Dallas. Departing his new wife, whom he left in the care of his parents, Sul joined his brother and reported for duty with what would be known as the "Sixth Texas Cavalry."[19]

Sixth Texas Cavalry

Because of his record and leadership during the US Civil War, Sul Ross was widely considered one of the most gifted officers who served on either side of the conflict. Always at the point of action, he was revered by his men, who knew he shared their dangers and hardships on an equal footing. The severe wounds he endured in the Wichita Village fight took years to mend and brought him discomfort for his entire life. Yet this did not cause him to shy away from his duty and obligation to his men. Once on active duty, he was promoted to the rank of major and dispatched in late 1861 to General McCulloch to lead an advance scouting force in central Missouri. Using skills learned on the Texas frontier, Major Ross and his unit were assigned to conduct reconnaissance and raids in the Union army's rear echelon. His resourcefulness and success resulted in eloquent reports of commendation from the commander of the Sixth Texas Cavalry, Colonel Warren Stone, noting:

> Major L. S. Ross, of my command, was called for to take a scouting party in rear of the enemy and cut off his [supply] train and annoy his rear. This duty was most gallantly performed by attacking a portion of the enemy's army at Keetsville, killing 25 of his number, capturing 9, and destroying much of his train and commissary supplies. The major returned with wearied, conquering heroes from the field without the loss of a man, although he met the very blaze of their guns only a few feet distant. I cannot too highly estimate the chivalry and gallantry of this intrepid, daring knight, nor too highly appreciate the ability of this officer, who although but a boy, has won imperishable honors as an officer in the border warfare of Texas on repeated occasions, meeting, as he has now done, the full appreciation and admiration of our executive, and securing his fullest confidence. It is with pride that I thus bear testimony to the distinguished merits of my brave major, L. S. Ross.[20]

Ross consistently faced danger and hardship during the war. In letters home, he chronicled detailed and vivid impressions of battles, his fellow soldiers, camp life, and combat. He penned, "I came very near being killed. Davis and myself were just together in front of my Battalion, forming them, and a bomb shell—fell and burst just by us, but never hurt either. For a long time they were flying thick and fast around our

Regiment, but I [am] convinced that they scare more men than they kill." In a letter to Lizzie, he discussed the dismal living conditions of his mid–March 1862, snow-covered encampment on the Missouri-Arkansas border. Food was scarce: "[W]e just have what we can pick up along the road, such as turnips, and parched corn—and it snowed most of the time—ground frozen hard." And after losing his bedding, Ross "lay three fence rails down on the ground [for a bed] & wrapped up in my saddle blanket, on them [to] try to sleep—my health is good but I am yet very much fatigued." In addition to describing the field in detail in his letters, Ross corresponded regularly with Lizzie about the management of their Brazos River farm, as well as financial concerns.[21]

After a brief leave to return to Waco, Ross joined friend and newly promoted Maj. Gen. Earl Van Dorn, fighting at Pea Ridge and Des Arc, Arkansas, and by mid-1862 he was promoted to colonel in command of the Sixth Texas Cavalry. Colonel Ross and his Texans were singled out for commendation for their bravery following multiple frontal attacks at the Battle of Corinth and the engagement at Hatchie Bridge. There were no medals, decorations, or commendations for acts of bravery in the ranks of the Confederate army—General Robert E. Lee had declined the creation of such awards. The only honors mentioned were in official dispatches to higher command and battlefield promotion as a result of leadership and "distinguished gallantry" under fire—both of which distinguished Sul Ross, as noted in the *Official Record* report from Gen. R. V. Richardson, commending the "gallantry of Brig. General L. S. Ross and his entire brigade of Texans."[22]

Skirmishing continued during 1863, when the twenty-three-year-old Texan became the ninth-youngest general in the Confederate army. His promotion and command greatly improved morale and re-enlistments. Ross's Cavalry Brigade consisted of the Third, Sixth, Ninth, and Twenty-Seventh Texas Cavalry. The combined force, noted for their aggressive fighting skills, played a significant role in the Mississippi and Tennessee campaigns of 1863–64 and skirmishes around Atlanta in late 1864. The hardships of fighting nearly every day on little sleep, in bad weather, and with poor food took a toll on both Ross and his men. In his *Fighting with Ross' Texas Cavalry Brigade, C.S.A.* (1976), author Homer L. Kerr provides a chronicle of the service of the Sixth Texas Cavalry in vivid detail. Battle intensified in mid-1864 during one period, when the Ross Brigade fought some 112 days straight. The stress of the constant fighting, poor rations, foul weather, and wounds resulted in a steady stream of hospitalized troops and desertion from the ranks. Ross was briefly captured by the enemy at the Battle of Brown's Mill, but he was able to escape due to a counterattack. His last days in the field were the Franklin-Nashville Campaign in the late winter of 1864.[23]

By March 1865, Ross requested furlough after being away from home for nearly two years. Granted a leave of absence, he returned home in very poor health, sick with a persistent fever, and most likely fighting a bout of malaria. As his unit prepared to cover the campaign into Atlanta, at Lick Skillet Crossing, six miles west of the capital, it would be the last time he would see the Sixth Cavalry in active service. During the course of the war, Ross participated in 235 engagements. He had seven horses shot out from under him, and unlike many of his friends, he was not wounded, yet did have, for the remainder of his life, reoccurring bronchitis and chills—and possibly a mild case of malaria. He was at home in Waco when he learned of General Lee's surrender at Appomattox, Virginia, on April 9, 1865.[24]

Reconstruction and Unrest

With the end of the Southern rebellion, twenty-six-year-old Sul returned to his family farm on the south Bosque River, west of Waco. Ross was not present with the Sixth Texas Cavalry when they formally surrendered in Jackson, Mississippi, on May 14, 1864, due to a ninety-day furlough that began on March 13, 1865. Due to his high rank, Ross was not included as a part of the blanket parole and amnesty protecting him and his troops from possible arrest. As a former Confederate general officer, he was concerned with any possible confusion or attempt to confiscate his property. He voluntarily applied for a special presidential pardon on August 4, 1865, via federal representatives in Austin who forwarded his documents to Washington, DC, for review. Pres. Andrew Johnson approved his petition on October 22, 1866, but Ross did not receive formal acceptance until July 1867. This document describes his prewar role in Texas and loyalty to Governor Houston, his CSA military record, and his post–Civil War perspective on the future of the state of Texas and the South:[25]

Austin, Texas   August 4, 1865

To the President of the United States,

Sir:

The undersigned, a citizen of McLennan County, Texas, late a Brig. Genl. Confederate States Army availing himself of the invitation extended in your amnesty and pardon for his participation in the late Rebellion of the southern States.

Your petitioner would state that before the act of secession by the State of Texas, he was in command of the state troops on the frontier, by authority of Gov. Houston, by this connection he would state, that he had no participation in the seizure of United States property at the Posts on the Frontier.

During the sitting of the Secession Convention of the State, official business required his presence at Austin, where he conferred freely with the Governor—and a few days before Gov. Houston was deposed was promoted by him to the rank of Colonel and Aide on his personal staff.

On the 16th of April 1861 he volunteered as a private in the Confederate States Army, was subsequently elected major and afterwards Colonel of the Regiment to which he belonged. On 22nd December 1863 he was commissioned Brig. Genl. in the Confederate States Army and served as such until the close of the war.

During the late struggle the undersigned used his best exertions in an honorable way to promote the success of the Confederate cause. He participated in two hundred and thirty-five engagements and shrank from no duty that devolved upon him as a soldier and as an officer.

He feels, should occasion require in the future history of the United States, that he can serve her as his country with the same devotion and energy and does most conscientiously say that he desires the prosperity of the Government and trusts that the wounds so unhappily inflicted during the late struggle may be speedily healed and all animosities forgotten.

He would further say that he regards the slavery question as finally settled and would view any attempt to reestablish slavery in the South as insidious and impolitic.

He believes that the people of the South should regard the question as settled forever and that it devolves upon the several states in their respective conventions to so provide in their organic laws—

Respectfully submitted,
L. S. Ross[26]

Conditions in Texas following the war reflected much of the same turmoil and dangers of the late 1850s. The absence of active Texas Ranger
units and the US Army allowed an increased level of Indian attacks and
incidents across the western frontier. The plight of the returning veterans
was captured by one eyewitness, Acie Sooner, in *Frontier Times*: "They
came home with their faded and tattered gray jackets, and with their
paroles in their pockets, presenting them to their children as a testimony
of faith and fidelity. Ragged and half starved, heavy-hearted and some
wounded, they surrendered their guns. . . . Their money was worthless
and their people were without government or law." Added to the Indian
troubles were the difficulties posed by displaced white and black farmers,
now homeless and landless. Further, problems arose from what Acie
Sooner termed "skallawags [*sic*] and carpet-baggers that infested Texas
at that time [who] were promising [former slaves] as much and in some
instances giving them forged deeds to parts of their late master's lands."
Postwar law enforcement across the state was very weak, and the Federal
Reconstruction authorities did little to settle unrest and lawlessness in
Texas. The conflicting expectations and dreams of newly freed African
Americans and of many Southern whites increased tensions.[27]

Notwithstanding, the first focus of the trim and willowy Sul Ross was
to regain his health and develop his small farm to support his family.
In spite of receiving his final pardon from Washington in July 1867,
under the rules of the federally imposed Reconstruction, he could not
vote or hold any elective or appointed public office. He used the period
to improve his farm and expand into cattle ranching with his brother
Peter—recalling in a speech before the Fort Worth Interstate Convention
of Cattlemen in March 1890, "I served a long and faithful apprenticeship
as a cowboy." With a shortage of postwar farm labor, the Ross family
employed about forty Tonkawa Indians as tenant or sharecroppers to
clear land for livestock and plant cotton—a system that gave the land-
owner a lien on the tenant's crop, with payment coming from annual
crop production less expenses. Due to the shortage of hard currency in
circulation in Texas and competition from larger cattle operations, and
with the dilapidated infrastructure in poor repair, the Ross brothers first
sold wild range cattle in Missouri—along the trails to and from Texas
they knew well from their days in the war—but they abandoned the
"ticklish business" of cattle sales due to a hostile environment north of

the Red River, rife with rustlers and thieves. The Rosses opted to drive their cattle to market in New Orleans (in spite of the fact that the north-bound Chisholm Trail to Kansas went through Waco), which paid two cents per pound on the hoof, bringing sixteen to nineteen dollars per head—at a time when most cattle drives failed to succeed. Avoiding the fate of the northern trails, the brothers returned to Waco with a nice profit. Prior to the end of Reconstruction, Lizzie and Sul would add four children to the household: Mervin (1866–83), Lawrence Sullivan Jr. (1868–1914), Florine (1870–1945), and Harvey (1873–1944). By the mid-1870s, the Ross family had accumulated more than one thousand acres and built a house in downtown Waco, a "town house" considered essential in order to be close to schooling for the children.[28]

In 1873 Reconstruction came to a halt in Texas. For nearly a decade, most white Texans had a visceral dislike for the federally imposed laws and controls and eagerly anticipated the day they could take back their local and state government from federal oversight. Some of the most pressing issues for Texans of the time included checking the wanton crime, introducing a new democratic government, and assisting with the recovery of agriculture across the state. Concerned with the poor agricultural markets in Texas, Sul became the corresponding secretary of the White Hall Agricultural Association of McLennan County. His only other memberships were with veterans' organizations and the Masonic Lodge No. 92, AF&M, in Waco. In the postwar years, farmers across the South, including Texas, once again became dependent on a one-crop system—cotton. According to Alwyn Barr in *Reconstruction to Reform* (1971), "By 1873 Texas grew more cotton than they had in 1860." Yet falling cotton prices, going below nine cents per pound, negated the production gains.[29]

With the end of Radical Reconstruction, veterans of the Confederate cause were now eligible to hold public office. The citizens of McLennan County on December 2, 1873, wasted little time in electing Sul Ross county sheriff. Naming brother Peter as one of his chief deputies, Ross set new aggressive guidelines to curb crime. Within two years, the sheriff's office had arrested more than seven hundred outlaws, horse thieves, and cattle rustlers—particularly those holed-up "Modocs" in the La Vega wilderness along the Brazos River. In late April 1874, the *Waco Daily Examiner* concluded, "[T]he people of Waco are determined to tolerate no more jail breaking foolishness," and with "Ross on the spot . . . dismissed all apprehension." Crime had expanded beyond livestock and property theft into stagecoach and bank robberies. One outlaw of some fame apprehended by Sherriff Ross was the "Bandit Queen"—the infamous Belle Starr—who was hiding in Waco after a series of robberies in Dallas and wanted on a warrant for horse theft. However, a growing concern across Texas (at first blamed on the lack of law enforcement during the Reconstruction period) was the lawlessness also perpetrated by alleged "good" citizens who, out of frustration, were quick to take the law into their own hands. Ross realized those engaged in mob rule held sway in frontier justice over the established law and due process. To curb the wave of postwar mob violence or vigilantism, Ross convened a statewide meeting of sixty-five county sheriffs from across Texas on August 14, 1874, in Corsicana, Navarro County, to form the Sheriffs' Association of Texas, mandated to condemn the lawless acts of mobs, enforce all laws, and pledge to "protect citizens to the extent of

Richard Coke immigrated to Waco, Texas, to open a law office. A lifelong friend of Sul Ross, he was the governor of Texas and active in the dedication of the A&M College in October 1876. Source: Texas Collection, Baylor University

our legal power." It is also likely that part of the intended outcome for Ross and his fellow sheriffs would have been to curb vigilante violence with racial motivations. Race violence was undoubtedly present in postwar Texas, as C. Vann Woodward noted: "The record of violence should not be hastily attributed to the Negro, for at least . . . in Texas white men killed much more often, in proportion to their numbers, than did Negroes." One of the biggest concerns at the time was rampant cattle and horse theft, which was seen by most in the public as an immediate hanging offense. Even Sheriff Ross had his prize "beautiful grey" racehorse stolen, but it was found by his deputy, Peter Ross, and returned. Many criminals soon realized it was safer to be arrested and jailed by the local sheriff than to face the hostile rope of a mob.[30]

Ross resigned from the sheriff's office to be elected as a delegate from Waco to the 1875 Texas Constitutional Convention, which had been roundly promoted by his close friend and mentor, the newly elected Texas governor Richard Coke. In the wake of the abrupt departure of provisional governor Edmund J. Davis and the Radical Reconstruction, Coke captured the tone of the Constitutional Convention: "Let the heart of the patriot throb with joy, for the old landmarks of constitutional, representative government, so long lost, are this day restored, and the ancient liberties of the people of Texas re-established. The virtue and intelligence of the country, no longer ostracised, now wield their legitimate influence, and the government of Texas henceforth is to be administered in the interest and for the benefit of the people, and to reflect their will."[31]

Members of the constitutional gathering represented a broad cross section of Texas citizens and leaders: twenty-three had state legislative experience, more than two dozen had been commissioned officers in either the Confederate or Union armies, twenty-nine were attorneys, and more than half were farmers and ranchers. Those who attended the September gathering in Austin were very interested in overcoming the perceived abuses and waste of the Radical Republicans. Thus, in keeping with the spirit of the times, the convention adhered to a strict principle of decentralization of government authority, conservative fiscal policies, and popular election of all officeholders in the executive branch. Once the convention was assembled and seated, Ross, who left his family in Waco, served on a committee to seat the officers of the convention, in addition to serving on select committees on frontier affairs, taxation, apportionment, and education. Ross supported unlimited suffrage (for males) and opposed a poll tax that limited voting by African Americans. The education committee of the convention drafted language and procedures for the creation of the A&M College, Prairie View Normal College, and Huntsville Normal Teacher's College. In a confusing twist involving politics, administrative policy, and decades-long upheaval regarding legislative funding, the new Texas state constitution declared the A&M College to be a branch of the University of Texas, which did not yet exist.

The overwhelming passage of the new constitution in 1876 set the pattern for state government for the next quarter-century. Texas was once again in the hands of Texans. However, the proceedings failed to resolve a number of pivotal issues that would impact the state over the balance of the century: agricultural assistance, prohibition, how to handle the railroads and trusts, education, water rights, and land-usage reform. A contemporary critic in 1876 provided an opinion of the new constitutional document in terms that were both vivid and readily apparent to Texans, 90 percent of whom were rural: "The harness is so small, the straps drawn so tight, the check rein pulled up to the last buckle hole, and the load to draw so heavy, that the legislative horse will be galled from collar to crupper in the attempt to work, and the State wagon will go creaking along the highway of progress, in the rear of the procession."[32]

The new A&M College of Texas, the fortieth institution funded under the covenants of the federal Morrill Act of 1862, thus operated under its own board of directors as an essentially independent and separate institution. From its earliest adoption, public higher education was a political football. In 1884 zealous and pro–A&M College board member, George Pfeuffer of New Braunfels (1879–83), as chairman of the Texas Senate Committee on Education, fought back against the political wrangling in Austin intended to undercut the college: "The legislature had scarcely met when we heard words of ridicule addressed against A. and M. College, and derisive sneers at efforts, and suggestions that it be abandoned as an educational institution and be converted into an asylum." Land speculators and lobbyists, promoting the establishment of the new university in Austin, worked to curb funding and political support for the A&M College.[33]

The Path to the Executive Mansion

Already a household name from his frontier days as a Ranger, Ross was considered for the office of Lieutenant Governor in 1878. Regardless of widespread speculation by the press, the next step that would place Sul Ross on the path to the governor's mansion was his election as state senator in 1880 for the Twenty-Second District in Central Texas. The rise of Sul Ross to public office was clearly influenced by his role in the statewide Sheriff's Association and his tenure as a delegate in the Constitutional Convention. In an article that was reprinted in newspapers across the state, the *Houston Telegram* provided a laudatory endorsement: "No purer, better and but few abler men live within the borders of broad Texas. A knightly gentleman, a Christian gentleman, a soldier, a statesman, a man of depth and breadth, a progressive man and a young man that's the kind of a man we want." Continuing his civic interest and duty, begun during the Constitutional Convention, he was appointed as the chairman of the finance committee in the Texas Senate and was also a committee member on education, internal improvements, military affairs, and agricultural affairs.

While Ross's health had improved, this was also a bitter time due to the death of his firstborn son in 1883. By the time he ended his Senate term, the Ross family added four more children: Frank (1875–1938), Elizabeth (1878–1932), James Tinsley (1880–81), and Neville P. (1882–1938). After returning home to his family in Waco, it was only a brief time before Ross's friends actively raised the question of Sul running for governor—a prospect he refused outright in 1884.[34]

In one of his last acts as state senator in April 1882, Ross cast a vote for an appropriation of state funding for a new capital building, with the cornerstone laid on March 2, 1885, after a massive fire had destroyed the existing two-story wooden structure in November 1881. Payment for the new capital was from a Texas grant of some 3.2 million acres sold at 50 cents an acre, with land set aside in the Texas panhandle, which for many years comprised the XIT Ranch. Final oversight for the largest project in nineteenth-century Texas history was by the commissioner of the General Land Office, Judge Charles Rogan, a mechanical arts graduate in the class of 1883 from the A&M College.[35]

As early as 1880, a group spearheaded by former Sixth Texas cavalryman and editor of the *Victoria Advocate*, Victor M. Rose (no known relation to A. J. Rose of Salado), promoted and encouraged his former commander to run for office. Honored by the encouragement from Rose, Sul Ross requested he "take no steps to bring up my name before the people [of Texas]." His main concern was an ongoing feud between Governor Coke and the editors of the *Galveston Daily News*, which, he concluded, would "thus induce it [the *News*] to wage an uncompromising warfare upon any man from Waco." He advised Rose he would return to his Texas Senate post. Then tragedy struck with the death of his month-old child, James Tinsley Ross, on December 30, 1880, followed by the loss of Lizzie's mother, Elizabeth Dorothy Tinsley. Concerned for his family in Waco, Ross declined reelection to a second Senate term and planned to enter the newspaper business, purchasing a half interest in the *Waco Daily and Weekly Examiner and Patron*. However, a deadlock at the 1882 Senate nominating convention in Hillsboro renominated Ross, in his absence, as a compromise candidate. Winning with little opposition, Ross returned to the Senate in Austin in late 1882 and sold his investment in the *Examiner* to avoid any conflicts of interest. Struggling with his own poor health, Ross's second term was marred by the death of his oldest son, Mervin Hellum Ross, age seventeen, of pneumonia on January 31, 1883.[36]

By Thanksgiving 1885, Sul had changed his mind on the governorship, but he did not officially announce that he would stand for governor until February 25, 1886. There was an immediate outpouring of statewide support for his campaign, especially from veterans, the Knights of Labor, the powerful Texas Sheriff's Association, the Farmers' Alliance, and East Texas farmers. He was nominated on the very first convention ballot. At the time, the election platform of the Democratic Party was a mix of agrarian issues, stances on grazing rights, and for sale of land to active, "not foreign," owner-occupied settlers, with a watchful eye on growing corporate land trusts and railroad operations.[37]

With Ross being a household name, the best the opposition could offer was that he was "pandering" to a few interest groups to gain their vote. "Ross did not think of himself as a politician," biographer Benner noted, "nor did other politicians consider him one of them." Thus, his appeal—in the tradition of "Jeffersonian democracy" that he who governs best governs least—was to the common man and not to the Democratic machine's antics. Although suffering a number of bouts with illness before and during the Democratic convention in Galveston and the fall campaign, Ross was nominated by acclamation. The childhood scrapbook of daughter Florine Ross includes an undated article from mid-1886 that reflected the sentiment of a majority of Texans: "Ross has a personal magnetism about him which wins men and attaches them to his person as by hooks of steel. His name and his history are without blemish as becomes the knightly gentleman whom the people will make governor next November if he lives." The sobriquet of "knightly gentleman" replaced "boy captain," and during the '86 gubernatorial election, it was used regularly in newspapers statewide. And the "if he lives" comment leads one to wonder if the unknown reporter was aware of Ross's sometimes fragile health.[38]

Avoiding the growing statewide debate over prohibition, Sul Ross won a sweeping victory for office by a nearly three-to-one margin (78 percent of the popular vote) over two opponents. The reception and inaugural ball at the brand-new Driskill Hotel on Congress Avenue in Austin was, at the time, the largest gathering of the power elite, veterans, ranchers, lawmen, and politicians in Texas. All went smoothly at the gala festivities until one of the guests was questioned at the entrance about his credentials for admission. In a story related by his grandson, Lawrence Sullivan Ross Clark '21, upon arrival, Sul's father, Shapley—well on to eighty years of age and a "tall and venerable" hardened frontier legend—was asked by the master of ceremonies to present an official inaugural ball invitation:

> "No Sir," promptly responded the old Captain.
> "Only those who have invitations are allowed to be present."
> The eye of the old veteran at first flashed, but appreciating the situation with a smile of humor, he said:
> "Well sir, if I am not allowed here, I believe I will go in and get my boy, Sul Ross, and take him back home and break up your ball."
> He got in.[39]

Gov. Sul Ross was one of the few postwar senior leaders of his generation to hold the governor's office in Texas. Following his two-term, four-year administration (1887–91), a line of younger, eager lawyers (a tradition of Texas attorneys general from the Democratic Party political machine) captured the statehouse. They were skilled in their trained legal professions but unconnected to and untested by the tribulations of the dynamics within the changing agricultural sector, the implications of the frontier in Texas, or the aftermath of war. Ross was often misjudged by the young upstarts and so-called progressives who wanted action and elements of swift change without having the breadth of background—political, commercial, and personal—that he and his generation brought with them to the governorship. No Texas governor after 1891 could boast life experiences and the ability to identify with the common man, the everyday Texan, quite like Sul Ross, who, for example, was routinely seen sitting on a bench in front of the state capitol in the late afternoon hours—just as he had sat as a teenager on the front porch of his father's hotel with young upstart Richard Coke back in Waco in the early 1850s to hash out the stories of the day—talking and bantering with Texans from all walks of life about their issues and concerns. This reservoir of experience and connection with the people of Texas, along with his God-given leadership talent and strategic thinking ability, provided the state with an incredible man of character, at the right moment and the right place.[40]

Governor Ross was what is often called "a legend in his own time." He had a "dazzling career" long before the rise of modern mass media hype or publicists who promoted the politicians of future generations. Few in the state of Texas had a combination of life experiences that rivaled the aura of the "boy captain" who had grown in expertise and wisdom to be a seasoned governor. One element among those detractors quipped that he was not a "pure" or "real" politician. Yet these rising political amateurs grossly misjudged the full meaning of his gravitas. In the words of his first inaugural address on January 18, 1887, before a crowd of citizens—and delivered from a makeshift stage in front of the ongoing construction of the new capital—Sul Ross prophetically captured the tone, opportunities, and challenges facing the state:[41]

> I have a profound hope, not clouded with the slightest doubt, that these great and vital measures will be undertaken with commendable temper, moderation, and fairness; and I feel confident that you will meet bravely, unselfishly, and loyally the great work confronting you; recognizing a common obligation to do full justice to all—the humblest as well as the highest—and make stronger the bonds which

should unite us as a people in a common, great destiny, commensurate with a State boundless in its resources, infinite its possibilities, and extending the largest freedom to pursuit in matter of religious concernment, social habits, and business engagements, with no respect of persons in regard to rank or place of birth—in unison with that political creed which peculiarly distinguishes our system of popular government.

The tone and confidence of the Ross administration were set. The newly inaugurated Governor Ross would prove to be a part of the transition and passage of the Texas frontier he had grown up on, fought for, and loved. He had a well-earned reputation as a fighter for what he believed and was a stalwart conservative. Texans in the late 1880s, as in the balance of the South, endeavored to broaden the economic base and reclaim the agricultural and commercial infrastructure that was destroyed during the war. To do this would require the attraction of new industry, increasingly large amounts of capital investment, the expansion of trade, ample educational facilities, and the improvement of agricultural practices, along with better access to consumer markets. Sul Ross was indeed not a politician in the truest sense of the term. This irritated his opposition, whom he routinely outmaneuvered, but endeared him to rank-and-file Texans. As a member of the 1875 Texas Constitutional Convention, he was a party to the conservative limited government and fiscal policies he was now elected and empowered to enforce. Compared to the executive power granted in other state constitutions of the era, the governor of Texas was a weak chief executive—which continues to this day. He was empowered to serve as commander-in-chief, execute laws, exercise the veto, represent the state in ceremonial events, and act as head of the party within the state. The Democratic Party of the era that endorsed Ross was conservative and exacted its power from its large agrarian base.[42]

In addition to the modernism implied by the post-Reconstruction "New South" theme that, it was hoped, would accelerate and diversify the Texas economy, new forces of conflict were at work in the transition of the "frontier" and rural sections of the state. Texas was truly in a period of transition; thus ensuring that a balance among forces would be critical. While there were scattered cases of vigilantism and other crime—including an increase in train robberies, leading the governor to offer cash rewards for the arrest of the responsible bandits—the state was no longer threatened by Comanche raiders and rampant lawlessness, as new frontier issues impacted the state. A majority of the Ross administration's challenges with the frontier dealt with land (who could own it and who could build on it with the support of state subsidies), grazing rights, the spread of barbed wire, fence cutting and "illegal enclosure," and the age-old problem of water rights.[43]

The future of the Texas frontier lands spawned disagreements between farmers and ranchers. In general terms, the better-financed ranchers wanted unfettered access to land for grazing, and the Grange–Farmers' Alliance coalition wanted fencing to keep cattle off their lands, better crop financing, and better access to markets. To assist agriculture statewide, the Texas Agriculture Experiment Station was established in 1887 to develop programs to help "farmers and stock raising," increase production, lower cost, provide the most current advancements, and expand markets. The idea to establish "experimental farms" to promote interest in agricultural education was proposed as early as 1877 by the Texas Grange—petitioning the legislature to create such a "teaching farm" at the A&M College. Cotton remained the dominant cash crop due to its resistance to drought and the higher return value per acre. Thus Ross worked with the legislature to offer assistance to farmers, address public land issues, and secure easier access to ownership. The legislature agreed and passed laws in an attempt to limit fraud, provide low-interest land loans, and develop new short-lease land laws.[44]

Cattlemen gradually agreed that there would be no stability until pastures were fenced, livestock branded, water rights defined, and more access opened to northern markets. Thus the invention and sale of improved barb wire by Joseph E. Glidden in the mid-1870s, the extension of railroad service into West Texas, and the discoveries of adequate groundwater and the windmill, in time, allowed a more peaceful and profitable advance into Texas's western open rangelands. However, within a decade, western range-fence wars, land disputes, and water rights spawned an epidemic of "wire cutters," dominated by feuds and local mob violence. Notwithstanding, the most important element in Texas and across the West was water, which led famed historian Walter Prescott Webb to conclude: "Water is more valuable than land."[45]

Three issues that were constantly just below the surface during the Ross administration were, first, the demands by agricultural organizations for regulation of the railroads; second, the obligation of the state to protect citizens from lawless acts of violence (and to bring violators to justice); and third, the unconnected issue of prohibition. Ross wanted railroads monitored and controlled "by statute" for the good of the people but not regulated to an extent that it hampered investment and new infrastructure in the state. The governor expected competition to allow for equitable freight rates, yet often the railroad manipulated both rates and schedules. T. R. Fehrenbach, in *Lone Star* (1968), noted: "The Texas government was in no sense hostile to commerce or business. Texans, like many 19th Century Americans, had a historical suspicion and antipathy to corporations, not so much because of what corporations did but because the idea was strongly held that no 'soulless enterprise' should be equated with human beings and given the full protection of the laws." The demand for a regulatory commission was debated constantly during Ross's time in office, yet a formal railroad commission was not created until the governor's successor, James Hogg, took office.[46]

Acts of violence continued statewide as Texas grew in population. The governor's strong stance against lawlessness dated from his time as sheriff of McLennan County and the formation of the Texas Sheriff's Association in 1874. To put the state behind local law enforcement officers, Ross issued a law-and-order proclamation in June 1887, authorizing rewards of $1,000 for the arrest and conviction of all individuals involved in a train robbery. To assist local sheriffs in curbing mob violence, a $500 fine was offered for each person who participated in a mob action resulting in the crime of murder. Sheriffs were advised to "put a posse in motion to intercept and arrest the fugitives." If local citizens were "unwilling or unable" to come to the support of the sheriff, he was to call on the governor for "such assistance as he may have at his command." The governor's message, carried statewide, linked strict enforcement of law and order with the future progress and prosperity of Texas.[47]

The governor's concern with lawlessness was echoed in a feature article in the *Austin Daily Statesman*, "The Little Cavalryman: His Utter Condemnation of Mob Law of Every Character," which was issued statewide after a string of mob violence and lynchings of both white and black men without a fair trial:

I am aware that it is sometime urged in justification of Lynch law so called that our laws are imperfect and not properly executed and because maladministration in the exercise of the poser belonging to the state and the counties to secure obedience, bad men under certain conditions may be relieved from punishment. This is unquestionably true and it would be strange if it were not since our laws are made by fallible human legislators, expounded by fallible human judges and executed by fallible officers. But this is no excuse for violating them such as they are.

The way to gain relief for the violation of law is not by inaugurating lawlessness. If so, we might as well tear down our temples of justice. The very worst law is better than no law; but those who have an interest in the country or the prosperity of the state; those who have property to be preserved by law and order; those who have liberties to be protected; those who have rights that they cherish are the last men in the community who should sanction to acts of violence. Punishment is not to be administered by way of vengeance.[48]

In the case of prohibition, a very tricky subject for the Democratic Party, Ross favored local option and was clearly against any laws to limit such free public choices. As Judith Benner concluded in her biography *Sul Ross* (1983), Ross felt that a small number of supporters hoped to "drown out the voice of reason." While roundly attacked in the media as "a saloon stump speaker," Ross noted, "No government ever succeeded in changing the moral convictions of its citizens by force." Notwithstanding, there was enough prohibition sentiment in the legislature to pass a proposed constitutional amendment to prevent the manufacture or sale of liquor in the state and to present it to the citizens of Texas for a vote.[49]

Given the polarization of the prohibition issue, the governor played no overt public role in the public debate, yet the "wet" opposition to the amendment, headquartered in Waco, was chaired by Ross's former statewide campaign manager, George Clark. US senators from Texas Samuel B. Maxey and John H. Reagan—both friends, fellow veterans, and political supporters of Ross—voiced strong support for prohibition. The halls of the US Congress were not reflective of the attitudes of rural Texas—particularly the more than two hundred communities of Czech and German Texans that stretched from the coastal plain to the Hill Country to East Texas and traditionally enjoyed their "spirited" drink. When presented to Texans, the prohibition amendment gained strong support from African American Republicans, but the amendment was defeated overwhelmingly by a vote of 129,270 for and 220,627 against. Prohibition would not resurface again as a heated political issue in Texas for more than two decades.[50]

The Ross approach to conservative spending practices resulted in a budget surplus, thus confirming his belief that the best government was the one that governed least. The surplus confounded the progressive opposition, who wanted no limits on spending. More often than not in a legislative setting, it was harder to deal with surpluses among elected officials than a looming fiscal deficit. Ideas on how to handle the excess money abounded, yet Ross maintained a positive influence upon the solons to save the treasury windfall for a rainy day. In another successful venture, the governor presided over the week-long dedication of the new state capitol on May 16, 1888. The dedication speech for the new capitol on behalf of the people of Texas was delivered by A&M College ex-cadet State Senator Temple Lea Houston, a member of the Corps of Cadets in 1877–78. Built from Texas red granite (from Burnet County), the massive new capitol building, standing 310 feet in height, rivaled the size of the capitol in Washington, DC, and was hailed as a clear indication of the Texas economic recovery. In fact, it was seven feet taller than the national capitol when measured from the grade line to the top of the statue, the "Goddess of Liberty," on the dome, and in 1888 it was considered the seventeenth-largest building in the world.[51]

The Empire State of the South

The first governor of Texas to actively promote the state to investors outside the Lone Star borders, Sul Ross first attempted to invite Pres. Grover Cleveland to Texas for the 1889 State Fair and Exposition in Dallas. When the president declined, he seized on a second opportunity to take the state message on business prospects directly to the East Coast, when Texas became involved in a 1.5 million–acre borderland dispute case with Oklahoma along the Red River in Greer County, under review by the US Supreme Court. To advocate for their case, the governor headed a delegation of Texans to "visit" with the US attorney general and took the occasion to meet with Pres. Benjamin Harrison—who he knew during his time in the Antelope Hills campaign in 1858—at the White House.

The most compelling testimony on behalf of Texas's claim of ownership was provided by Ross's aging father, Shapley, who provided details, maps, and boundary information dating back to 1847. However, the case was held in favor of Oklahoma. With all their efforts exhausted and after a grand dinner with the Texas congressional delegation hosted by Senator Richard Coke, the delegation departed Washington by Pullman train up the coast to New York City to visit former president Grover Cleveland.[52]

The East Coast media coverage and promotion of Texas—fueled by a local fascination with both Sul Ross's frontier days as well as business prospects in the Lone Star State—proved a tremendous success in presenting the opportunities in the state to easterners enthralled with the lore and wildness of the "West." This was further reflected in a steady stream of magazine articles from the pulp press, promotional literature to attract new immigrants, and volumes, both fiction and nonfiction, that filled the market, such as the 1889 novel *The White Mustang: A Tale of the Lone Star State*, by Lieutenant R. H. Jayne, whose colorful narrative of life on the frontier fueled the pressing East Coast urban interest in the West (though reflecting the dominant stereotypes of the time), as is evident in the following passage:

> The red men [sic] were only four in number, so that the first glimpse of their assailants showed them the uselessness of making a stand. Firing their guns, they flung themselves, as far as possible, on the opposite side of their animals, and, with fierce whoops, sought to throw the cowboys into fatal confusion by dashing among and around them. But the plainsmen were too experienced in such warfare to be affected by the hullabaloo, and, drawing their revolvers, they emptied them right and left with amazing rapidity.[53]

Texas was presented to eastern investors and would-be southern settlers as a land of opportunity, with prospects for future capital investment (land, railroads, and seaports), trade (cotton, cattle, and lumber), and tourism (with "tourism" as a veiled attraction not for visitors but for immigrants to settle and improve the vast lands within the state's boundaries). Ross, responding to reporters' questions and rumors of commercial and trade friction between the North and South, dismissed these notions as "impractical" and speculative political rhetoric. Addressing President Cleveland and a group of New York investors and bankers,

Governor Ross was clear in his message regarding the progress of and opportunities in Texas: "We have come a long way. The State of Texas, with her good laws, good schools, light taxation, and cheap and fertile lands, is already inviting an influx of capital and immigration that is contributing to build up her power, wealth, and numbers at a compound ratio."[54]

Upon the governor's return to Texas, following his grand tour de force in the North, Texans widely approved of his message, with the May 25, 1890, *Austin Daily Statesman* noting, "[M]ore was learned about Texas than ever known before. The enforcement of the laws, the happiness and prosperity of the people, the protection given property and life . . . the State is in a better condition in every way now than it has ever been in its history. He [Ross] is recognized in the North as a remarkable man. His life is known, and he is considered a marvel in having succeeded in developing from a ranger boy [captain] into a governor."[55]

CHAPTER 2

Called to the College

Lawrence Sullivan Ross can be understood only in terms of the
immense prestige and public esteem which he brought with him
to the office of president of the Agricultural and Mechanical
College of Texas . . . not only did he hold the public's confidence,
but he proved to be a very efficient and effective administrator.

Henry C. Dethloff, A Centennial
History of Texas A&M University

The power to discriminate, to build up one place and tear down
another, to build up one individual or firm and tear down another,
is a power that should not exist if it can possibly be avoided.

Richard Coke, August 24, 1890

Sul Ross won reelection to a second term as governor by near acclamation, with more than 70 percent of the popular vote, opposed only
slightly by the prohibition candidate Marion Martin of Corsicana. The
issue of railroad regulation trust-busting continued to be widely debated,
as Ross's attorney general Stephen Hogg continued to build his career
on claims that he could prevent the corporate monopolies and railroads
entering the state from unjustly taking Texas land grants and charging
unreasonable rates. Other key issues in 1888 included improved public
education, tax reduction, and protection of voting rights statewide.
Governor Ross was not the firebrand that Hogg wanted him to be, and
Ross was quick to remind Hogg and the Texas State Legislature that the
goal should clearly be to regulate—not destroy—the railroad, as a small

vocal minority advocated. Ross knew, as did many across the state, that the ills of the railroads indeed needed to be corralled, yet not at the expense of future growth, the attraction of new capital investment, and the industrialization of the state's economy. Notwithstanding, the vocal farming sector opposition clamored for a state regulatory "commission" to control the railroads.[1]

Some background information on railroad expansion in Texas is critical to understanding both the site location and the future growth of the Agricultural & Mechanical College of Texas after the opening of classes on October 4, 1876. At the end of the Civil War, there were only a dozen short-line railroads, aggregating less than five hundred miles of active track. Most existing tracks in Texas radiated from the Galveston-Houston area, and the farthest north any line ran was a small-gauge track (standard gauge was added in 1876) to Millican, a railhead for cotton and produce shipments, in southern Brazos County. Thus, following the passage of the legislative act on April 17, 1871, to establish the A&M College of Texas, three commissioners were named by the governor to locate a suitable site for a new institution, with there being three primary criteria (1) located on high, well-drained ground; (2) positioned near a plentiful source of freshwater; and (3) located on a transportation line accessible from the (then) major population areas of Texas: Galveston and Houston, Austin, San Antonio, Corsicana and Dallas, and Waco–East Texas in general. Gov. Richard Coke convened the first A&M College board of directors meeting, which he chaired, on campus on June 2, 1875, to inspect the site and building program.[2]

The proposed college site four miles south of Bryan, the county seat of Brazos County, was largely considered because of the available transportation. The first postwar railroad constructed northward from Houston via Millican was the Houston and Texas Central (H&TC), which by early 1871 passed the "proposed college site" before reaching Corsicana by December and Dallas in July 1872. This was completed only weeks before the site selection commissioners visited Bryan. The H&TC, after reaching Dallas, merged in 1874 with the Missouri, Kansas, and Texas (the "Katy"), built southbound from Kansas City, and was in competition with the International and Great Northern (IGNR), owned by the syndicate headed by tycoon Jay Gould. For decades, the portion of the trackage from Houston to Bryan and on to Dallas was referred to as the H&TC. Thus the railroad line that allowed Gov. Richard Coke and his party to come by rail from Austin to dedicate the new college campus in early October 1876 was the result of a spur line extended from the H&TC west of Hearne, known as Valley Junction, to Austin in early 1876.[3]

The furor over the judicious regulation of the railroads briefly diminished in the late 1880s, with the governor's concern and his attention during his last two years in office focused on education, the advancement of agriculture and ranching across the state, and care and housing for all indigent citizens and disabled veterans. Education at all levels was a key area of concern. The average duration of formal education in Texas was eight years. This was well behind other states, and a key reason for this was the predominant agriculture economy, the shortage of good schools and teachers, and a lack of funding. Ross's role in education dated from his days as a member of the Texas Constitutional Convention of 1875. He voted to appropriate no more than $40,000 to the A&M College for its "immediate and successful operation" and championed the establishment of an "industrial school" to teach the vocational trades. One motion to increase access to education came in the form of a proposal, which took more than a decade to implement, to have the state provide free textbooks. In his first message to a joint session of the Texas Legislature in January 1886, Ross expressed "profound regret that our reformatory efforts to save neglected and forsaken children, have not keep pace with our programs in common school education." Thus, legislation championed and signed into law by Governor Ross included an asylum for mental patients, a state home for orphans, $50,000 in funding for an "Institute for Deaf, Dumb, and Blind Negro Youth," enhanced veteran's land grants, and a state rehabilitation prison in Gatesville for Texas youth, as well as an appropriation of $100,000 for drought assistance for West Texas.[4]

"You Have Done Well"

Ross was one of the last governors of the state to have been a Confederate veteran. His concern for Confederate veterans was a hallmark of his last few years in office, which was met with little attention by the general public. He felt the state should express their gratitude for veterans' service, providing housing and caring for the homeless and disabled as well as their widows, noting that Union veterans living in Texas received federal pensions. Ross's efforts to establish the Confederate Veterans House and fund its operations continued for the balance of his life. As a ranking veteran and the titular head of veterans across the state, it was obvious to him that only action at the state level with some limited local support (offered by some county commissioners) could address the concerns of particularly elderly and disabled veterans of the lost cause. Thus it would have been considered derelict if he had not used his influence and stature as governor to address the needs of veterans, moving to establish a hospital and affordable housing for them as needed. His efforts were stalled by the Texas constitution of 1876, prohibiting state appropriations to any "individual, association of individuals, municipal or other corporation whatever," except in cases of "public calamity." The statute was partially circumvented with a broad interpretation of the state Land Grant Program of 1881, which provided land (that could be sold) to veterans. This was further advanced when land grants to the railroads were halted. Charity organizations, as we know them today, did not exist, and there was no federal funding for the indigent in the 1890s. Thus Ross was able to gain approval for an appropriation to build a home for veterans in Austin, reminding the legislature, "[S]urely Texas ought to afford one home for the defenders, as the old soldiers of the Confederacy can look nowhere for help . . . if this duty is neglected, the state prosperity will only make more glaring her ingratitude."[5]

To slightly distance himself from seeming too overt, Governor Ross placed his chief of staff, Maj. Henry M. Holmes, in charge of the veterans' home project. This attracted attention because Holmes, born in Bristol, England, and an immigrant to Waco, was a prewar family friend of the Rosses. With family and roots in Connecticut, Holmes departed Texas in late 1861 to go north and enlist in the Union army. He fought in a number of campaigns, was taken prisoner at the Battle of the Wilderness (May 1864), and released in a POW exchange after four months. Following the war, he was stationed with the Twenty-Fourth Infantry at Fort McKavett and discharged in 1871. When the war ended, he returned and settled in Mason, Texas; entered into business, land development, and farming; and was elected justice of the peace in 1872. Prior to moving to Austin, he played a prominent role as a prosecuting attorney in the bloody 1875 cattle rustling feud known as the "Hoo Doo War"—*hoo doo* being a nineteenth-century expression for bad luck. Known and recognized by all as "the Major," Holmes and his family returned to Mason at the end of Ross's term as governor. From 1891–93, he was known as a vocal advocate in settling unresolved Indian depredation cases and claims regarding kidnappings and horse thefts dating back to the late 1860s. He would be one of Sul Ross's most trusted confidants and friends up until his death in August 1895.[6]

To supplement the legislative stipend for veteran hospital care, Ross informed former Texas Confederate groups or "camps" across the state that donations to the "Confederate House" and medical care would be needed to offset rising costs. Major Holmes set up an informal organization with the administrator of the veteran's hospital so that they could receive moderate donations. While philanthropy was not yet a big part of social norms at the time, one such donation came from the cadets and staff at the A&M College, with Ross acknowledging the timely contribution:[7]

> Executive Office of the Governor
>
> Austin, April 28th 1890
>
> Proj Louis L. McInnis
>
> My dear sir,
>
> On my return, I find yours of 24th Inst. with S/D [sight draft] for $51.65 donation to Confederate House. Kindly sent by Mrs. McInnis as a contribution from the officers & students of the A&M College. This will be delivered to Col. Shelly at once and I desire to express my hearty thanks for this aid to remember the old Confederates. They tender their gratitude to Mrs. McInnis & the liberal donors.
>
> Respectfly [*sic*]
> L. S. Ross

The Ross governorship was a period of continued economic growth and fiscal prudence in Texas, marked by the character, honesty, self-reliance, and dignity he brought to the office. Furthermore, he worked to enhance Texans' access to public education as well as to enhance indigent care and reduce crime and election fraud—opposing those who wanted a poll tax. The attempt to limit voters was vocally proposed by Senator A. W. Terrell, who targeted both African Americans and Mexican Americans for disenfranchisement. As with his days as sheriff in Waco, the governor was very vocal in his "condemnation of mob violence of every character and urged the people to be fearless and prompt [in the] vindication of the supremacy of the law wherever and by whomsoever they maybe assailed." The *Austin Daily Statesman* proclaimed on the eve of his departure, "You have done well . . . he was wise, conservative, and patriotic, as a man he was without reproach." Thus, as the state and the Democratic Party entered a new tumultuous political era of progressive ideals and change, it was not surprising that the "little cavalryman" was repeatedly encouraged through the mid-1890s to run for a then-unprecedented third term and restore decorum to the image of the state and the governor's office. Flattered, Ross was nevertheless adamantly opposed to any such idea.[8]

Florine Ross was the eldest daughter of Sul and Lizzie Ross. A socialite in Austin during Ross's governorship, she eventually moved to the college to assist several student organizations. She married Prof. Henry H. Harrington in 1892, and their first son was named Sul Ross Harrington. Source: Texas Collection, Baylor University

Imbued with the importance of education from an early age, Ross was the first governor to champion education *for all Texans*. His efforts to provide care for the indigent with the "care of colored lunatics [the then-current term for those with impaired mental health] and for the colored deaf, dumb, and blind asylum, [at a cost of] about $650,000 annually," was in concert with his goals to improve educational programs. While there was opposition to providing ample funding for the education of African Americans in Texas, Ross became an advocate of education, beginning with the Constitutional Convention of 1875 and during his tenure in the Texas Senate. As governor, he used his often-limited options to fund higher education, including allocations for Prairie View Normal College, established to provide education for African Americans. To counter those attempting to limit education for African Americans in Texas, in the last months of his term, he released a detailed printed circular and an analysis of student participation, tax revenue, and funding.[9] To fight against those who opposed funding proportionate programs, Governor Ross argued, "Although colored tax payers pay but one thirty-third of the taxes collected for school purposes, they receive the same proportionate share of the school funds that the whites do." He further stated, "The negro shall enjoy equal rights before the law," and he openly combatted and opposed ongoing efforts by some legislators, such as Senator Terrell in Austin, to impose a poll tax and property ownership requirement as a condition to vote. While post-Reconstruction era race relations were often tense and contentious, the leading African American educator and spokesman in Texas, Edward L. Blackshear (future president of Prairie View College), was vocal in praising Governor Ross for his firm stand on education: "It is a certain fact, as testified to by the noble governor, a man whom all classes and races in Texas love and delight to honor, it is, I say, a certain fact the Negro is advancing in all that constitutes a Christian civilization."[10]

The Road to A&M

In early 1890, Sul Ross was at the height of his popularity and political career in the Texas governor's office. Roundly respected and admired, even his opponents praised his conduct in office. As early as April, some encouraged him to buck the tradition of two terms and seek a third term as governor. His popularity, even-handed governing, and expanded political base made the prospect of remaining in Austin a real possibility. However, his young and eager attorney general, Stephen Hogg, had already made it known that his next goal was to be governor of Texas, as had Lt. Gov. Thomas B. Wheeler, who nevertheless soon dropped from the race. There were hints that if he so desired, Ross could be a shoo-in for a US senatorial seat in Washington, which he declined. After all, the options of staying in Austin or going to Washington would both prevent his return to farming and ranching and his family in Waco. His father, Shapley, died in September 1889, making Sul Ross and his brother Peter the heads of the family and fully responsible for their investments in McLennan County.[11]

Sometime in late May, after his return from New York City, Ross had a confidential conversation with his close friend and then president of the A&M College board of directors, Archibald J. Rose of Salado, on the image and growing problems at the institution and concerns about its future well-being. The chairman of the faculty and chief administrative officer of the college, Louis L. McInnis—who Clarence Ousley characterized by saying, "[H]e gave to the institution singular devotion and highly intelligent service to the College almost from its beginning"—proved in 1887 to be an effective leader of the small campus. By 1888, the college's academic requirements and programs transitioned from a three-year to a four-year degree-granting curriculum in eleven academic departments: agriculture, mechanical engineering, mathematics, English and history, civil engineering, horticulture, drawing, chemistry, veterinary science, languages, and military science and tactics. In addition to degree programs, the college retained a basic vocational training schedule to grant "certificates of proficiency" in machinery, blacksmithing, carpentry, surveying, and dairy farming. Legislative funding was in short supply, cadet housing was crowded, and facilities were in need of repair and upgrade. A minor crisis due to an acute deficiency of water was briefly averted by drilling a couple of deep wells.[12]

Agrarian Crusade

The prime influence in Texas during the decade prior to the turn of the twentieth century was the vocal agrarian movement that organized to improve all aspects of farmers' lives, from the improvement of crops to the best conditions to profitably market produce. The recovery of the farming sector during the years following the Civil War was dismally slow, due to a lack of capital, poor markets and unstable market pricing, runaway freight rates, and a shortage of farm equipment. Ross cautiously opposed all new regulations that could impact the agriculture sector, and he signed the Texas antitrust legislation, which initiated the most proactive and progressive aspects of the Ross years. To highlight the changes in agriculture across the state, Clarence N. Ousley, an 1881 graduate of the A&M College of Alabama in Auburn and editor of the *Texas Farm and Ranch Weekly* (and, beginning in 1890, managing editor of the *Galveston Daily News*) was active in promoting the A&M College. However, the leading advocate of farm and ranch issues statewide was Archibald J. Rose of Salado, who, as noted by Robert Calvert, was "the most important granger in Texas." He was a lifelong champion of farming improvements and the expansion of public education and agricultural colleges for all Texans. His views on the farmers' movement and education would have a direct, lasting impact on the A&M College and its role in the enhancement of farming and ranching across the state. The Briscoe Library in Austin has a treasure trove of Rose's primary documents, including remarks penciled on a Big Chief Tablet. Grange Worthy Grand Master Rose specifically remarked on one item that he simply titled as "Agriculture."[13]

Agriculture

Farming is the noblest calling of man.

From the products of the soil all classes are fed and made to thrive. Without the farmer they could not exist. The farmers produce the wealth of the nation. But they are like the fountain heads of the crystal stream that continuously pours out their sparkling fluid—sending them forth to increase the Plan adopted by the Grange will do this and nothing short of this will ever do so.

Every encouragement should be given the farmer to encourage agriculture in all its branches and every legitimate means should be used to enable them to retain from the farm the profits made there. There are other reforms necessary that must be made by the farmers. There must be closer economy by them until they can afford ready money and it is an unjust thing not to give full value in exchange for these things. There is no question but that the best interest of the country demands that after meeting the necessary expense of marketing the products of the farm and releasing their supplies that the balance should remain upon the farm and not continue to flow into commercial centers.

It is a pleasant thing to contribute to the comfort and hapiness [*sic*] of the human family. This pleasure is increased in proportion to the appreciation shown by the beneficiaries.

It is a great and good work enough by the farmers in producing for the world all the necessaries to sustain life, and the material from which they are to be clothed. To pay for luxuries—again there must be more system and more industry by many who consume too much time around their grumbling.

Following his second inauguration, Governor Ross recommended both support and funding for higher education. In the spring of 1888, the governor called the legislature into a special session to consider a number of items, including education. Faculty chairman McInnis and the A&M Board drafted an itemized funding request totaling some $100,000. This bold proposal for funding (the highest to date at the time) was not unusual, given that it was normal to request more appropriations than were expected to be granted. Following standard practice, the legislature reviewed the request and ultimately approved a $44,500 allocation. Texas A&M was pleased and adjusted its priorities to concentrate on its dorms and inferior wood-burning stoves for heating, outdated gas lamps, an assembly hall, overdue repairs, and some much-needed improvements to the campus water supply. The biannual visit by the joint Senate and House legislative committee made special note in their final report of the college's persistently poor water supply, concluding, "[The campus] buildings are not insured, thus a system of water works [and a new well] may save thousands of dollars of property damage." To reduce the risk of wood-burning stoves and gas lamps, it was strongly recommended that an electric power plant be constructed on campus. In early June, Governor Ross traveled to the A&M campus for commencement exercises and special drill performances by the Corps of Cadets—featuring the first public appearance of the Scott Guards, the cadet honor guard that was precursor to the Ross Volunteers. Following the graduation of sixteen students in June 1888, enrollment for the 1888–89 school year declined slightly to some

180 cadets. The good cheer of funding and graduation soon dissolved into an undercurrent of discord and tension on campus.[14]

Rumors of recalcitrant faculty fighting and factionalism, financial mismanagement at the college (which later proved unfounded), unrest among the cadets, and tinkering by the board of directors proved fatal for the McInnis administration. The commandant of cadets, Lt. William S. Scott, informed Chairman Rose that the faculty was replete in "disgraceful squabbles." Cadet correspondence housed in the Cushing Library echoed the same feelings as Lieutenant Scott and the discourse of professors; Cadet Lucius Holman, concerned with the operations and unrest at the college, wrote home, "[T]his school is going down faster than I ever saw . . . they are not managing it rite [sic]."[15]

A Scare at the A&M College

About a week ago the students rooming in the Mess Hall building were thrown into a state of consternation at the sound of a terrible explosion in the third story of the building. The facts, as they came to us, are as follows: Two students who lived in Bryan are [sic] permitted to return home from college on Friday night and remain with their parents until Monday morning. So last Saturday a week ago, while in Bryan, a fellow student knowing they were in town, went into their room to be to himself where he could study and seek repose.

It was cold. He determined to make a fire. The student put paper in the stove, laid on the kindling, struck the match, and before he could say "Jack Robinson," he was thrown violently against the door some eight feet from the stove. The stove was carried to the ceiling in the "twinkling of an eye," and the window sash lay in shattered pieces on the ground below, a distance of sixty feet. The student was somewhat mutilated. His hair was singed off close and he was terribly burned about the face and eyes.

The cause of the explosion was a pound of gunpowder which the young men from Bryan had placed in the stove to prevent accident of any kind that might happen while absent from their room. Excitement ran high at the time of the explosion. Bedsteads, mattresses, books and students were seen tumbling out of the third story windows, and it was thought that the State of Texas would be minus one of her public buildings. We are not informed as to insurance, and we will not comment on the propriety of having gunpowder or dynamite in the A. & M. College buildings.

Source: L. L. McInnis Scrapbook, Cushing Archives, ca. September 1885

The first cracks in the McInnis tenure at the college began with the resignation (later proved to be a forced termination) of the agent or secretary of the board, Thomas M. Scott (no relation to the army's Lieutenant Scott), in late February 1890. There was outside pressure from both the Grange and the Farmers' Alliance concerning the quality of the agricultural programs at the college. McInnis seemed to quickly address their concerns and recommendations. Many of the ills pointed out by outside detractors could be solved with an increased appropriation from the legislature for new facilities and dorms. However, by spring, campus politics had evolved into a behind-the-scenes effort, led by faculty members William Bringhurst, George Curtis, and Charles Fountain, to foment dissatisfaction and discredit McInnis. Unrest seemed to be settling down prior to the spring graduation. However, following an editorial in the *Bryan Eagle* that predicted "radical changes" at the college, by early June, more than half of the seventeen-member college staff and faculty either resigned or were terminated. Governor Ross was a special guest for the campus graduation of the class of 1890 and final review in mid-June, but there is no confirmed information that the unrest was discussed with him at that time.[16]

Changes were also underway regarding the composition of the Texas A&M board of directors. In 1888 Christopher Garrett and George Dilley, two staunch McInnis supporters, left the board. The governor then appointed J. D. Fields of Manor, L. L. Foster of Austin, and John Adriance of Columbia. A. J. Rose, a director since 1886, was selected as chairman of the board. Longtime board member William Cavitt of Bryan was the only sitting director not appointed during Governor Ross's term in office. Whether by design or chance, as Henry Dethloff notes in the *Centennial History of Texas A&M*, "This then was now a 'Ross's Board.'"[17]

Chairman Rose was in frequent contact with Faculty Chairman McInnis, advising, "[T]hings are not in the best shape at the college." Thus, at some point in May or June, a scenario was considered by the board to conduct a reorganization of the administration at midyear at the college, in preparation to relieve those who were considered problem staff. This would be accompanied by a search for a new chief administrator—with the reinstated title of president—whose prime duties would involve the administration of the school's affairs. Knowledge of financial matters, as well as a solid understanding of agriculture in Texas, along with political connections in Austin, would prove helpful. Yet the prospect of Sul Ross going to A&M would not attend to his desire to return to his farm and family in Waco.[18]

There were other, more personal aspects that Ross considered when making his decision. At the end of his gubernatorial term in January 1891, he would be fifty-three years old, and the prospect of seeking elective office or starting new ventures in Waco seemed out of the question. However, he harbored two major concerns: First, there was the issue of his health. Four years in Austin had not improved his bouts with recurring fever, possible malaria from his cavalry duty in the Mississippi swamps, and a constant string of colds. These conditions were further complicated by lingering pain and periodic paralysis (most likely a recurring neurological condition) and discomfort from the severe wounds he sustained in the Wichita Village campaign in 1858. The second concern that led him to strongly consider the presidency at A&M was that he had four children who needed access to higher education. In early 1891, Harvey would be seventeen years old, Frank would be fifteen, Elizabeth or "Bessie" would be fourteen, and the youngest, Neville, was eleven and not far behind. Sul's eldest son, Lawrence Jr., was twenty-two and

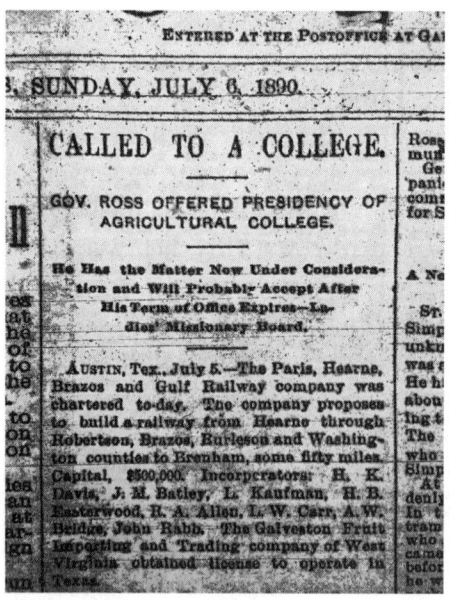

"Called to a College" was a feature article in newspapers statewide on July 6, 1890, announcing the offering of the presidency of the A&M College to Governor Ross. Source: Author's collection

had taken a job in Austin. Florine, at the age of twenty-one, had plans to attend school in Waco. As president of A&M, Ross's children would have reduced fees or no tuition and a fine education. The boys would attend A&M, and Bessie would attend school in Waco with family.[19]

In early June the board of directors held their meeting at Prairie View Normal School near Hempstead, Texas, but Governor Ross was not in attendance due to accepting an invitation to attend graduation ceremonies at the A&M campus. A majority of the matters covered at the board meeting, attended by members Rose, Cavitt, Foster, and Adriance, involved the operations at Prairie View Normal and one primary administrative action concerning the future of the A&M College. The position of chairman of the faculty, held by Prof. Louis McInnis, was abolished effective July 1, 1890. The first and only official written mention of the creation of the position of "president" in the board minutes occurred at the end of the meeting. In the interim, the board approved English professor William Lorraine Bringhurst "to take temporary charge of the books, papers, accounts and money and property of the college on and after July 1st, and until the selection of the President." On June 7, the board ordered Bringhurst to jointly fill his teaching position and the office occupied by McInnis in Old Main, to "familiarize himself with the duties." McInnis was without a job, and despite his best efforts, he was not rehired at A&M, exiting to enter private business in Bryan as a banker.[20]

On July 1, 1890, at its fiftieth called meeting since 1875, the board reconvened on the A&M campus, with members Rose, Cavitt, Foster, Fields, and Adriance in attendance. After a number of brief administrative items, including accepting the resignation of Walter Wipprecht, a special chemist at the Agricultural Experiment Station, the board entertained a motion to elect Gov. Lawrence Sullivan Ross as president of the A&M College of Texas, "to take effect at the end of his present term of office as Governor." Rose and Cavitt had strongly lobbied for Ross to resign in July or August to immediately come to the campus. Ross refused, with the board placing Bringhurst as the interim chief agent of the college in the newly created position of vice president. In a final, rather anticlimactic, yet very important action, the board named a small committee to investigate the cost of bringing electric lighting to the campus and determine "if as many as 200 sixteen candle power electric lights can be placed in the College at a cost of not exceeding $500."[21]

With rumors circulating in Bryan after the McInnis dismissal in early June, the A&M board sent a formal letter to Governor Ross and simultaneously released it to the press, timed to hit the highest statewide circulation in the Sunday editions:[22]

The Galveston News—Galveston, Texas, Sunday, July 6, 1890

CALLED TO A COLLEGE

GOV. ROSS OFFERED PRESIDENCY OF AGRICULTURAL COLLEGE

He Has the Matter Now Under Consideration and Will Probably Accept after His Term of Office Expires

Austin, Texas July 5.—The Governor took the following under advisement today:

Hon. L. S. Ross, Governor of Texas –

Dear Sir: We the undersigned constituting the board of directors of the A&M College of Texas, take this method of notifying you we have unanimously elected you to the office of president of the college, to take effect at the expiration of your term of office as governor. In taking this step we deem it proper and right to briefly state the reasons underlying our action, which are as follows:

1. That the government of the college has been changed so as to divorce the purely professional and technical work of the teachers from any connection with the general business management and disciplinary authority with the view of securing the best executive and administrative ability in the general management of the institution. The president will therefore be charged with the business management and disciplinary authority of the college.

2. We believe that you possess in a high degree the qualifications essential to success in the administration of the affairs of the institution, and that as its president you would be afforded the opportunity of rendering a service to the people of Texas, second in no respect to any you have heretofore preformed during your long and honorable career, either as a private citizen or a public official. Your identity of interest with the agricultural class specially and your knowledge of their conditions and needs, in our judgment, render it peculiarly appropriate that in retiring from the office of chief executive of this state, you should become head of the institution around which centers

the hopes of the great body of people of the entire state of Texas, and the purpose of whose existence is to inculcate the dignity of intelligent labor and disseminate a scientific knowledge of agriculture and mechanical arts.

3. We believe that your election to this office will meet with the hearty and unqualified approval of the people of the entire state, and that they will regard your acceptance of this call to their service as an additional evidence of your devotion to their highest and best interests.

Awaiting a reply at your earliest convenience we have the honor to remain respectfully—

A. J. Rose, President
W. R. Cavitt
L. L. Foster
John D. Fields
John Adriance

Pride of the State

The response to the Ross appointment in the major newspapers in Dallas, Galveston, Houston, Bryan, and Austin was overwhelmingly positive and reported as exceeding all expectations for the future of the college. Local residents, who had the most to gain commercially from a successful and growing college, demonstrated their approval with a large nighttime meeting in downtown Bryan, organized by Mayor Clifford A. Adams, to draft a petition of support for the Ross nomination. Statewide, editorials stressed that the governor's "firm executive hand guided by a just mind" was exactly what the college needed. The cascade of positive approval surely impacted Ross's decision. As had happened before in Ross's life, as biographer Judith Benner rightly noted, "the job sought the man."[23]

During the balance of July, while a tremendous amount of preplanning and conversation had gone on behind the scenes with the governor and board members, Ross carefully considered the appointment and his obligations in Waco. Numerous offers were extended to Ross, including those from friends and admirers in Mississippi, who hoped to lure him to their state with the offer of a large cotton plantation. Except for an unconfirmed job offer from St. Edwards University in Austin, whose cornerstone laying the governor had officiated in September 1888, two additional unnamed proposals were received from commercial entities with good salary potential, yet it was suspected these were even farther away from Waco than the A&M College.[24]

The lure of running for elective office apparently was, in fact, a very low consideration by the governor, in spite of the fact that in his last months as governor and over the next three to four years, he would receive vocal partisan support and numerous calls to again enter the political arena. The concern for his family and his fragile health—unknown but to a small group of friends and immediate family—warranted a departure from public office, as he confirmed shortly after coming to A&M in a confidential letter to the Major. The elective option did not appeal to him because he was "becoming too much in love with rest of body & mind to be sorely tempted by the applause of [elective office] a fickle populace."[25]

In early August, Ross and Rose again had a long conversation, prior to a called board meeting at the Driskill Hotel in Austin, that confirmed the president's salary in the amount of $3,500 (the governor's salary was $4,000) and ensured he would have complete authority on campus, a suitable campus residence would be provided, and his children would be allowed to attend college at little or no expense. Interestingly, there is no indication that any detractors or the media drew attention to the fact that the college board of directors that nominated Ross was one of his own making—however, this would become a politically charged topic of discussion months after he accepted the presidency.[26]

Rose and Ross were fully aware of the appointment of "former governors" in Texas. The news media took little notice of the fact that Gov. Oran M. Roberts held power when the law that created the University of Texas was enacted. In addition to presiding over the convention of Texas secession, he was hired at the University of Texas by the first board of regents he had appointed. While his appointment was considered "popular" at the time, one observer noted, "it bespoke a connection between politics and school that lingered long." Furthermore, little notice was made, then and now, that the first University of Texas president (chairman of the faculty), John W. Mallet, along with nearly all the principal faculty, were devout former Confederates: Leslie Waggener, the first

English professor; Robert L. Dabney, professor of philosophy; and law professors Robert S. Gould and Roberts.[27]

The month-long wait for an answer was ended on August 8, 1890, when Governor Ross released a detailed letter of acceptance to the board and published his views on the college and agricultural education, the need for discipline, the value of military training, and the importance of the college in preparing its students for the future challenges facing

Table 2.1. Postwar Confederate generals serving as college presidents

Gen. Ellison Capers	Chancellor, University of the South (Sewanee)
Gen. Henry Clayton	President, University of Alabama
Gen. Josiah Gorgas	President, University of Alabama
Gen. Daniel H. Hill	President, University of Arkansas
Gen. G. W. Custis Lee	President, Washington [and Lee] College*
Gen. Robert E. Lee	President, Washington [and Lee] College*
Gen. Stephen D. Lee	President, A&M College of Mississippi
Gen. L. L. Lomax	President, Virginia Polytechnic Institute
Gen. Mark Lowrey	Founder and president, Blue Mountain College
Gen. Lawrence S. Ross	President, A&M College of Texas
Gen. Edmund Kirby Smith	President, University of Nashville
Gen. Alexander P. Stewart	Chancellor, University of Mississippi

*The name was changed in October 1870.

Texas. Furthermore, his emphasis on the need for relevant-quality agricultural programs was a clear signal to both the Grange and the Farmers' Alliance regarding their concerns on the future of the college. Thus it was Ross's goal and obligation "to secure for the institution a commanding eminence that will make it the pride of the State."[28]

Sul Ross would join a group of a dozen former general officers in the Confederate army, including Robert E. Lee, to become president of a major academic institution in the South between 1875 to 1900. In terms of other Texas governors, one predecessor, Oran M. Roberts, taught law at the University of Texas and one successor, Pat M. Neff, became president of Baylor University in 1932 (see table 2.1).[29]

GOVERNOR ROSS' LETTER ACCEPTING THE PRESIDENCY OF THE AGRICULTURAL AND MECHANICAL COLLEGE OF TEXAS[30]

Executive Office: Austin, Texas   August 8, 1890

To President Rose and Members of the Board of Directors
A. and M. College

Gentlemen—Respectfully acknowledging the high honor, I make this formal declaration of acceptance of the presidency of the Agricultural and Mechanical College. I hope to meet your reasonable expectations by assisting the harmonious, intelligent and combined efforts of the officers and teachers in the several departments to make its efficiency such as to give it a high rank among the kindred institutions of the country. That the proper care, training, and education of the youth of the State is of vital importance to its welfare needs only to be mentioned to be appreciated, and I have always believed that their minds, hands, and hearts should be trained in unison, and that this trinity must be recognized and applied to prepare them for a freer, wider, and more intelligent choice of pursuits.

In order to accomplish the wise ends for which this institution was established it should properly equip boys for their future career by the fullest development of their powers with reference to their wants of life, and acquaint them thoroughly, both theoretically and practically with the duty, the dignity, and the nobility of labor. There is a great field opening in our State for practical technical employment and a growing demand for services of those fitted for labor in every branch of scientific knowledge, and we are now compelled to draw upon the skilled labor of other countries to fill the most lucrative, honorable, and important positions in every industrial enterprise. In face of this fact, there can be no exaggeration of the value of an institution which will afford the direct advantage of conducting the student from the simplest mechanical principles to the complex order of artistic ingenuity by enabling him to combine principles, construct models, and call into activity his ingenuity for designing, while a practical knowledge of the use of tools can be acquired in one half the time necessary under the ordinary method of obtaining a trade knowledge as an apprentice, kept at such work only as proves most profitable to the employer.

Agriculture in our country is the admitted basis of public wealth, and we must look to it as the chief source of our prosperity. The machinery of a prosperous agriculture once put in motion brings in its train a vast number of other public enterprises, creating new demands for skilled employment, and the skilled hand gives dignity to these pursuits and places a higher estimate upon their value.

Instruction in agriculture and horticulture; how to plant, tend, harvest, and store the products of farm and garden; how to care for all the various kind of stock found on well regulated farms will inculcate a taste for these pursuits, and induce the young men to seek employment in the country, to the development of a self-reliant manhood, instead of wasting their lives, as is frequently the case, in the over-crowded professional ranks in the cities, by being educated into a fitness for such employment only as require an abstract mental training, and ignore altogether that which is practical. The young men of the State can acquire at the institution a knowledge that will prepare them to achieve the highest and best results in any station through the reliable factors, education, industry, and a proper moral instruction, by the application of plain moral precepts to every act of life.

In addition to this, the military feature of the College is of transcendent importance, though probably not appreciated. The arguments in its favor are numerous; but far in advance of all others, and what is sufficiently important to at once decide the matter, its conduciveness to health. The outdoor exercise, the erect position and expanding chest give the lungs the free play so after the cramped position necessary to the school room; the pleasurable excitement accompanying the drill, the strictness of attention required to secure precision and accuracy of movement in performing the evolutions, are highly conducive to bodily health, grace, and strength, and perform a very active part also in the inculcation of habits of promptness, regularity, and order, and aid materially in preserving proper discipline.

To you, as Directors and personally, I am heartily thankful for
this evidence of your confidence; and invoking a continuance of your
co-operation to secure for the institution a commanding eminence
that will make it the pride of the state.

I am, most respectfully,
Your obedient servant
L. S. Ross

A&M Ex-Cadets Respond

Louis L. McInnis, after his dismissal in favor of the board's reorganization of the leadership and staff of the college, received an outpouring of
letters and visits from friends and former A&M students across the state.
Former A&M College board chairman Judge Christopher C. Garrett of
Brenham noted, "I am afraid the board has made a mistake." Others
soon had the same sentiment. McInnis had been at A&M since its earliest days and had survived the purge of the disruptive "Crisp Affair"—a
faculty dispute regarding the promotion of Cadet John C. Crisp to the
rank of senior captain (known today as the Cadet Corps commander) in
the Corps, during the Thomas Gathright administration in 1879. Thus
McInnis's long tenure on campus and popularity with cadets for more
than a decade resulted in many of the "old ex-cadets" being opposed to
his dismissal.[31]

Among those who had maintained contact with McInnis after graduation from A&M was Edward B. Cushing '79, a railroad executive, who
dashed off a telegram to his friend and mentor, "If the Houston Boys can
serve you in any way—command us." Cushing and, ironically, the sitting
president of the A&M Alumni College Association, Walter Wipprecht
'79 (who had been dismissed along with McInnis), stepped forward to
offer a plan to obtain a signed petition of support from the ex-cadets
statewide, calling for McInnis's retention on the college staff or that he
receive a gubernatorial appointment to the A&M College board. The
energetic ex-cadets, whose early history is chronicled in Adams's *We
Are the Aggies* (1979), were unaware of the full circumstances, detailed
conversations, and letters between McInnis and A. J. Rose, which made
it clear in writing that the A&M board would hold him harmless, that it

was "the best interest of the college that prompted this action," and that there was "no chance for [McInnis] to remain at the college."[32]

The second option was a board seat, due to an assumption that board member L. L. Foster would exit the board to become the commissioner of agriculture under the incoming governor James Hogg's administration. The plan was to have one of the four A&M alumni in the legislature, most likely the recently elected Rep. Charles Rogan '79 (one of the original first six students to enroll at the A&M College of Texas in October 1876) present a petition from the ex-cadets to the new governor on McInnis's behalf. However, as further details of the unrest and changes at the college became public, many A&M ex-cadets softened their stance and support of the professor, reflected in a note to Cushing from alumnus Walter W. Moore '85, indicating that he "would qualify my signature [on a petition] . . . provided Mr. McInnis will agree *not* to make war on Gov. Ross."[33]

The prestige of Governor Ross caused pause among the ex-cadets, including Cushing. McInnis had recently secured a position at the First National Bank of Bryan, and Cushing advised him that "your appointment just now would cause discord on the A&M board." After further reflection on the board's selection of the new president, Cushing concluded, "The board having made the change used good policy in selecting Gov. Ross for president as he is personally popular and naturally could be more agreeable to the public at large than almost anyone else!"[34] But this would not be the last to be heard from Louis McInnis.

In the fall of 1890, the A&M College had a new spirit of excitement that garnered attention statewide. News of Governor Ross's acceptance of the presidency resulted in an influx of hundreds of student applications, of which only 316 could be admitted—notwithstanding the fact that the campus accommodations were geared to about 250 cadets. Room was made for the overflow, and this triggered efforts to add new campus facilities. Eager to add improvements to address the growth, the A&M board submitted a budget request to outgoing Governor Ross and the legislature totaling $128,000 for new dormitories, a new mess hall, a chemical laboratory, a carpenter shop, a veterinary hospital, and a bathhouse. After some active lobbying by the board and the governor, the college received some $66,400—the largest annual appropriation received since the college had opened its doors in October 1876.[35]

Governor Ross concluded his Austin administration with his next career in clear sight. The fall gubernatorial campaign pitted Attorney General James S. Hogg against prohibition candidate Webster Flanagan. Hogg, portraying his campaign as "the peoples' choice," lambasted the domination of Texas railroads by "foreign" (i.e., out-of-state) corporations and championed the creation of the statewide railroad regulatory commission. This stance endeared him to the farm bloc, who longed to control what continued to be seen as overbearing manipulation of freight rates by a growing number of unregulated railroads across the state. Angered at Hogg's agitation, the railroads funneled money to Hogg's opponent, Jay Gould, the powerful owner of the International and Great Northern Railroad (I&GN) consortium, which controlled most of the rail service in the state and threatened to build no more mileage in Texas "until such time as capitalists could feel more security in their investments in the State."[36]

As outgoing Governor Ross concluded his last months in Austin, his farewell address to the legislature on January 13, 1891, highlighted the priorities of his four-year tenure in office. Most observers did not consider Ross to be an aggressive reformer, by any means; instead, he was a transitional governor—the last of the post-Reconstruction redeemer era—in an atmosphere of change, especially compared with the wave of progressive politicians, events, and legislation that followed his administration. He left a clear record of economic growth and promotion of the state to new investors, maintained a tight fiscal policy, addressed the opening of Texas's western lands, and curbed the lawlessness associated with fencing. He remained a strong advocate of public education, and one who had tremendous compassion with the plight of all indigent Texans and disabled veterans "without distinction of creed or party, or direction of denominational or partisan character."[37]

Ross took no active part in the 1890 governor's race. Following the inauguration, there were numerous galas, including a "complimentary german" (a reception and dance) for Miss Florine Ross, age twenty, Sul's oldest daughter and active Austin socialite, deemed by the *Austin Statesman* as "one of Austin's most brilliant accessories." Stephen James Hogg, Texas's first native-born governor, was sworn in on the steps of the new state capitol. "Hogg in a sense marked a new generation," noted Alwyn Barr, "less bound by tradition, for he had not fought in the Civil War himself, but was the son of a Confederate general." After the ceremonies, the Ross family departed Austin by train for the A&M campus. The transition from the governor's mansion and the seat of state government to the rural and remote campus was indeed a major change of pace and lifestyle.[38]

Campus Arrival

Arriving at the cold and wet campus to little or no fanfare in early February was a shock to the Ross's oldest children, who had greatly enjoyed an active social schedule in Austin. After life in the capitol, the campus resembled a frontier outpost. Harve, age eighteen, "stomped" back to Austin to stay with his older brother Lawrence, who worked at the Texas General Land Office, and popular socialite Florine "fled outright," departing to stay with an aunt in San Antonio. Not to be distracted by the glum conditions found in their new campus home, Ross wrote his former chief of staff Major Holmes that he, Frank (age fourteen), and Nev (age eight) would "soldier" on and make the best of the situation. While his first visit with the A&M cadets was deemed very successful, Ross expressed concern with the surprising level of sickness among the students, filling the campus hospital for all of February 1891.[39]

Ross would soon find out that there was an implied history of the so-called sickness on campus. While never proven, detractors and concerned parents of the college had, since the opening of the college, blamed many of its problems and slow growth on the rumored "unhealthy location" in Brazos County. However, the most probable cause of numerous episodes of "la grippe" and the spread of measles was not the location but the cadets' overcrowded living conditions, generally poor hygiene due to a lack of potable freshwater, and a shortage of medical services. The crowding and poor infrastructure on the A&M campus would continue, in spite of the addition of a new dorm and more water wells during the early Ross years, through World War I and the nationwide outbreak of influenza in 1918, after which the water supply, new dorms, a natatorium and bathing facilities, and campus-wide electrical service were greatly upgraded.[40]

Agricultural & Mechanical College of Texas

President's Office

College Station, Texas   February 2, 1891

My dear Major, [Henry M. Holmes]

I have this morning assumed charge of the A&MC, so far as I can tell, my presence is very acceptable to all parties and, in short talk made to the young men this morning, seemed to take very well. When we arrived everything looked cheerless about the new home. The house had been long vacated, was damp, and rain coming in steady fall. No beds, no comfort in any respect, and if you have seen Lizzie and the children when I inducted them into their new quarters their condition and hopeless forlorn looks would have elicited your sympathy.

Harve stomped and went back to Austin, but soon returned and Florence fled outright and is paying Annie B and Miss S_____ a visit. Frank, Nev, and I were the only soldiers who were willing to accept the situation and made the most of it. Things soon brightened up however. I have good carpets put down, the house warmed up and everything fixed up in good style, and now all are fully satisfied.

The school is full of sick, 15 cases of measles and "la grippe" prevails to an alarming extent everywhere in this part of the state. I find the work in details somewhat annoying, but not difficult, and very soon have things running smoothly here. I think I shall like it.

Have you noticed the criticisms of Hogg? They are giving him the hot end of the polls already. What will they do for him before the end of his term. Tell Mrs. Holmes and May I long to see their gentle kindly faces once more, and trust we may meet some time and all have a good time recounting over trials, joys, and troubles. Write and tell me what you are doing and how you take the change. I have had many very fine complimentary letters about my administration from strong men of the state here and at Washington City. They pronounce it the most successful Texas has ever had. Coke is specially [*sic*] complimentary. Write me often. I hate to part from you and haven't gotten over it yet.

Your friend, L. S. Ross

Political Tergiversation

Early 1891 was a pivotal period for the course and structure of public higher education in the state of Texas. The selection of Gov. Lawrence

Sullivan Ross as president of the A&M College, located south of Bryan, somewhat neutralized much of the discord in Austin against A&M. However, supporters of the fledging new university in Austin dug in politically to influence the state legislature to fund the University of Texas at the expense of the A&M College, Prairie View Normal, Sam Houston Normal, and the newly designated medical branch in Galveston. In the weeks during the transition of Governor Ross from Austin to college president, a detailed book authored by J. J. Lane, titled *History of the University of Texas: Based on Facts and Records* (1891), was rushed to press to argue the case for the total dominance of higher education in the state by the seven-year-old UT. The manuscript disclosed a great jealousy surrounding the founding of the A&M College with federal funding provided in the Morrill Act and the "bitter and often partisan contention in the halls of legislation . . . of [the] sometimes extravagant demands for the Agricultural and Mechanical College, or branch at Bryan." As governor, Ross had publicly stated on numerous occasions that he clearly was for a successful UT; nonetheless, there were those who viewed his exodus to Bryan as indicative of his stance to enhance and "save" A&M over UT. Any additional Texas legislative funding for A&M and Prairie View was viewed as money that could and should go to expanding the Austin institution—as Lane observed, "the attitude of the Texas legislature [toward higher education] . . . presents some remarkable displays of political tergiversation."[41]

The A&M College faced constant attacks by individuals and lobbyists—political and nonpolitical—in Austin, among them land speculators and politicians who schemed to benefit from the development of commercial lots, hotels, and student boarding homes around the UT campus. (These complaints went well beyond those of the Grange and Farmers' Alliance regarding the composition of the agricultural courses at A&M.) The grievances repeatedly referenced the Texas constitution, which stated that the A&M College was a "branch" of the university. The fact that the university was opened seven years after the establishment of the college had no bearing or merit on efforts to curtail the growth of the college. Many antagonists of A&M, dating from as early as 1881, echoed J. J. Lane's argument for the "removal of the A. and M. College from Bryan" and the consolidation or "amalgamation" of the college and university into one Austin campus, leaving the Bryan campus as little more than a demonstration farm and/or an adjunct of the prison system or state lunatic asylum. These attacks were also focused on diminishing programs at Prairie View, Huntsville, and Galveston. Gov. Oran M. Roberts (who was subsequently employed as a professor of law at the university after he left office) attacked the college, noting that the cadets "instead of learning anything of agriculture . . . are being educated as lawyers [there was no law school at A&M], and doctors [there was no medical program at A&M], and the old Commoner thought it an outrage and a shame to run such a sham at the expense of the State."[42]

Ross, while governor, had worked and advocated to ensure the funding and expansion of all Texas schools of higher learning. In the case of Prairie View, Ross had "advocated colored education" since the time of his service on the education committee of the 1875 Texas Constitutional Convention. He continued his support of Alta Vista, a black college that focused on producing secondary educators for public schools, as a state senator, making sure that the A&M College mandate and

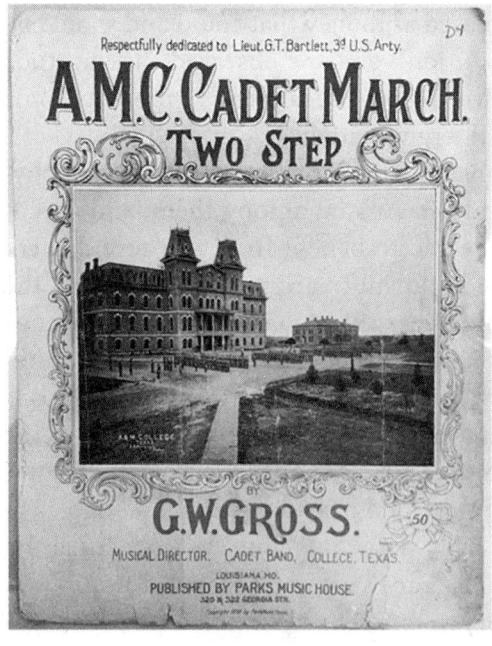

The "A. M. C. Cadet March," predating the "Aggie War Hymn" by more than two decades, is one of the earliest known songs played by the Texas Aggie Band and was introduced to the Corps of Cadets in the mid-1890s. Source: Jeff Dunn

structure would be an appropriate model and fit for the new African American–based institution. Once Prairie View was opened in 1879, the school struggled to attract and retain students due to harsh economic conditions that proved difficult to overcome. The Prairie View campus at Alta Vista in Waller County was placed under the management of the president of the A&M College, and the campus was administered by a "principal" approved by the A&M board of directors, who oversaw coursework that was similar to that of A&M. In addition to economic impediments, many African Americans during the post-Reconstruction period did not want to farm and were drawn to urban areas or exited Texas completely—thus, the Prairie View mission shifted its emphasis to training teachers. A large group moved to Kansas to eke out what they hoped would be a new and more prosperous life. Tenant farming and sharecropping proved not to better the economic conditions faced by poor blacks and whites during the last quarter of the century. Any exodus from Texas was greatly overshadowed by a growing number of immigrants from the lower South and Europe.[43]

Agricultural and Mechanical College of Texas

President's Office

College Station, Texas   Feby 13th 1891

My dear Major

Your kind letter was like the invigoration of good wine. It cheered all hands but not like your genial & much missed presence would have done. Well, I am setting down to a steady gait. No prancing or flourishes, but a complete acceptance of the situation and a determination to make the most of it. The change was radical but not greater than I anticipated. Every one becoming better satisfied and as you predicted, I think, the Cadets are my friends & the Board who have just concluded their meeting were much pleased with the fact that everything have [sic] a new aspect about the institution, and all for the better. Save this sickness which continues very much but not serious. From 30–60 in the Hospital every day. The measles took quite a run, and is holding the fort with unabated persistence.

We have not yet been honored with the Legislative visiting committee. Expect them soon however. The board was confronted while here with the fact that there was a deficiency of money—$5,000—occurring under McInnis administration of the finances. It does not appear that there has been any wrong done, or that there was a misapplication of funds. The Board simply cut out more work for him and made larger appropriations than their resources would warrant.

I believe now if you & Mrs. Holmes & May were here with us we would all like this change first rate as it is. I have been so much accustomed to seeing you all around that life seem incomplete without you. So far as the politics goes, I don't say you will be surprised when I tell you that with the expect an occasional copy of the Capitalism which Vanderhurst send Florence we don't see a new paper over a week. Haven't seen the [Austin] Statesman since leaving Austin and the [Houston] Post only once or twice. I have seen and heard enough however to know that friend Hogg is resting in no flower bed of roses with a flattering prospect of more thorns than roses.

Harve is still trying to find some employment and is so opposed to becoming a cadet that I have concluded he would do no good were he forced to enroll. He evidently wasted his time & my money while in Austin. Frank has taken a high stand in his classes and is a great favorite with cadets, professors. Nev & Bessie are going to school with the wife of the Chaplain who is an Episcopalian Minister and a good man in every way. They have a large family of children of their own and we found enough with my two to make Mrs. Biddle a very good school. Florence is still on a visit to San Antonio and Seguin. Don't know when she dates her proposed return. As usual I have left that matter to my frau.

I hope you have fallen into a necessary line of practice and are content. In due time your country will come to the front and I would suggest that you hold fast all good real estate which you may have. If there were a railroad to Mason [Texas] we would like to run up in the summer to see you all. We will spend as much time as we can in summer away from here for fear of fever & chills.

Love to all   Yours truly   L. S. Ross

Legislative Oversight

Within weeks of settling in on the campus, Sul Ross and the A&M board of directors were advised that a select legislative visiting committee would soon inspect the college as a part of biannual oversight visits to Prairie View Normal School, Huntsville Normal Teachers College, and the Galveston Medical School. Detractors of the A&M College and a select few political enemies hoped to use the occasion of the inspection to erode popular support, as well as siphon legislative funding away from the institution. It is unknown if Ross read the book by J. J. Lane. One additional vocal detractor looking to degrade the college along with the legislature was former professor Louis L. McInnis.[44]

In a detailed correspondence found in the Cushing Library Archives, McInnis addressed former A&M College faculty, board members, and staff; his friends; and his legislative contacts in Austin, hoping to poison the "visiting" oversight committee and (negatively) influence their final report back to the legislative leadership in Austin. Clear evidence of McInnis's meddling is found in his letters with State Senator Henry A. Finch of McKinney, Texas. Following his inability to be appointed to the visiting committee, Finch, writing on Texas House of Representatives stationery, assured McInnis in late February he would personally work behind the scenes to create a poor image of the college and ensure a negative outcome of the committee report, boasting: "I have been careful to protect you and taken such action as I believe will be calculated to bring notice of the joint committee that something is wrong and that an investigation will follow. I have, I believe moved discretely [*sic*] but I believe with effect."[45]

These efforts to "discretely" discredit A&M and President Ross failed, as the visiting committee returned a positive report to the legislature and Governor Hogg. In their correspondence, Ross pointedly concludes to Major Holmes that this would effectively prevent Hogg from making changes to the membership of the A&M board of directors. Ross, the old warrior, whom many in Austin constantly underestimated, was undeterred, telling Major Holmes that even if a new board was appointed, "I will capture the new ones," retaining his control, as was the case with current board.[46]

There is a twist of irony associated with McInnis's attack on Ross and the college—particularly concerning the board and how he had been summarily dismissed. Ross defended the former chairman of the faculty over a reported shortfall of some $5,000 at the college in 1889–90. Although the board's finance subcommittee, chaired by John Adriance, a year earlier in July 1890 had reported to the full board (and governor) that all accounts were "checked and found correct," the board—which later determined it was their fault for overextending funds they did not have—still called the dismissed McInnis to answer questions before the board to review the accounts. Ross, after reviewing a report from the auditors, was emphatic that to the best of his knowledge there was no wrongdoing and, seemingly unknown to McInnis (or unappreciated, if known), Ross defended his predecessor.[47]

There is no question that Louis McInnis gave great service to Texas A&M and its students during the college's formative years. His more than five-decade association with the college was significant; as engineering professor Charles W. Crawford recalled, "[H]e remained a staunch friend and supporter of the College." Yet, from 1890 until 1894, he harbored deep-seated ill feelings against Sul Ross and the board of directors—but not against the many cadets during his tenure or the A&M College he had helped found. And in 1905, Gov. Thomas Campbell, fifteen years after it was suggested by a number of ex-cadets, appointed McInnis to a three-year term on the A&M board of directors—just in time to be involved with campus disturbances and unrest, which became known as the great "Troubles of '08."[48]

Agricultural and Mechanical College of Texas

President's Office

College Station, Texas   [no date; circa early March 1891]

Confidential

My dear Major

I have had the Legislative visiting committee here for several days and they came poisoned against the college and my management but when they left I have good reason to think they were so far convinced that their report so far as I am concerned will give the governor grounds for a war upon us, which I am sure was contemplated.

He may finally attempt to review us through the agency of our objectional [*sic*] Board. It is believed he intends to change the present one for some cause. If he does this & doesn't look out, I will capture the new one. When a man is contentious of rectitude, as I am, he is safe in any event.

Hope this letter to President Cleveland will suit your ideas. Had mislaid your letter & forgotten when you desired to go. You can add that in the space left

All well L. S. Ross

As the spring of 1891 drew to a close, President Ross returned to Austin to gather with old friends and drop in on "the old den" and Governor Hogg. Ross received a very warm welcome from all—even the newspaper reporters—and Hogg seized on the occasion to make the most of the popular former governor's goodwill. Hogg appeared to Ross to be under considerable strain, juggling the duties of his office. Being the governor of Texas was not like being the attorney general, where Hogg had been insulated from the public and day-to-day conflicting political squabbles. The political dynamics, vocal interest groups, and constant legislative intrigue were, he soon found, vastly different and time-consuming. Thus, to gain a bit of popular support, Hogg ushered Sul Ross arm-in-arm upstairs in the capitol and into the House gallery to watch the floor debate, so they could be seen together. Sul revealed in his report to Major Holmes that he felt their appearance together "caused some little flutter." Hogg's artificial gesture was little more than political posturing and showmanship. Throughout his administration in Austin, Hogg and his supporters felt threatened by the gravitas and magnitude of the statewide popularity of Sul Ross.

Returning to make preparations for the June commencement ceremonies, Ross and his family at last settled in their new home—and all his children returned to the homestead.

Agricultural and Mechanical College of Texas

President's Office

College Station, Texas   March 10, 1891

My Dear Major

We have nothing new to write you from college. All are well and reasonably happy. Florine still at Seguin. Harve gone to Waco to attend to some farm matters, and look up some business enterprises or engagement for himself.

Was in Austin a few days ago. Met many warm friends & received hearty hand grasps from all. I dropped into your old "Den" and found things looking mixed. The old man playing the role of Private Secretary looked jaded and seemed listless and unhappy—Hogg came out and met me cordially and extended invitations to his House & the freedom of the office. He is bearing unmistakable marks of great care & anxiety.

He took me by the arm & asked with much urgency that I go with him into the upper Gallery of the Representatives Hall and see & hear the proceedings & members—our presence together in the Gallery and the frank and friendly intercourse between us evidently caused some little flutter for the time being. I look for an opposition to be speedily organized against his administration.

All the newspaper men were glad to see me and were not slow to say what they thought of my administration in contrast with his— especially Thornton—who with his usual perverse disposition seemed disposed to defend & champion Hogg in all his acts. This seemed strange enough in consideration of his previous opinions all around. Of course I did or said nothing to anyone to invite criticism of our Governor, and in every act have been one of his most loyal subjects, and I do hope he may have a peaceful administration.

It is extremely funny, to find that Cone Johnson & Hogg have fallen out about the [Railroad] commissions bill, the former thinking the latter had thrown him overboard for Terrell.

Write us fully of your present & prospective movements & give our love to Mrs. H. & May.

Yours truly, L. S. Ross

Soon enough, the political winds in Austin once again drew Ross into statewide election wrangling. His family was at last settled on the A&M campus, and the new president focused on his priorities for the college. An increase in statewide population due to immigration, the rise of populism to challenge the status quo, and conflict within the long-standing Democratic ranks created uncertainty as to who should head the Democratic state ticket, thus creating fissures in longtime loyalties and ambitions and deflecting public interest in and concern about higher education.

CHAPTER 3

Schemes of Ambition

Governor Sul Ross used to tell [the cadets] that Coronado's men while wandering on the Staked Plains were perishing from thirst when some Indians found them and guided them to water in one of the forks of a long river. And because it had saved them, Coronado's men named the stream Los Brazos de Dios.

J. Frank Dobie, Texas Folklore Society[1]

Each state [will establish an] endowment, support, and maintenance of at least one college where the leading object shall be, without excluding other scientific and classical studies, and including military tactics, to teach such branches of learning as are related to agriculture and the mechanic arts, in such manner as the legislatures of the States may respectively prescribe, in order to promote the liberal and practical education of the industrial classes in the several pursuits and professions in life.

Morrill Act of July 2, 1862, section 4

At last, the A&M College of Texas was on the right track. The excitement created by its famed president only enhanced an already growing enrollment and established a positive image for the institution. Attacks and criticisms would periodically be directed at the college, yet its leader was fully capable of handling any and all detractors. Sul Ross embraced the Corps of Cadets and its military traditions and training as a prime means to develop both a well-educated student and a graduate who had an appreciation for duty and honor, saying, "the military feature of the College is of transcendent importance, though probably not appreciated." Ross engaged the cadets with stories of the frontier, ranging from the legends of wandering conquistador Coronado's expedition to his war scraps and campaigns in the Antelope Hills. Texas A&M archivist Ernest Langford '13 noted, "Tradition has it that [Ross] used to sit in his first-floor office [in Old Main] on Sunday mornings with his feet on his desk, rolling his own cigarettes, and be open for visits from cadets and staff." There would, however, remain those outsiders who decried the military regimen while the president worked to educate his cadets, staff, patrons, and those outside the college regarding the uniqueness and excellence to be achieved with a regimented environment and education.[2]

In the early 1890s, the A&M College campus was a bleak, barren, and remote site—little more than the raw frontier villages Sul Ross had known well during his youth. The only difference was that the college had a railroad station and a few large buildings. A feature columnist from *Leslie's Illustrated Newspaper* attempted to put the best face on the bland campus, with its few scattered structures dotting the open prairie. In 1891 the campus was occupied by two permanent buildings—Old Main (1875) at the center of the campus and Gathright or Stewards Hall (1876)—which were the only significant structures standing for more than a decade. They were surrounded by single-faculty residences, barns, woodsheds, and outdoor toilets. The five two-story "cozy" residences (1877), according to the first 1895 A&M yearbook, the *Olio*, were known as "Down the Line," and were constructed behind and south of Old Main, facing to the west. At the south end of the housing row, there was a small pond over a dammed area where natural clay had been removed and fired in 1873–75 to make the bricks for the construction of Old Main and Gathright Hall. In the mid-1880s, two new dormitories were added—Pfeuffer Hall (1887) and Austin Hall (1888). The rooming capacity to house cadets varied with the availability and the time of year.[3]

There was no electricity until late in 1890, no running water, no trees, and no improved roads or sidewalks. The *Texas Health Journal* noted that the "great and increasing work" of the college made "one feel proud of the progress"; however, the main drawback to the institution was that "they have no system of waterworks, and we say, but little water." Bryan Electric service provided connections for 150 sixteen-candle lights for five hours per day at a cost of $1,600 yearly. Up until the formal depot and station were constructed in 1883, the H&TC railroad stop was little more than a platform. A caliche and ash pathway was the welcome mat running from the railroad, at "West Gate," to the steps of Old Main. The train station, the location of the first campus post office, had a tall pole and elevated hook to snag incoming mail bags from the passing trains. Passenger schedules varied with the seasons.[4]

The remoteness of the college was marked by limited transportation between the campus and Bryan, five miles away, accessible by foot, bicycle, horse and buggy, or at intervals by a train ride on the Houston & Texas Central Railroad. However, when the numerous cross-country traveling circuses rolled into Bryan, with or without approval from the commandant, cadets always seemed to find a means to go to town. To the excitement of all, the "College Bicycle Club" (CBC), a craze much like baseball that was sweeping the country, was organized—yet the cyclists still had to navigate the campus's irregular paths and dirt roads. Notwithstanding, the CBC was governed by a constitution and bylaws and chaired by a "Roadmaster." It grew in prominence and membership among the cadets, staff, and faculty, including Charles Hutson, Dean Kyle, P. L. Tilson, Miss Mary Bittle, Charles Puryear, Frederick E. Giesecke, Miss Bessie Ross, and Miss Rita Sbisa. Not until June 1910 did the campus have "rapid transportation" with the introduction of the narrow-gauge, gasoline-powered "Bryan-College Interurban" trolley—running north from the campus up College Main Street to Bryan. Generally operated on the hour, single tickets were ten cents and round-trip fares were fifteen cents.[5]

Consolidating the university's leadership roles, Ross served both as president and treasurer for fiscal matters. He posted a bond of $20,000 to manage the college accounts, began a new bookkeeping system to prevent the misleading double counting previously encountered by Professor McInnis and the A&M College Board, developed a budget for the college, and selected the banks of his choice to manage college funds. As part of his duties, President Ross was further designated by the board as the titular "president" of Prairie View, working with the Hempstead campus "principal" on budgets, staffing, enrollment, and facilities. And, with the board's approval, he formed a two-man committee with board member William R. Cavitt of Bryan to revise and update the

A&M College catalog. As historian Henry Dethloff concluded, "There was little question that Ross . . . was the sole and absolute control over fiscal and administrative affairs of the college."[6]

Agricultural and Mechanical College of Texas

Military Department
Gov. L. S. Ross
President
Lieut. B. C. Morse, U. S. Army
Commandant
Headquarters Corps of Cadets
College Station, May 13th 1891
His Excellency
Governor James S. Hogg

I extend to you & Mrs. Hogg an invitation to visit us during the commencement exercises of the A & M College to begin June 7th & to last to the 9th. We expect a large crowd from all parts of the State and I promise you a most cordial greeting & a hearty welcome, and guarantee to you both a pleasant time.

Will be in Austin in a few days and add my personal solicitation to the present writing.

Very respectfully
L.S. Ross, Presdt A&MC

Continued good relations with Governor Hogg and key legislators was a hallmark of Ross's success, marked by numerous invitations by the governor to visit the college. Ross's confidence during his first few months at A&M is indicated in a letter to the major following a hearing, held by the legislature in Galveston after the final College commencement ceremonies in early June 1891: "I received unmistakable manifestation of kindly feelings from all hands. I came away with good will for them all alike." And even with the weight of the governor's office off his back, supporters were active in encouraging Ross to run for the US Senate seat or another term as governor. Once again, Ross's health and the well-being of his now partially blind son Frank, a freshman cadet in the A&M Corps, weighed heavily on any decision.[7]

During the summer, plans were made to expand the electric service, improve the roads, and ensure the quality of the campus water supply. The foundation for the presidential residence was laid, and work began on new mechanical engineering shops. In the meantime, legislative committees continued to probe the operations at the college—generally without any clear or binding evidence of mismanagement. President Ross confidently and boldly stated, "I have more than justified expectations of all concerned."[8]

Agricultural and Mechanical College of Texas

President's Office

College Station, Texas   June 21st 1891

My dear Major

I have just returned from Galveston where I had gone in response to a summons from the Legislative committee. When they interrogated me, both sides claiming to be my friends, said they did not want to mix me up with the Sooty grist going through the mud machine, and accordingly I was excused. This was kind, and as I received unmistakable manifestation of kindly feelings from all hands, I came away with good will for them all alike.

It appears that the Tyler crowd are more than holding their own, and their policy will doubtless be to protract the investigation by injection of inclement & worthless matter to such a length & expanse that the peoples will wonder & grow mad that such fuss & so much money is being spent to so little purpose.

Geo. Clark has pulled out, & gone to Washington, and Alexander will give up the chase in a day or two. This will leave Gerald & Felix Robertson, who will fall easy victims to the superior shrewdness of their opponents. The Committee was growing weary & disgusted, and taking it all in, it is going to be the grandest farce that was ever presented for the delectation of a suffering public. The Tyler crowd will have much mud & tar sticking to them when it is over, but that is too much in the nature of congeniality to do very great harm or to provoke any considerable criticism. On the other hand, I expect to hear Gerald & Geo Clark cursed from Dan to Beersheba. This is my estimate of the situation. Wait & see how nearly it will be verified.

The question of politics as presented to me only strikes me forcibly in one direction. Many portions are sounding me to see if I would like to be Governor either the next time or subsequently. My reply has not been encouraging. Sometimes however I think it would be pleasant in enabling us all to be reunited again, but at the same time, I have no expectations in that line. *I am well pleased here*, and from all I can learn have more than justified the expectation of all concerned.

The Boys went home well pleased and the prospect is flattering for a large increase in numbers next term. The Board is preparing to build me a handsome & comfortable house, and this, with very satisfactory monthly salary, makes the situation far from uninviting. I have never, as you know, felt any desire to the US Senate. The labor would I fear be too great for me, and I am fortunately not ambitious enough to assume the duties of a place without the full determination to make a success as fast as possible. It has always been my misfortune, however, to respond to my country's call when my services were in demand unmistakably and hence I do not know what would be my decision should such honor be freely & voluntarily conferred upon me. (A thing not likely to occur I admit) but I do not know that I will never make that personal effort & struggle on the part of any one, to secure the prize, which to me is by no means glittering or over exciting—purely and simply, because I am too lazy, & becoming too much in love with rest of body & mind to be sorely tempted by the applause of a fickle populace.

Florine & Harve are over in Austin & the balance of the gang are here. Frank is about to lose entirely the sight of one eye and as the other is in sympathy to some extent. I shall send him away to an oculist. He stood fourth in a large class and was made Corporal by the Commandant for superior military bearing & efficiency. This is a serious blow to his hopes, and unless something can be done to relieve him, I fear the worst will speedily ensue.

All are well & send love to all. God bless you all.
Yours as ever L. S. Ross

Texas Democratic Politics in Transition

With the post-Reconstruction period and rise of the new southern Democratic Party in Texas, Gov. Richard Coke had championed the crafting of the Texas constitution of 1876. Following Coke's election to the US Senate, the Texas Democratic Party split into a number of factions, yet it would continue to dominate statewide politics from 1877 through the 1960s. The cross-currents of political loyalties and priorities continued throughout the decade of the 1890s. While out of office, former governor Ross remained engaged in the behind-the-scenes debate on key issues facing the state, while also being a keen observer of the jockeying over who occupied the governor's mansion and controlled the legislature's agenda. The future of the A&M College was clearly tied to Ross's ability to improve the image of the college as well as to increase legislative funding to expand campus facilities and staff. The political dynamics were many and diverse, centered primarily on who controlled the Texas Democratic Party—with the political power, prior to 1900, centered in the office of the governor. Political factions were both regional and philosophical.[9]

The old-line Democratic guard faction was headed by Coke, Reagan, Hubbard, Ross, Clark, Rose, and others who comprised the Jeffersonian, fiscal conservative wing, steering toward limited government, anti-prohibition, pro-agriculture, and measured tolerance but concern over the growing impact of railroad expansion across the state. By early 1890, the Grange and Farmers' Alliance, while often in conflict over the same membership base, stepped forward to capture the political high ground by exerting influence and patronage on the Democratic nominating conventions across the South in general and in Texas in particular. Governor Ross was one of the last of the Civil War veterans and the generation of post-Reconstructionists to hold major statewide office. In spite of his repeated statements to friends, the Democratic Party organizers, and the media that he would not seek or be drafted for a third term as governor, loyal supporters would advance his name to accept one of the US Senate seats representing Texas—which he also repeatedly declined.[10]

The second Democratic faction was made up of the progressive-leaning faction headed by James Hogg, who rode into office on an anti-railroad plank to create the Texas Railroad Commission, which was heralded to address the antitrust abuse, rate manipulation, and land-grab schemes of the railroads. This faction gained strong backing from the Grange, Knights of Labor, and Farmers' Alliance. Fred Gantt, in *The Chief Executives in Texas* (1964), noted:

> The Galveston Daily News commented editorially that it meant the overthrow of the older leaders and turn the Party over to the "kids," with the "biggest kid in Texas" [Hogg] heading the ticket. Hogg won in 1890 and the railroad commission entered into law. Reform-minded

voters statewide returned only 22 of the 106 members of the Texas House in 1890. Thus the weakness of Hogg's coattails and a divided party in 1892 is demonstrated in the fact that he squeaked by his opponents, elected by only a plurality to become a minority governor for his second term.[11]

The "Tyler crowd," from East Texas, as referred to by Ross, had for a number of years produced winning candidates, beginning with Oran M. Roberts in 1878. Hogg, a product of Wood County, in the early 1880s served as district attorney and practiced law in Tyler before moving to Austin. Regional political power came from the recovering cotton economy in Northeast Texas. The city of Tyler was also placed on the state ballot in 1881 as an alternative site to Austin for the location of the new "university." It failed by a two-to-one vote. The forty-acre "university" campus finally opened in Austin with eight professors and 220 students in September 1883. Party divisions would soon lead to new challenges to Texas progressive Democrats.[12]

Dissatisfaction and broken ranks among competing factions of Democrats allowed for the rise of the Populist Party. "A good many Texans," noted Randolph Campbell in *Gone to Texas* (2003), "had found the 'New South' [rhetoric] an empty promise and wanted something better." Discouraged farmers and new immigrants were attracted to the Populists, who further singled out the railroads as a unifying target to rally support. While Hogg captured voters by insisting that the Railroad Commission be established, Texans in the early 1890s did not fully grasp the magnitude of the railroad. According to C. Vann Woodward in the *Origins of the New South*, the prospect of vast tracts of southern lands was a "powerful magnet to attract Northern and foreign [primarily English] capital." Many of the railroads were "paper roads," built on speculative corporate stock options and prospectus (most chartered outside Texas) just to collect land grants, political favors, and cash subsidies—with the *Galveston Daily News* running a headline, "Has the State Been Swindled?" Not until the issuance of a 1936 US Congressional investigative report on "The Western Range" was the full magnitude of the railroad land grab, greed, and power disclosed. In the case of Texas, a dozen railroad companies received 33,153,818 acres—an area larger than the state of Indiana. In 1930 the General Land Office first reported 35,777,038 acres (estimated as much as 38,900,000 acres in early 1893) granted to railroads. Upon resurvey, it was found that the railroads had received 3,623,160 more acres than allowed by law, and the state eventually recovered this excess of the state's total sovereign land of 164,191,308 acres, or 20 percent. Compare this with the only 3,000,000 acres set aside for the new state capitol in 1887, and it is little wonder why the Populists clamored for the regulation of railroads and, if necessary, statewide ownership of the industry.[13]

In 1892 Hogg was opposed by two rising factions—one led by a corporate railroad attorney, who was vehemently against the Texas Railroad Commission, and the other led by former governor Richard Coke and Sul Ross's gubernatorial campaign manager, George Clark. When the seated Democratic Convention locked out Clark and his supporters, he bolted from the halls of the convention to run as an independent candidate. Thus the two opposing camps were soon labeled "Bolter-crats" and "Hoggocracy." Once again, Clark's supporters, labeled "calamity howlers," worked to undermine Hogg, angering US Senator Richard Coke, who returned from Washington to campaign for Hogg. This seemed to do no known harm to Ross and Coke's longtime relationship; Coke's main concern was Clark's refusal to support the party's nominee, thus undermining the "established party system" in Texas. The second faction that opposed Hogg in 1892 was led by Judge Thomas L. Nugent, the standard-bearer for the Texas Populist Party, who tended to oppose prohibition. In the 1892 race, Hogg received only 44 percent of the vote— elected by only a plurality, the first minority win in Texas gubernatorial voting history. The final voter tally was Hogg 190,486, Clark 133,395, and Nugent 108,483.[14]

Colonel Edward House

During this period, all Texas gubernatorial candidates of the era were nominated by party conventions, which, due to a high degree of manipulation of balloting and party planks, increasingly came under criticism. George Clark, who bolted Democratic ranks to run on the statewide ballot, was an exception. The system allowed a few corporate attorneys and special interest groups the ability to manipulate the outcomes. However, for more than a decade beginning in 1888, no single individual exercised as much behind-the-scenes influence on the gubernatorial nominees as wealthy independent political operative Col. Edward M. House of Houston and Austin. As an advisor to every governor from Sul Ross to O. B. Colquitt, House orchestrated the successful guberna- torial nominations of Hogg, Charles A. Culberson, Joseph D. Sayers, and Samuel W. T. Lanham. Once they were nominated, he directed each candidate's victorious campaign for office. From 1886 to 1903 the majority of officeholders in Texas for governor, lieutenant governor, and attorney general had East Texas roots and were all impacted by the political influence of Colonel House (see table 3.1).[15]

Table 3.1. *Texas officials, 1886–1903*

Dates	Governor	Lieutenant governor	Attorney general
1886–90	Lawrence S. Ross*	Thomas B. Wheeler*	James S. Hogg†
1891–94	James S. Hogg†	1891–92, George C. Pendleton* 1893–94, Martin M. Crane	Charles A. Culberson
1895–98	Charles Culberson*	George T. Jester*	Martin M. Crane
1899–1903	Joseph D. Sayers*	James N. Browning	1898–1901, Thomas Smith 1901–1903, Charles Bell

* Confederate veteran
† Son of a veteran

Colonel House's title—bestowed by a grateful Hogg—was honorary only. He rarely attended the political conventions when in session, elected to watch from the sidelines, and shunned all elective or appoint- ive offices. Godfrey Hodgson, in *Woodrow Wilson's Right Hand*, notes the astute and discernible Texas operator had an "extraordinary influ- ence on the state's electoral process and careers of its politicians . . . a quite exceptional flair for making the system work for the distinctly mixed group of men." He soon moved to New York City to package and craft the nomination of presidential candidate Woodrow Wilson in 1912. House's strategic skills and ability to detach himself from the heat of the political battles of Texas Democratic political circles for more than a decade proved a winning formula. Not only was Wilson elected, but House was charged as the principal advisor and reviewer of new cabinet post nominations and hundreds of federal patronage positions. His recommendations resulted in the first Texans to ever enter the presidential cabinet: David Houston, former president of Texas A&M (1902–5), as secretary of agriculture; Albert Sidney Burleson (an A&M College ex-cadet, 1878–81), as postmaster general; and Thomas Watt Gregory, as attorney general.[16]

Agricultural and Mechanical College of Texas

President's Office

College Station, Texas   August 9th 1891

My dear Major

   As this is Sunday I have concluded to devote a part of my pious meditations to you and family. I have my full in supervising the construction of several buildings and watching over the affairs of the College generally. The special appropriation entailed more work on me than I supposed would result. The House being built for our use is very nice and comfortable one, and when finished hope you, Mrs. H and May will come down and see us. Florine is now on a visit to Bonham and Frank has gone down to see Dr. Rutherford partly on pleasure but chiefly to have his eyes examined by an Occulist [*sic*] there. Harve has returned from Austin and expects to find employment in Houston under Kinsman Moore who started a Collar factory etc etc. Bessie received a letter from Mrs Holmes today and is now making her reply. Lizzie is very much pleased with her new home now and, as I have gradually gotten hold of the reins, I find work more agreeable and pleasant. I tell you at first it made me turn grey very fast.

   From present outlook I will have a fine attendance from the best families of the State. They write that their sons come on my account. Our friend Walter Tips by this mail gives me notice to expect his boy, also Reagan and his secretary of R'y [Railroad] Commission send a Boy-

   I hear very little from Austin but think [Richard Moore] Dick Hill is broke world without end. They have gone over on the foot-hills above Barton Springs. Friend Hogg too seems to be having rough sailing, but I guess the Machine will keep him running in the same old groove. What are you doing? Hope time is dealing gently with you all. Don't get impatient and surrender present advantages whatsoever they may be in prospect for something better unless certain of success. I think I shall be compelled to run up and see you all next summer. Dorsett keeps me in remembrance and I like the old fellow better and better as time jogs by.

Haven't been up about Waco for a long time, and my farming interest there will probably pan out worse and worse. Will put in a little time there next week. I paid the Int. on the land note as per your suggestion. Hope our cactus patch will bear fruit some of these days, not sanguine however. Write me a long gossipy letter. We think of you all every hour of every day, and scarcely ever sit down to the table without having some of the family refer to Major or Mrs. H and May.

God bless and keep you all at all times.
L. S. Ross

A Fine Attendance

Students from across Texas, soon to be in the uniform of Texas A&M's Corps of Cadets, flocked to the campus in September 1891, again creating a challenge in terms of overcrowding and insufficient facilities to care for those interested in A&M. Newly arriving students were required to be fifteen years of age or more—with the college accepting new and returning students for enrollment as late as mid-November. A new forty-one-room, three-story dormitory (in later years named Ross Hall) opened, while the fourth floor of Old Main was converted to additional cadet rooms. The fall 1891 semester opened with an enrollment of 295 cadets by October 12, with some 30 prospective students turned away, according to President Ross, "for one cause & another—most failed to pass our application" process. Ross spent time among the cadets daily, and beginning with the new fall semester, he personally interviewed all incoming students at his first-floor office in Old Main, in addition to visiting with the existing cadets to discern their deportment and suitability for the college and Corps. Faculty members were then assigned to determine if the prospective student was ready for college, in addition to determining their proposed academic field of study. Once enrolled, entering students reported to the commandant, Lt. Benjamin C. Morse, to go over the rules and regulations and be assigned their quarters and cadet company. As the fall semester progressed, Ross confided to Major Holmes, "At times I have some petty annoyances with the Boys, but they have conducted themselves splendidly with very few exceptions."[17]

Agricultural and Mechanical College of Texas

College Station   Oct 12th 1891

My dear Major Rose

I have mailed you for approval a number of vouchers, which please send at once to Austin in care of Mr. Hollingsworth. I expect to be there Thursday evening. Have some business with Gov. Hogg & want to meet him Friday before he gets away to Dallas if possible. Everything flourishing. The Barracks up story & half, shop walls already up. Well down 900 ft. 10 inch pipe.

Residence's frames are up and carpenters busy on it. The first time contractors seem to be in a hurry. The applications still come in. 295 matriculated & about 30 turned away for one cause & another. Most failed to pass. One application from Guatemala which I have agreed to take.

Will write you at length in a few days.

Very respy——
L. S. Ross, Pres.

Modifications of the A&M College catalog served to enhance the academic curriculum in both agriculture and mechanical fields. The course hours required to complete a degree were increased, and extra hours were required in English, math, and science. Fees and expenses were held stable, with the 1891–92 session costing $140. Additional expenses included $18 for the regulation, cadet-gray cloth uniform. President Ross, writing Major Holmes, expressed enthusiasm that "I have a fine attendance from the best families of the State"—including the son of Texas Railroad Commissioner John Reagan.[18]

Within months of Ross arriving at A&M as president, the college began the most extensive building period it had enjoyed to date. In addition to a new president's residence, priorities included new "barracks" or dorms, an expanded mess hall, a natatorium, as well as mechanical shops, barns, and a creamery. Given the concerns with overcrowding, the most pressing project was the completion of a three-story, forty-one-room dorm with wood-burning stoves. While improvements to faculty housing predated Ross in the late 1880s, he advocated the upgrade of on-campus quarters as an essential step in expanding the faculty and staff. President Ross directly worked on these projects, down to the details of each, as noted by his concern about the safety of the chimneys in a letter to the architect:

December 11, 1891

To: E. T. Heiner, Houston

There is a very grave question about the chimneys on the dormitory building at this place. As called for in the plans the flues must be twisted round so far that they will come entirely off their base of support in some of the chimneys even where they would clear the valleys and hips when run up straight. The two front ones at the ends the whole chimney will have to be brought entirely off its base in order to better clear the roof timbers, and that in a height of about four feet. That will make a very bad chimney it seems to us and should be avoided if possible. Can you find time to come up and look over the work and see if you can make suggestions which will get us out of the difficulties noted? The masons are nearly through with the work now and will want a decision as soon as possible. In the longitudinal section of the building does not drawing show arches in the cross walls for supporting the post from the roof? The [president's] residence will be ready for occupation by Monday I believe, and the [mechanical] shop is nearly complete.

L. S. Ross

The Scott Volunteers

Enhancing the public image of the A&M College was a top priority of President Ross. He wanted to secure a positive public perception of the institution. More so than others, he realized that the Corps of Cadets was a key feature of the college. While there had been and still were a

few military-oriented prep schools in Texas, none matched the A&M
Corps of Cadets in terms of sheer size and appearance. Former students
or "ex-cadets" scattered around the state in agricultural and industry
professions were proud to have worn the "cadet gray." Thus, beginning in
his first year as president, Ross was keen to enhance the college's image
and recruiting plans by creating events for cadets across the state.[19]

College Station, Tex., September 28, 1891

To: Hon W. C. Conner, President Texas State Fair

My dear sirs and friends—

　　We have here at the Agricultural and Mechanical College a splendidly drilled cadet company [the Scott Volunteer's] and they are very
desirous of attending the fair for a few days as an organization. They
would, I am sure, reflect credit upon our state and probably add some
little interest to the many attractions presented at the fair. They number twenty-nine officers and privates. Can you extend them any courtesies? They are young men of the very best families of our state and
would doubtless keep in grateful remembrance any consideration
shown them, soliciting an early reply.

I am respectfully, etc.
L. S. Ross, President

The most prominent element of the Corps of Cadets was a "select body
of military" cadets selected from the ranks to form an honor guard that
would one day be known as the Ross Volunteers. The origins of the volunteers, the oldest continuous student organization in Texas, began in
1887 when a faculty committee chaired by Louis L. McInnis authorized
"a crack military company" based on merit, drill expertise, and deportment. The initial name of the company was the Scott Volunteers, named
for Col. T. M. Scott, who at that time was a business manager and agent
to the A&M board of directors. In their formative years, the volunteer
drill presentations were limited to the annual commencement exercise.
Governor Ross and his daughter Florine witnessed the Scott Volunteers
at the 1890 graduation ceremonies.[20]

In July 1890, with the departure of Professor McInnis and numerous staff, including Colonel Scott, there was a brief moment of confusion as interim vice president Bringhurst, according to departed former commandant Lt. W. S. Scott (no relation to Colonel Scott), in a fall 1890 letter to McInnis, would not permit them to reorganize "unless they changed the name of the company." Lieutenant Scott, who held bad feelings for both Bringhurst and the college board, knew the reorganization of the volunteers was in the hands of the board. The volunteers were allowed to practice and drill, and the board deferred the name change until the arrival of the new president.[21]

In February 1891 the thirty-member company of cadets (who dressed in distinctive all white, trimmed in black and gold fashioned from naval dress uniforms of the era, including white pith helmets) was renamed for the new president—the Ross Volunteers (RVs). Miss Bessie Ross, the president's youngest daughter, was selected as the "sponsor" of the Ross Volunteers. Cadet RV officers wore a wide crimson silk sash tasseled in gold. Following the death of President Ross, the name of the organization was briefly changed in July 1898 to the "Foster Guards" under the administration of Ross's successor, Lafayette L. Foster, and changed again in April 1902 under A&M Pres. David F. Houston to the "Houston Rifles." However, in September 1905, incoming president Henry Hill Harrington, the son-in-law of Governor Ross, requested the board give the company the permanent name of Ross Volunteers, "in honor of this great soldier, statesman, and college president who knew and loved his cadets." Thus, for more than a century, the Ross Volunteers have served as the premier cadet company on campus, providing the firing squad for Silver Taps ceremonies as well as honors, provided after 1940, at the annual campus Muster each April 21. Shortly after World War II, the RVs were designated the official honor guard of the governor of Texas and perform ceremonial duties at each governor's inauguration on the steps of the capitol in Austin.[22]

Agricultural and Mechanical College of Texas

Office of the President

College Station, Texas   Dec. 20th 1891

My dear Major

As this is Sunday I have concluded to devote a few lines to you and Mrs. H. We are now in our new house, which is in every way more comfortable & convenient than the Mansion, and we feel much more at home, and have hung the latch string on the outside for you & the Madam to make an early pull. We have room for you at any time, with hearts warmer than ever, four new fireplaces and they are hot. When ills betide you or the blues seize you run down & spend a few days. Nev poor boy, has been quite sick with a fever which broke out among the Boys in November & brought upon us 19 cases in all, two proving fatal after the boys were carried home. It was doubtless caused by overcrowded conditions and low stage of cistern water in consequence thereof.

Since Dec. & the late rains falling about the first, we have had no new cases. The college has a poor reputation for health in general esteem and this will likely prove detrimental for a time to its prosperity. Nev is very weak but is regaining his health & strength as rapidly as could be expected. We thought his case very dangerous at one time. My affairs are working so harmoniously & in such perfect accord that we begin to feel much attached to all hands. At times I have some petty annoyances with the Boys, but they have conducted themselves splendidly with very few exceptions. Have just had a letter from John Moore telling me that in a recent trip through the West he found the people very desirous of having me back in the Executive office, and by the same mail came one from Kendall of the D&D Institute urging me to let my friends know that I would accept the senatorship [*sic*] as there would probably be a deadlock etc. Now I have just read his fulsome praise of Hogg's administration extracted from his recent report, and was rather disposed to question the sincerity of his allegiance. However in his & other cases, it does not take many minutes for me to so reply that they can find little to rejoice over or complain of. Good hearted John Moore writes from a pure desire, and would doubtless gladly aid me to the extent of his abilities in any of my ambitions.

The Hogg & Chilton crowd finds little comfort in the Press I imagine, and their lives are likely to fall in state more under general plans in the end. It looks as if Mills had the Senatorship secured. Don't understand Culberson's move in finally rejecting the place offered by Harrison & then announcing for Senator against Chilton. Does it mean that he expects to be beaten and then fall heir to the sympathy of the people ala Mills as a stock reserve for Coke's place. I think there is some kind of understanding between Culberson, Mills, & Coke. Some think Mills will run against Hogg for Gov. & let Culberson beat Chilton & then Mills take Coke's place, as the latter wants it no longer—so he says—Anyway the Hogg gang are not now happy over the outlook. And things that may be brewing will hardly prove wholesome to them. Geo. Clark is swinging round the circle stirring up the monkeys & having lots of fun., and is concocting a lot of devilment for the administration to chew over. Don't think he wants an office, but if no one else runs, he may try Hogg? This is guess however as I have known nothing of his plans or purposes for many Moons.

I am going in the going down to the Jas Davis Ranch on a camp hunt, and will take Frank along. Of course we expect a splendid time. Harve has been at work for quite a time getting $2.25 per day, and is as steady as an Old Veteran at the business. Write often and give my love to Mrs. H. and to May.

God bless, all well but Nev
L. S. Ross

Note that Sul Ross would continue the custom of a midwinter hunting trip for the remainder of his life.

The Spring 1892 Political Season

The observation by Sul Ross about the upcoming political wrangling in his December 1891 letter was a very prophetic preview of the dynamics ahead in the '92 governor's race. In his first year, Governor Hogg had not solidified a political base and was threatened by a number of challenges, not the least of which was Ross himself, who repeatedly was suggested as a candidate by friends and the media. When Ross's former campaign manager, George Clark of Waco, declared his intentions to run for governor, his campaign slogan was "Turn Texas Loose"—a head-on attack on Hogg's alleged overregulation and legal restrictions, felt to restrict business and investment in Texas. In response to the attack from Clark, the Hogg "machine" and supporters turned their attention once again to Ross and, by extension, the A&M College of Texas. A corporate railroad attorney and vocal anti-prohibition advocate, Clark—no stranger to a good fight—was a revered Civil War veteran, having participated in more than a dozen major campaigns and being wounded four times in battle, including a near-fatal wound at Gettysburg during Picket's Charge on July 3, 1863. Following the end of Reconstruction, he served as attorney general during the Coke administration. Ross wrote a private letter to Major Holmes on December 20, 1891, providing insight into the political details and competing personalities of the era.[23]

Statewide interest in a possible Sul Ross candidacy for governor attracted attention to a translated letter printed in the newspaper *El Ciudadano* of El Paso:

> El Gobernador L. S. Ross ha escrito la siguiete carta:
>
> College Station, Texas, Febrero 26 de 1892.
>
> Hon. C. B. Gerald,
>
> En contestacion a la carta de vd. Debo decirle que no soy candidato en nigun sentido. Las manifestcio nes que vd. Nota que hacen algunos de mis partidarios nacen de su pura buena voluntad hacia mi. o no he en manera ninguna, ni directa ne indiectiamenta, significado el desso de permanecer es cete puesto por un tarcer perido. Yo debere sostener para el al Hon. George Clark. Habuendo estado relacionado con el social y amistotamente como su vecino desde la guerra, yo puedo manifestan con toda su fuerza mi confianza en su ilustracion, patriotismo e incorruptible interes que abriga por los mas altos y mejores intereses del pueblo texano.
>
> Vuestro respetuosamente
> L. S. Ross

While potential opponents mounted, including Charles Culberson, Roger Mills, and Frank Chilton, members of "the Hogg gang" were "not very happy with the outlook." Concerned with Ross's role, implied endorsement of his friend, and assistance with the Clark campaign, the Hogg camp launched a barrage of rumors and attacks in newspapers across Texas, targeted at the reputation and honor of Sul Ross and his position at the college. With Ross constantly encouraged by friends and admirers across the state to stand for reelection, the Hogg camp was fearful that Sul Ross would enter the '92 governor's race. If he had decided to run, both Clark and Nugent would most likely have thrown their support behind Sul, which would ensure the defeat of Hogg. Thus, Ross was fully aware of the angst among Hogg's followers and the "devilment" the vocal Clark created as he campaigned across the state, seemingly humored by his old campaign manager's ability to "stir up the monkeys and have lots of fun" at the expense of Hogg's overconfident campaign. Hungry for news (and controversy) to fill the papers, editors were more than willing and eager to provide coverage, including Ross's reply in the *Galveston Daily News*, which the paper headlined "The Man Whom Texans Honor Writes as he Fought."[24]

"It Was a 'Fat Take'"

The primary attacker from the Hogg camp, Judge Alexander William Terrell, is somewhat of a mystery, given the many parallels between his and Ross's careers. Both were veterans and former brigadier generals in the CSA and served their first statewide elected position as state senators. Senator Terrell had been a part of the planning committee for the new capitol and was invited to stand with Governor Ross at the dedication, along with former governor Oran M. Roberts and Temple Houston, youngest son of Sam Houston. Terrell had very little dealings with Ross, either as governor or immediately after his term. Having played what he felt was a prominent role in the establishment of the University of Texas in 1882–83, this was a means for him to both attack Clark via Ross and plant the seeds of discourse in the next legislative session to reduce funding for the A&M College. Considered by many opponents as "a heavy-handed anti-monopolist" and a demagogue for stirring up discontent, Terrell was attacked by party stalwarts in his bid in 1887 to be elected a US Senator, and John Reagan won by a wide margin. By endorsing Hogg and attacking Clark and Ross, it is also possible that Terrell hoped to endear himself to the vacillating progressive wing of the party, divert legislative funding from A&M to the new university in Austin, and thus better position himself to be governor in 1894.[25]

One main difference between Ross and Terrell is that Terrell spear-headed a rabid fight in Austin to disenfranchise African Americans, poor whites, and citizens of Mexican heritage by constantly introducing laws that limited their voting rights. By advocating a mandatory poll tax at both the local and state level, Terrell hoped to also expel as many African Americans as possible from Democratic Party ranks, with the objective of controlling local primary elections. In contrast, Ross advocated for universal voting for all Texans of voting age, no poll tax, and a constant review of inequities in the judicial system. Demonstrating his concerns related to biased conviction, Ross granted more than twenty pardons to African Americans while governor.[26]

In the context of the era of the 1890s, it must be remembered that mass media or communications did not exist. There was no radio or television. Other than private letters and telegrams, printed news was conveyed by newspapers. In Texas, there were only ten large-circulation papers and more than three hundred smaller, mostly weekly papers. Some small towns, such as Bryan, often had two or three newspapers, and as a whole, Texas had a flourishing foreign-language press with eighteen German publications, eight Spanish publications, and two Bohemian publications. Agriculture was a pivotal topic of debate, leading to a wide circulation of nineteen agricultural journals, including the *Texas Farm and Ranch*, *Texas Livestock Journal*, and the *Southern Mercury*. There were nine publications geared toward African American readers. Articles (and their rejoinders) were printed, reprinted, and passed from paper to paper and often "in the news" for weeks. Most newspapers were owned by local investors, politicians, and businessmen. There were no syndicated media conglomerates. Thus Texas papers were likely to be very politically partisan—especially in the editorials—and there was little to no concern for fact-checking or libel laws. And no topic was more volatile than highlights of candidates, campaigns, and their claims during each election season.[27]

Whatever Terrell's calculated motivations, which began as a continuous campaign speech for the Hogg campaign, they were widely reported by the newspapers statewide. Clark claimed Terrell had "forgotten all of the proprieties of political discussion," and his "foul breath" remarks grew into personal character attacks "on those very close to him." His attack on Sul Ross, who at the time had no active role in the campaign, did not go unanswered. Ross's response filled papers statewide:

College Station, March 27, 1892

ROSS SCORCHES TERRELL

The Man Whom Texans Honor Writes as he Fights.

To: the correspondent of the Galveston News, Austin, Tex.—Sir:

Yours of even date tendering the columns of your paper for such reply as I might wish to make to the unprovoked attack of Judge [Alexander William] Terrell upon me in indirect reflection upon the honorable board of directors who tendered me the presidency of the Agricultural and Mechanical College is at hand, and I return my thanks for the courtesy. It occurs to me the [Galveston Daily] News in stating the facts has left me little to say, except it be to add that when I accepted this work with a salary of $3,500, I declined two other desirable offers each with a salary much greater. This should acquit me of mercenary motives.

And touching any political or official phase of the charge, I could say nothing to give additional force of weight to the rant that I retired from the duties of the executive office with the united commendation of press and people.

The only thing in connecting with this charge troubling me in the least is to define the motive for forcing upon me a quarrel by one against which I have never spoken an unkind word and at a time when I was taking no part in the political canvass further than to say, in answer to the direct inquiry from my friends that I was not and would not be a candidate for governor but expected in the exercise of my right as a citizen to vote for neighbor and fellow townsman Judge [George] Clark.

Now, sir, crimination and recrimination never was a proper method of settling any controversy among men and I have no time and less inclination to engage in such pastime with a man who, far as opportunity and ability goes, comes up to the full measure of Macaulay's description of the Italian [Machiavelli] statesman.

"We see a man whose thoughts are words having no connection with other . . . who never wants a pretext when he is inclined to betray. His cruelties ring not from the heat of blood or the insanity of uncontrolled power, but from deep and cool meditation. His passions, like well-trained troops, are impetuous by rule, and his most headstrong fury never forget the discipline to which they have been accustomed. His whole soul is occupied with vast and complicated schemes of

ambition, yet his aspect and language exhibit nothing but philosophical moderation. Hatred and revenge eat into the heart, yet every look
is a cordial smile, every gesture a familiar caress."

"He never excites the suspicion of advisories by petty provoca-
tions. His purpose is disclosed only when it is accomplished. His face
is muffled. His speech is courteous till vigilance is laid asleep: till a
vital point is exposed: till a sure aim is taken, and then he strikes. He
shuns danger, not because he is insensible to shame, but because in
the society of his thoughts timidity has ceased to be shameful. He
cannot comprehend how a man should scruple to deceive him he does
not scruple to destroy. We would think it madness to decline open
hostilities against a rival whom he might stab in a friendly embrace"

He is such a man—political bankrupt, and his reputation "for ways
that are dark and tricks that are vain" is so notorious that the gallant
old Confederate hero, General John M. Clayborne, and many other
warm friends of Governor Hogg throughout the state are seriously
questioning the loyalty of his friendship for the cause he so vindic-
tively disposes. It may be that in this instance being forcibly reminded
of his experience in the late unfortunate war, he has determined to try
in his old age to make up by bluster and mock courage what he lacked
of an honorable record during its continuance.

If so, I assure him that until he refutes the open charge of arrant
cowardice which his neighbors, Judge Sheek and the noble old veteran, General DeBray, who reported in the columns of the [Austin]
Statesman to have made in recent political address at Austin and
which Judge Clark and others are daily making from the rostrum—
until he confronts these reported accusations, the chastisement of his
insolence would reflect less credit upon anyone than to strike in anger
a—- women.

L. S. Ross

Ross's letter to the *Galveston Daily News* created quite a ruckus statewide.
He soon confirmed that the Terrell attacks were instigated by Hogg.
Rumors from Austin indicated that Terrell demanded "satisfaction"—
in an earlier era, the standard call for a duel. According to news from
Austin sent to Lizzie, Terrell wanted "to challenge" Ross for his attack on
his record and valor (i.e., "he lacked of an honorable record") during the
late "unfortunate war." Some spoke of a duel, yet no such event occurred.

Ross boasted to Major Holmes that after "my execution of Terrell," he had received many letters "thanking me for so artistically skinning him." Sen. Alexander Terrell's attack was on both Sul Ross and the A&M College. As a vocal supporter of the University of Texas, the senator used his position in Austin to lobby against funding for A&M. When both Terrell and Ross were sitting state senators in the early 1880s, Ross blocked Terrell's efforts to set aside millions of acres, citing that it was not a good action for the people of Texas and only for the benefit of the university. When Ross became governor in 1886, the two cut off all communication. Furthermore, Terrell's efforts (along with other speculators in Austin who lobbied the state legislature) to direct more funding to the university was based on his efforts to capitalize on personal real-estate holdings and investments in downtown Austin around the university campus—as the university grew, his land holdings would grow in value. This conflict of interest was singled out by an *American Statesman* editorial: "Judge Terrell has put his money into town lot speculation [in Austin] . . . the land boom he helped to start in full swing, Terrell was in the swim up to his whiskers . . . he pocketed the big profits . . . It was a 'fat take.'"[29]

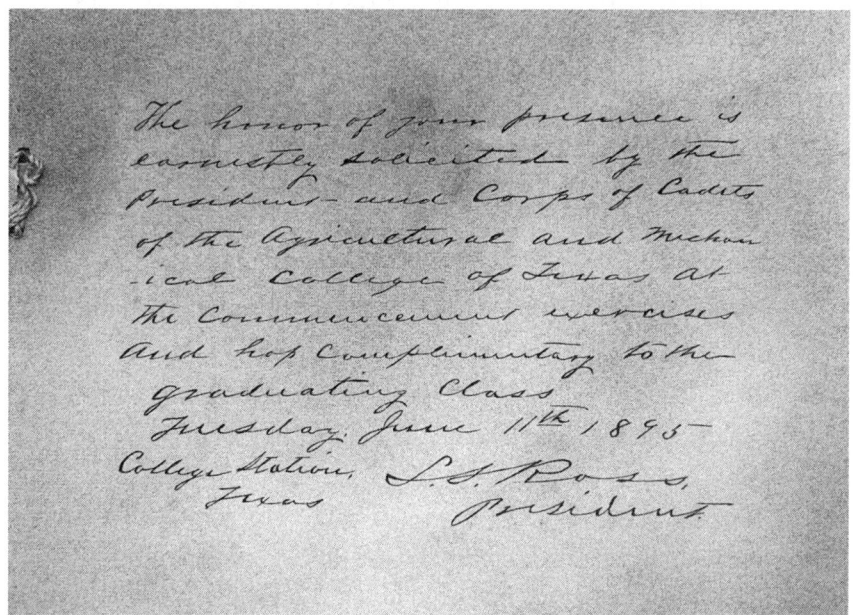

A&M College graduation invitation sent by President Ross in June 1895. Source: Author's collection

In the wake of the Ross-Terrell-Hogg political exchange, Ross was constantly watched by those who sought to determine his future political intentions. The politically charged exchange between Ross and Terrell caused quite a stir in Austin. Many observers and political hacks of the '92 governor election considered the role of Ross as pivotal to Clark's victory, notwithstanding the remote possibility that Ross would enter the race. While Ross endeavored to remain out of the limelight, his every move or "rumored" activities were watched. A case in point is the stir created by his rumored visit to Austin in early April, triggered by an erroneous report in the *Galveston Daily News* that on the morning of April 8, an "L. S. Ross, college" had signed into the guest book at the Avenue Hotel. It was common in that era to publish the hotel arrivals in the local newspaper; yet those who signed in were not verified, and in this case, the hotel manager had no knowledge of Governor Ross as a guest. Nonetheless, word of the former governor's so-called arrival spread rapidly in the capital, with "a number of his admirers," including his son, Lawrence Ross Jr., who was employed by the Texas General Land Office, stopping at the hotel to greet him. Yet Sul Ross was not, nor had he been, in Austin. The *News* noted that the commotion was created "by the enemies of both Ross and Clark who wanted to create the impression that General Ross [had] slipped into the city on a political mission and slipped out" unnoticed.[30]

The *News* reporter in Austin followed up the story with a special delivery telegram message sent to College Station to clarify Ross's location:

> Austin, Tex., April 8—To Governor L. S. Ross, College Station:
>
> "Have you been in Austin to-day [*sic*]? Answer at once: important."
>
> Shortly before 11 o'clock tonight [P.M.] the following reply was received:
>
> College Station, Tex., April 8—To the *News* Correspondent, Austin:
>
> "I have not." L. S. Ross[31]

Even in his rumored absence, Sul Ross attracted media attention.

Terrell biographer Lewis L. Gould noted, "[F]ew of his contemporaries really liked him as a person, and many distrusted him," concluding that in his war of words with Sul Ross and the embarrassment of the controversy, "Terrell had gotten the worst of this exchange." The state-wide exchange of letters, editorials, and jabs from the political campaign trail resulted in a massive behind-the-scenes effort by Colonel House to calm the Democratic ranks, neutralize Clark, and consolidate Hogg's position in advance of the convention. The heated statewide campaign included a number of joint head-to-head appearances. A rally in Cleburne attracted more than twenty thousand partisans and plenty of antics from the speakers' platform: "They were so unruly that only a few people actually heard the candidates, but Hogg did something there that Texans talked about for years. A few minutes after Clark paused in his speech and poured a glass of water, the massive Jim Hogg picked up the pitcher and drank from it!—to the delight of his followers." The race was close, and Clark was a viable challenger to Hogg. To draw the majority of the Democratic Party together, House brokered a deal to place Charles Culberson from East Texas on the ticket for attorney general. As Ross watched the newspaper editorials and political deals unfold, he confided to the Major, "[M]y prediction be verified, Clark is a goner." (Ross also personally conveyed his concerns to Clark.) Yet, still over five months from the November general election with Clark's chances all but dashed, Ross remained loyal to Clark and gave the Hogg camp no rest as to his intentions.[32]

Agricultural and Mechanical College of Texas

President's Office

College Station, Texas   April 20th 1892

My dear Major

I was mighty glad to hear from you again. Didn't' know what had become of you. Was afraid you had gotten sick. Have been down in Houston and went to see [Dr. Robert] Rutherford, poor fellow he is a complete wreck. Don't believe if he gets well he will ever have much mind. I thought surely he would die in a few days. He had not known anyone for days, save possibly Mrs. R. She said he had called out my name but speaking so incoherently for days that she could not understand what he said. When I walked into the room he looked steadily at me for a second then eagerly held out his hand and seized mine, at the same time saying in a strong clear voice, "Now I have my wish." He held me hard and fast for 15 or 20 minutes, and went off into delirium, when I left as quickly as possible. Mrs. Rutherford writes today the "They say he is better," but evidentially she is not hopeful.

Well we had a time for a few days after my execution of Terrell. Lizzie heard from Austin that he would challenge me, and this I could see made her very uneasy. I am told by Johnson of the [Houston] Post that *Hogg was the instigator of Terrell assault.* I should not have noticed it but for his card exempting Roberts from . . .—which seemed to "rub it in" and add insult to injury. When my letter was published and even yet I am in receipt of letters almost daily thanking me for so artistically skinning him. So far I am decidedly the winner of the fight. Don't know what will be the result. I think Hogg will capture [Henry] McCulloch and the [Farmer's] alliance, that Reagan will quit the Ry Commission, take the field for Hogg. With the view of running himself for Governor next time, that they give him his place to [William] Wortham, and thereby make room for Henry McCulloch and that David Culberson will join with the promise of Coke's place.

That will be kept out of the canvass against Hogg by as assurance of no opposition from any Hogg man for the long term etc. These are my conjectuers [*sic*]. If my prediction be verified, Clark is a goner. Don't think he had any chance anyway and told him so. He won't get 100 votes in my judgement. I would give anything reasonable to see him beat Hogg and get the place, or even lock the Convention, but *dear he* cannot do either.

His is a hurrah campaign, and while he has a majority of the businessmen, the county will not vote for him. The [Farmer's] alliance and . . . will aid Hogg. If Hogg gets it again he will probably decapitate me or make my position so unpleasant that I shall have to retire. He can do this by selecting certain men for Directors. The College has been greatly improved in my respect, and no one will be able to rob me of that credit any way.

All well here, and send much love to you and Mrs. Holmes.

God bless and preserve and protect you both,
Your friend,   L. S. Ross

United Confederate Veterans

General Ross's stature among the citizens of Texas would remain a constant throughout his life, and his place among Confederate veterans in Texas was beyond reproach. At the time he took the presidency of A&M, there were other Texas Confederate veterans, many who outranked him from the late war, who remained in powerful elected office in Texas, such as senators like Richard Coke and former general Samuel B. Maxey. Yet no veteran commanded respect and honor quite like Sul Ross, as the titular head of Texas veterans. His actions to help indigent veterans and their families, as well as the establishment of the "Confederate House" in Austin, was appreciated by all. A champion of the home for widows and orphans, the governor was unable to attend the formal dedication, "he not being well enough," in large part due to his reoccurring neurological problems stemming from his 1859 wounds. To recognize Ross's gravitas in April 1892, he was selected as the statewide commander of the Texas Division of the United Confederate Veterans Association, or UCV. The UCV, similar to the American Legion or the Veterans of Foreign War (VFW), was in charter and in spirit a fraternal organization to foster periodic reunions and provide assistance to disabled veterans, particularly amputees, as well as their widows and families. Since there was no federal program to assist the southern disabled, in 1894, the State of Texas created a special appropriation for veterans.[33]

The 1890 national census estimated there were some 429,000 living Confederate veterans, of which 15.5 percent lived in Texas. These included both native-born Texans as well as scores who had moved to the state after the war for a fresh start. Texas was generous to Confederate veterans and the widows of Texans who died during the war, allowing them, in a program that continued through 1883, title to 1,280 acres of available land. The UCVs remained active in Texas from 1892 for about a decade, as the ranks of the aging veterans were quickly reduced after the turn of the century. To foster goodwill, a series of more than 1,200 local gatherings and reunion sites or "camps," where veterans and their families congregated to picnic and socialize, were identified across the South. More than one hundred communities in Texas, the most of any state, established camps with distinctive names. Ross was honored with having four UCV camps—New Boston, Denton, Henrietta, and

Bonham—named after him. There were no camps named for Terrell, Hogg, or Clark. Upon his unanimous reelection as UCV commander on San Jacinto Day 1893 in Houston before hundreds of elderly veterans—"many of whom he had led into the very jaws of death"—the scene was described as wildly "enthusiastic":

> The nominating committee having charge of General Ross entered the hall. The scene was a stirring one. The veterans mounted their chairs, threw their hats in the air and yelled themselves hoarse at the sight of the "little cavalryman." This was continued for five minutes and General Ross could do nothing but bow his thanks. He was visibly affected at this demonstration of love and affection on the part of his comrades, and well he might have been, for it was an ovation of which any man might have felt proud.[34]

Even while numerous Confederate veterans dominated public office across the state throughout the 1890s, the UCVs shunned candidate endorsements. Any such activity was left to the individual veteran. As a political block, they commanded no numbers in strength, except for their requests to maintain funding for the Confederate House in Austin.

President Ross's selection required little of his time away from the college, except for an annual convention and periodic invitations to address camps around the state. A volunteer command and communications staff headed by Gen. Henry B. Stoddard of Bryan was established to run independently of his day-by-day attention.[35]

It is clear that, even without his selection to head the Texas UCV, Sul Ross was one of the key leaders of the Texas veterans, and the network of relationships and contacts they fostered accounted for an unwritten political power base that lasted long after 1895. And while Ross privately confided to Major Holmes on more than one occasion that his support of George Clark over Hogg would result in him being "probably decapitated by Hogg or my position so unpleasant that I shall have to retire," he lamented on the eve of the November 1892 governor's election, "[I]f such is my fate . . . I will take my chances for something else." Somehow Ross knew—in spite of the campaign fireworks and personal attacks—that even Hogg, the son of a Confederate general, would not actually go head-to-head and publicly discredit such a well-known and respected Texan.[36]

Galveston Daily News April 21, 1892

Ross Assumes Command

General Orders From the New Confederate Veterans' Commander

Bryan, Tex., April 20—The following general orders were issued yesterday from headquarters:

Headquarters U. C. V. Division of Texas, Bryan, Tex., April 19, 1892

General Order No. 1

In compliance with my election under the constitution adopted by the Confederate Veterans assembled at Dallas, Tex, on April 6, 1892, I hereby assume command of all the confederate camps in the division of Texas.

L. S. Ross

Major General

Headquarters U. C. V. Division of Texas, Bryan, Tex., April 13, 1892

General Order No. 2

H. [Henry] B. [Bates] Stoddard is hereby appointed and assigned to duty as adjutant general and chief of staff.

J. J. Adams is hereby appointed aid-de-camp and acting assistant general.

L. S. Ross

Major General

Numerous invitations arrived weekly, in hopes that Ross would attend and keynote a UCV camp meeting of the "old Confederates." When not able to attend, he was able to dispatch members of General Staddard's UCV staff to honor the many requests.[37]

Agricultural and Mechanical College of Texas

President's Office

College Station, Texas   June 23, 1892

T. O. Moore

My dear sir:

   After thanking you for your very kind invitation I desire to assure you, that I should esteem it a very great pleasure to meet the old confederates of yours of our state on the occasion of your meeting and I shall certainly endeavor to so shape matters as to do so. My time will be engaged with the duty of supervising, however, buildings, and repairs about the A&M College, preparations to this next sessions work, and because I cannot promise definitely to attend the harmonious gatherings to which I am invited but hope to be with you & your friends.

Fraternally—L. S. Ross

In addition to invitations from veterans' groups, President Ross received numerous requests for presentations and personal appearances from civic groups, colleges and universities, and political candidates. In his early months at A&M, he attempted to limit his travel so that he could concentrate his efforts on the campus. Ross was very punctual in replying, and oftentimes his reply would be read at the requesting event and published in the newspaper. The *Austin Statesman* kept a close watch on events at both the A&M College and the University in Austin, and was ever ready to print any threads of news. On the eve of the University of Texas commencement in June 1892, they offered the following:

> A letter from the "Little Cavalrymen" shows so far as he is concerned the best of relations shall exist between the University and the Agricultural and Mechanical College:

College Station, June 12, 1892.

Dr. Leslie Waggener: [President]

My Dear Sir—

I regret that I cannot attend the commencement exercises of the University. I have witnessed your magnificent expansion with sincere gratification, and regard the University as the crowning glory of our state. I have authorized Prof. Harrington to represent me on the occasion and commend him to your kindly courtesy.

Very respectfully,
L. S. Ross, President

Hunting, Fishing, and Ticks

Regardless of the political pressures and demands at the college, Sul Ross routinely reserved time to hunt and fish. A product of the open frontier, he looked forward to stealing a few days and camping under the stars. With no defined seasons or bag limits, hunting was a year-round avocation—for deer, fish, squirrel, ducks—and not limited to just the president but also of great interest to his sons and the A&M staff and cadets. While guns were outlawed on campus, aside from an occasional shotgun for local ducks, few strictly adhered to the regulation. Almost all travel from home or on business resulted in individuals carrying firearms. Train transportation was relatively safe, yet stagecoach travel was always prone to holdups by bands of highwaymen looking to make a quick buck. As sheriff of McLennan County from 1873 to 1875, Ross spent a great deal of time ensuring the safety of coach lines in the region, yet the crime persisted into the 1890s.[38]

Sul Ross's letters are filled with numerous brief mentions of hunting trips, either accompanied only by his African American coachman, Jesse Parks, to the Navasota or Brazos River bottom, or with family members (and his prized hunting dogs) to prearranged campsites for fun afield, followed by the camp-wide evening meal and socializing. If residents of a location learned of his proximity or overnight intentions, it was cause for a community-wide camp meeting—not of Ross's making but from locals attracted to see and hear the governor. In such situations, as he recounts to Major Holmes in July 1892, he was thrust into the role of quartermaster to help feed the "guests" to the best of his ability, and he never shrank from doing all he could do to make provisions available and a meal for all.[39]

With little or no use of ice in the field to preserve the meat, wild game and fish were prepared the day taken, especially in the hot months of July and August. Camp cooks provided ample coffee and biscuits, and in one case, Ross faced a larger-than-expected dinner party and found one hundred pounds of bee honey in a hive to enhance the dinner.

His only complaint was that "[t]he ticks were simply fearful."[40]

Agricultural and Mechanical College of Texas

President's Office

College Station, Texas   July 22nd 1892

My dear Major

Presume you have heard of Mrs. Dorset's death. Had a letter from Dr. and B. They were pretty distressed and no doubt her death creates a sad breach in their family circle. Don't think Dr. is doing much practice and fear they are limited in funds to a serious extent. I hear Dr. Rutherford has quit his late near approach to mental disarrangement, if not death, has quit drink and gone to work to regain his former prestige and usefulness in Houston. The sheriff thinks he won't drink anymore, and everybody rejoices.

I have been kept very busy superintending some new buildings being erected, making contracts and repairs for next session and have not found time to go anywhere except out on a camp hunt and fish for two days.

Caught enough fish and I killed large deer. The only trouble was when the citizens of the vicinity heard I was along they flocked around until we had dinner one day for 25 men. Fortunately I found a Bee tree which they all cut and from which they got 100 lbs. of honey. This, with the deer meat, gave some of them the only meal they seemed to have had for quite some time. I think they would gladly vote for me to renew the trip at my earliest convenience. The ticks were simply fearful and I have a scratching time for almost a week.

Crops here are splendid and we have had excellent fruit, such as peaches, pears, etc. And the finest melons I ever saw grown in

Texas. So you see Darkies and White folks hereabouts are fat and sassy. Florine is busy arranging for the wedding and we are looking forward to your and Mrs. Holmes and May's presence at the coming pleasure of the occasion.

I am simply disgusted with the political affairs of our state. Hogg seems to have the nomination again. Have had letters from General [George C.] Pendleton [Lt.Gov. 1890–92] and other candidates for nomination to congress in our new District urging me to permit the use of my name as a satisfactory compromise all around.

Pendleton thinks the third party dangerously strong, and likely to defeat our Democratic candidate should he be an unfortunate selection. I have firmly declined, as I want to stay here, if I can, until Frank graduates. He is doing splendid, but has been a little sick. Bessie is over at Seguin with Aunt Beahan. Harve has been assisting Hass at Artesian Wells and made some money. He don't seem to shrink from hard work so it pays. Lizzie has had a slight bilious spell but is getting up again. Most of the kin folks will attend the wedding and we shall expect your family—

Write often, yours as ever,   L. S. Ross

Prairie View

In addition to his A&M College duties, Sul Ross was also the president of Prairie View. In an organizational mandate of the state legislature dating from the inaugural of the Thomas Gathright administration in 1876, Prairie View in Waller County was a component of the A&M College, with the chief administrator of the Hempstead campus known as the "principal." Having been on the educational committee of the 1875 Texas Constitutional Convention, Ross was well aware that the Texas constitution of 1876 called for equal education for all Texans, stating in Article VII, Sec. 7, "Separate schools shall be provided for the white and colored children, and impartial provisions shall be made for both." The constitution further established an Agricultural and Mechanical College to take advantage of the federal appropriations of the Morrill Land Grand Act of 1862. Notwithstanding his use of the then-common term "darkies" in the letter above—highly objectionable by current standards—Ross expended considerable effort toward ensuring that this aspect of the law was carried out, especially regarding the continued funding of higher education for African Americans.

To ensure educational provisions for African Americans, on August 14, 1876, the state legislature established a college "for the benefit of colored youth" and designated it a branch of the A&M College at Bryan. Following a search for a location, an old plantation was purchased for the new college and renamed "Alta Vista Agricultural College for Colored Youth," opening on March 11, 1878, in Waller County near the small town of Hempstead.[41]

The new college opened under its first principal, L. W. Minor, but was able to enroll only eight students. Pres. Thomas Gathright, charged with oversight, at first attributed the low enrollment to the fact that "there was no demand for higher education among blacks"—which was a poor rush to judgment by the career educator from Mississippi. Other factors impacted the opening, such as the remote location of the fledging campus, the cost of tuition (considered high), and a growing sentiment that students wanted something more than an agricultural education. Classes were discontinued in late 1878. Endeavoring to maintain the Alta Vista school, Orlando N. Hollingsworth of the Texas Education Commission prompted Gov. Oran M. Robert and the Sixteenth Texas Legislature to redirect the mission of the school toward a teacher's education curriculum, in order to address the growing demand for secondary school teachers across the state. The college thus was reopened and renamed the Prairie View State Normal Institute, appropriated $6,000 per year from the University Fund, along with a matching grant from the Peabody Education Fund. And thus the college was reopened on April 19, 1879, under new principal E. H. Anderson, with sixteen students, growing to more than sixty by the end of the term. Prairie View remained a branch of the A&M College.[42]

Sul Ross, as a state senator in the early 1880s, quickly learned the highly politicized nature of yearly funding of public higher education in the state. The Austin lobby (driven partly by land speculators around the new Austin campus) supporting the recently opened University of Texas felt it was fair game to attack and cut the legislative appropriations for the A&M College, Prairie View, and Sam Houston Normal for the benefit of the new university. The attacks on public college funding continued during Ross's governorship, yet he pushed back against the Grange, along with the lobbyists who questioned the funding of classical subjects and teacher's courses in land-grant institutions. The legislature, having funded Prairie View during its early years out of the University Fund, informed Governor Ross that such appropriations were no longer available and that any funding in the past (a cumulative sum of $27,000 since 1879) had been misappropriated and was now considered a warrant (or loan) payable back to the state comptroller. Ross was undeterred and made arrangements to support higher education needs through general revenue funds. Notwithstanding, Prairie View principal Laurine C. Anderson (1885–95) supplied a broader vision for his college to meet the challenges. The introduction of new courses in industrial and mechanical education and an experiment station, along with new funding from the second Morrill Act of 1890, were welcomed by both Prairie View and the A&M College.[43]

However, what seemed like a welcomed solution was soon attacked by African American Republican politicians, led by Galveston party organizer Norris Wright Cuney, whom Ross labeled a "bloody-shirt shrieker [*sic*]." This led to the drafting of a petition to the US government to withhold the needed Morrill funding from A&M on the basis that black-oriented schools had not received equal treatment. There were surely areas of inequity, such as teacher pay, classroom facilities, and available teaching supplies, but the fact remained that during this period, for all the shortcomings that are so apparent in retrospect, Texas was lauded by some as highly progressive and responsive to the educational needs of all Texans. A leading African American educator in the state, E. L. Blackshear, noted in an April 1890 *Austin Statesman* editorial, "It is a certain fact, as testified by the noble governor, a man whom all classes and races in Texas love and delight to honor, it is, I say, a certain fact the Negro is advancing in all that constitutes a Christian civilization." And Thomas Fortune, editor of the *New York Age*, noted the following after a tour of the state: "In many respects I think Texas is the best state in the South for Afro-Americans."[44]

Ross swiftly responded to Cuney's call for federal interference and prevailed, with the publication of a detailed document on Texas "Democratic" support of education for all citizens—black and white—addressed not to Texans but instead to a larger audience. Addressed "For the Information of the People of the United States" and titled "Education of the

Colored Race," it reviewed the increased pro-rata cost per student. The 134 percent growth of the student population won the day. Washington released the new funding, and the Texas Legislature passed a measure dividing the federal grant of 1890 on the basis of one-fourth for Prairie View and three-fourths for A&M, ignoring the recommendation by President Ross that the split be a fairer division of one-third and two-thirds. Notwithstanding, Ross was steadfast in his strong stance on the importance education for all Texans: "The question of higher as well as ordinary education of the colored race is one which demands attention of the university regents, as well as the legislature, under the requirements of the law providing for a colored branch university."[45]

A positive result of this confrontation was the selection of Ross's longtime friend and Democrat ally Edward L. Blackshear to assume the chief administrative post at Prairie View (1895–1915). Politically astute, Blackshear worked closely with Ross and the A&M Board to expand the facilities and programs of the school. While Republican politicians across the state lobbied for a separate black "university" on par with the one in Austin and apart from Prairie View, Blackshear (who had supported such a university proposal in 1892) knew there was no additional state or private funding, and the best use of the funds on hand was to expand the current programs. George Clark, in his memoir, *A Glance Backwards*, recalled the political dynamics of higher education during the 1892 governor election: "Even the Negroes who voted as a rule voted for Governor Hogg. I was told afterward that they had been promised a 'university' in Waller County at Prairie View." With the approval of the A&M Board, Blackshear, in an effort to address an increasingly urban and industrial society, reorganized the college's academic departments, expanded the curriculum, and improved the library, while also adding faculty and new dorms.[46] Responding to African American leaders and political observers in Austin, Blackshear, who at the time was the leading black educator in Texas, was quick and candid to stress the growing need for industrial and mechanical training.[47]

Republicans, some disgruntled Grange members, and lobbyists in Austin attacked Ross during the 1890s on purely self-serving political grounds. However, supporters of a broad base of public higher education as well as African American leaders and educators applauded President Ross for his ongoing efforts to improve Prairie View—at times in opposition to members of the A&M Board. Ross's efforts to enhance education and assistance to the black community dated from his time as state senator, when he advocated for adequate services to be provided for the indigent and mentally ill, while also backing more funding for education for all Texans. As governor, Ross fulfilled this promise by establishing state facilities to address these needs. During his years as sheriff in McClellan County, he openly abhorred all forms of mob violence, and as governor, he went so far as to travel by train from Austin to Richmond, Texas, in August 1889 with the Texas Rangers and militia to calm racial unrest. There was no known organized Ku Klux Klan active during the 1880s and 1890s in Texas, nor was Ross ever a member—quite the opposite, in fact. As governor, he outwardly confronted and denounced all who fomented trouble. This was widely known and appreciated by the black community. Governor Ross pardoned and commuted more African Americans than all the previous governors combined. Furthermore, he routinely hosted black religious and education leaders at the president's residence on the A&M campus, and he routinely visited the Prairie View campus to meet with the staff and students.[48]

Agricultural and Mechanical College of Texas

President's Office

College Station, Texas   Nov 5th, 1892

Dear Major

I was truly glad to hear from you & yours. I believe I was due you a letter & have from time to time promised myself the pleasure of paying my obligations in full. Harve has been pretty steadily at work with the well crew & running the engine. The well is down 1336 feet & work has been suspended temporarily for pipe to cut off quicksand. The job has given me much trouble by its slow progress. We have a fine body of water but not sufficient flow. Is up to within 92 feet of the top.

Frank is doing well in his studies & has the reputation of being a good student. Bess & Nev are going to a private teacher here, and seem to be doing well. Lissie has had much trouble recently with her eyes. Don't know what ails them. She has tried glasses without apparent relief.

Florence & Prof Harrington are keeping house at the place I formerly lived, and are snugly fixed up in every way. They expect Birdie Dorsett this evening for the promised visit. Harve thinks of going on the Farm next year. I proposed to give him all he could make. It should pay him about $1200.

I am afraid your prediction about Clark's majority will not be verified. I don't think we are going to get a fair count in many places where they are strongest & where Hogg's white friends are in power. They are considerably split up. I find the leading ones of Prairie View are against [Norris Wright] Cuney, and in favor of Hogg. I noticed when Clark gets up a big rally, his crowd is carried from other strongholds, which leads me to fear his strength is not real, and that his vote will not "pan out" in larger votes than in the primaries.

I have not taken active part in the canvass [election], but have not concealed the fact I should vote for Clark. And I am informed by a Dallas friend the [James B.] "Farmer Shaw" says my advocacy of Clark will cost me my place as President of A. & M. C.

If such be my fate I shall "bow" with becoming resignation and take my chances for something else. I am glad you read my address at Dallas. I am getting a good many compliments from friends on the subject. Glad May found time to pay you a pleasant visit. I know you all had a good old fashioned Methodist love feast. Your spontaneous effusion in the party line is very good & appropriate.

Give my love to all—Your friend as ever

L. S. Ross

President Ross was correct that the last-minute votes George Clark expected did not "pan out." Hogg won the election for a second term, and his supporters did not soon forget the heated campaign of '92. Hogg's staunch supporter and advisor Terrell was removed from an active role in Texas politics following his presidential appointment by Pres. Grover Cleveland, who had returned to the presidency after an absence of one term. In early 1893 Terrell was named American Minister (i.e., ambassador) to Turkey. Thus Terrell's absence and Hogg's departure at the end of his second term as governor removed most challenges for the Colonel House "crowd" to orchestrate statewide leadership in Texas until well after the turn of the century.[49]

Still, Ross and his staff took time to consult with other land-grant institutions, especially in the areas of agricultural experimentation and extension activities that connected the college with the citizens of the state, as shown in the following letter:

Agricultural and Mechanical College

College Station, Texas November 29, 1892

Hon. J. P. Lane, Norman, Ok.

Dear Sir:

Your communication of the 26th instant to the president of this college having been received and referred by him to the board, we wish to express our gratification at your proposed visit, and to unite with the president of the college and the directors of the experiment station in extending you such courtesies as may be necessary to acquaint you fully with our college work and to make your visit pleasant to those of you who may honor us with your presence,

Respectfully,
A. J. Rose, President Board of Directors
L. S. Ross, President A. and M. College
Geo. W. Curtis, Director Experiment Station

In many respects, 1892 was the most challenging year of Sul Ross's tenure at A&M—largely as a result of events that occurred off-campus. Improvements to the campus and the esprit de corps of the cadets was becoming very evident to outside observers. As enrollment grew, new facilities were added and the image of the college improved, and Ross subsequently found himself engaged in political election-year confrontations that were generally not of his making. The '92 governor's race saw the Texas Democratic Party split into the combative Hogg versus Clark factions. It thus became the most contentious statewide race since the election of Gov. Richard Coke. As such, Ross was drawn into the fray, causing him to defend both his reputation and that of the A&M College. And he did not waver from the challenge.

CHAPTER 4

Military Peacockery

The prescribed course in military science embraces lectures, drill,
guard mounting and guard duty, inspections, musters, reviews,
dress parades, target practice, competitive drill, battalion drill, and
as no student can graduate from the institution without a certain
proficiency in the military department, which is measured by the
high military standards required of the entire Corps of Cadets.

Texas House Journal, March 4, 1893

The Corps of Cadets contributed singularly to making the Texas
A&M University of today a truly unique institution of higher
learning. The Corps created a highly organized, responsive,
cohesive, and generally well-led student body from the earliest
days of the institution. This in itself marks a distinctive quality
in A&M's development, in view of the fact that most student
bodies have been and are disorganized, heterogeneous and usually
unresponsive groupings.

Henry C. Dethloff, A Centennial History
of Texas A&M University, 1876–1976

With the culmination of the 1892 governor's race, Ross turned his full
attention to the continued improvements at the A&M College. Detractors continued to question the role and viability of Texas A&M. In early
January 1893, President Ross was informed the Texas Legislature would
once again send a "visiting" committee to review the programs and status of the college. Rumors soon surfaced in newspapers, particularly in

the Dallas *Texas Farmer*, that "grave charges against a noble institution are vaguely hinted at but nothing specified." The editor, Col. Bill Shaw, was deemed to be "frazzled out by the recent political contest," thus directing his editorial comments to what he deemed mismanagement and "military peacockery" at the A&M College. The *Texas Farmer* had wide distribution to Grange members and politicians of the day who were interested to know how "the wind was blowing." The Grand Master of the Texas Patrons of Husbandry, A. J. Rose, described its mission as follows:

> The Texas Farmer publishing company was organized in 1882 by the patrons of husbandry. The object being to have a paper devoted to the farmer's interest and as a medium of communications. It was to stand on the watch tower and at all times keep the people informed of what was transpiring that affected their interest and the best interest of the country for good or for evil. It sounds the warning voice of approaching danger and as far as possible to point out the evils of the day and how to correct them. It is with pride and pleasure to me to state that performing these duties the paper has been as true as the needle to the pole.[1]

Thus the longtime blunt attacks by the *Texas Farmer*—following its "devoted farmer's interest"—centered around an ongoing debate that the college was not teaching enough pure agricultural and farming courses to properly prepare graduates for farm and ranch careers. The decade-long views of the Grange toward the role of the college, while officially professing to be "a strong defender of institution . . . while somewhat impatient at times at the slowness of getting a system of agricultural education underway" were persistent. The lack of a base of academic knowledge for agricultural education and the open-ended terms of the Land-Grant Act became "painfully apparent" at all the new "A&M" colleges nationwide. Sul Ross noted during his last year as president, reflecting on the progress and evolution of the two-decades-old college: "They [the founding board and faculty] have [been] given the new educational scheme but little thought or study and there was little in experience of the past to guide them. There were no models for imitation [yet] public apathy retreated . . . as men became enlightened in the subject." A foundation for a solid base of agricultural education was not mitigated until after the passage and implementation of the Hatch Act (1887), which established a system of agricultural experiment stations across each state and a $15,000 annual federal appropriation "in connection" with the parent A&M college. Texas A&M thus fully embraced the experiment station concept and the much-needed funding, yet detractors in various agricultural organizations still looked for reasons to criticize the college, including the military aspects of the Corps of Cadets.[2]

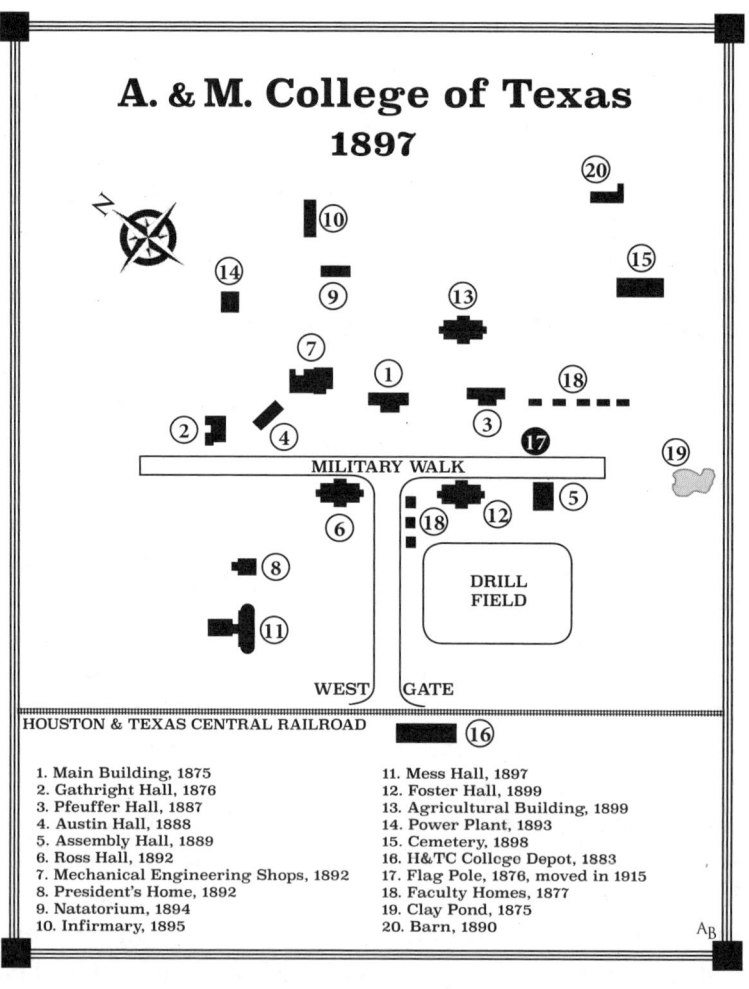

Map of the A&M College of Texas, 1897. Source: Author's collection

Criticizing the A&M course curriculum as heavy in the "classics," the *Texas Farmer* characterized the college as "one ounce of agriculture hyphenated with three-quarters ounces of mechanics," cloaked in "spindle-shanked dudeism at one end and elaborate military 'peacockism' at the other." By early 1893, the "military features" of the college fostered by President Ross and commandant Lt. Benjamin C. Morse had proved pivotal to an increase in morale, better overall discipline, and reduction of hazing, as well as an improved public image. Interestingly, the *Brazos Pilot*, published in Bryan, was very "defensive in the war threatened on the institution," noting, "The military feature of this and other agricultural colleges is something anomalous, while not particularly objectionable is not especially commendable—that we know of . . . we have nothing to say, but when it comes to attacking it [the Corps and the college] we shall take a hand." The *Galveston Daily News* signaled the pending challenge to Ross and the college with a front-page headline: "An Attack Likely to Be Made on the A. and M. College with a View to Knifing General Ross."[3]

The underlying tension created by those who opposed the college far exceeded complaints by the Grange and, as Sul Ross and supporters of A&M knew, was purely political and not substantive. The attacks from Austin began in mid-February 1893, while, in a rare absence from the campus when class was in session, Sul, his wife, and his daughter were in New Orleans for a few days, attending the annual Mardi Gras "carnival." Ross returned to three primary issues being floated "to attack" (as predicted by the *Galveston Daily News*) both his presidency and the college: (1) behind-the-scenes efforts, dating from 1881, to enhance funding for the University of Texas by cutting support for the A&M College during the upcoming legislative session; (2) the notion that cadets, if fully immersed in agricultural courses, should be "paid" an hourly wage for any work done related to their studies on the college farm, according to the *Texas Farmer*, to be able "to pay the greater part of [the student's] expenses for board, clothing, and books," so that economically disadvantaged students could attend the college; and (3) a continued effort to generally discredit Ross and the A&M College. The legislative appropriations reductions were also targeted toward Prairie View Normal in Hempstead and Sam Houston Normal in Huntsville.[4]

Given the official federal nationwide statistics compiled by the US Department of Agriculture (USDA) in 1893, much of the politically motivated criticism by the Grange was baseless. Political opponents wanted only to discredit A&M in general and Sul Ross in particular. And the news media had little incentive to review the substantial hard data. The documented results on the A&M College of Texas were compelling. By 1893, A&M had turned the corner when compared with similar land-grant institutions across the country. In terms of faculty, AMC, with a staff of twenty-nine, employed more full-time professors than forty-one of the forty-eight other programs. Long after the college expanded to a four-year agricultural curriculum, some eight colleges were still on a three-year schedule. In 1893 the USDA reported that there were 17,623 students enrolled at the forty-eight land-grant institutions, yet only 3,160, or 18 percent, were enrolled in agricultural programs. Unbeknownst to the Grange and critics, at AMC, 56 percent of the cadets were enrolled in agricultural studies, ranking it the ninth highest percentage nationwide. The primary limiting factor for increasing student enrollment and improving programs in agriculture at the college was funding for dorms, quality faculty, textbooks, and equipment. The average funding to all land-grant colleges was $77,000, and this number was skewed by the seven largest programs; thus, omitting these large programs, the average of the other forty-one programs (including A&M) was $53,000. Funding at A&M in 1893 was $51,155—and thus on par with the national average.[5]

The aim of these attacks was far from altruistic and purely aimed at fueling the political discourse and doubts prior to the opening of the 1893 legislative session. No mention was made of the service and success of Texas A&M former students (five of whom were members of the Texas Legislature), the stability and growth of the facilities and faculty, or the emerging contributions of the Texas Agricultural Experiment Station, which helped farmers and ranchers statewide. The Experiment Station, in conjunction with research by A&M faculty and staff, exerted a profound influence on Texas agriculture and was very active in addressing the pressing concerns of farmers and ranchers on critical impediments to production, providing solutions and methods for curbing screwworms and cattle ticks, increasing hog production, reducing alfalfa root rot, improving means of soil analysis and fertilizer usage, and educating farmers on the economics and marketing of the state's leading crop—cotton.[6]

A Life Worth Living

The visiting Texas legislative committee arrived at A&M in early February 1893. The "Report of the Joint Committee on State Institutions of Learning" noted a number of concerns with the college, yet as a whole, it was an independent confirmation of the positive impact President Ross

Table 4.1. Profile of the 1892–93 A&M College faculty and staff

Faculty	Staff
One president	One cook
One surgeon	Two dishwashers
One steward	One woodchopper
One stockman	Four janitors
One board secretary	One stenographer
One assistant meteorologist	Seven labors
Ten professors	Two head waiters for professors
One chaplain	One second cook
One shop foreman	One baker
One commandant	Two storekeepers
One bookkeeper	One head janitor
One adjunct professor	One milkman
Two associate professors	One campus foreman
Five assistant professors	Two head waiters for cadets
One assistant director	One second baker
One assistant chemist	Five waiters
One hospital steward	One drummer
One campus assistant	One bugler

Source: Austin, *Texas Journal*, March 4, 1893

was having on the A&M's image, statewide contribution, and improved infrastructure. The five visiting legislators interviewed many of the sixty-six faculty and staff members (a total combined biannual payroll of $111,663) individually and in groups, met with the entire Corps of Cadets in the College Chapel to obtain feedback, toured all aspects of the campus, and even solicited feedback from local Bryan residents (see table 4.1.).[7]

Representatives heard complaints from both the cadets and staff involving the quantity and lack of variety of food in the mess hall, the "unanimously condemned" campus laundry service, the need for more dormitory rooms, and concerns regarding poor medical personnel and facilities for "treatment of the sick." There was some concern, due to the cadet recruiting success, about overcrowding on campus, given the fact that some 270 cadets occupied a total of 110 campus rooms. The housing of some faculty and staff in dormitory rooms, necessitated by a lack of faculty housing, only made matters worse. Notwithstanding, the discipline of the students was considered "sufficiently strict to keep order" and was maintained by the military organization under the commandant. All findings of the legislative visit were valid concerns and perennial campus challenges during the mid-1890s as the college grew annually and became more popular under Sul Ross.[8]

The independent report, submitted in early March to the Speaker of the Texas House of Representatives, chronicled the culmination of the biggest period of new campus construction, infrastructure improvements, and overall growth since the founding of the college in 1876. The committee gave the A&M administration approval for the judicious spending of the state appropriations to complete the president's residence, three new frame cottages for professors (for a total of sixteen single-family residences), a two-story addition to the mechanical shop, a new brick creamery and cheese building, a gymnasium, and a new dormitory. Furthermore, there had been continued efforts to ensure a safe water supply. The blacksmith, wood, and machine shops were deemed by the visitors to be "well equipped and in very good condition" and were to be expanded to the "fullest development." In terms of agricultural programs and stables, the report lauded the campus dairy and quality care for livestock.[9]

Heraldry of the colors and "AMC," as presented in 1895. Source: Author's collection

Efforts to improve the appearance of the once bleak campus were noticeable. The *Galveston Daily News*, which had often published a harsh view of the A&M campus environs, noted that due to the "magic touch" of the college "florist" (i.e., landscape manager) Professor Ebertspacher, "there are no prettier grounds in the state—the surroundings are such as to make life worth living."

As part of the Texas legislative visit and inspection, President Ross was requested to offer comparative data on tuition and fees from other "agricultural and mechanical colleges" organized under the Morrill Act of 1862 from across the country. Information about the cost to students and college management, as well as information about legislative appropriations, was helpful in curbing exaggerated legislative claims in Austin about the operations at the A&M College. Expanded details and data about Mississippi A&M College are provided in the article because Texas A&M was routinely compared to this institution.[10]

Agricultural and Mechanical College of Texas

L. S. Ross, President   A. J. Rose, Pres't Board of Directors

College Station, Texas   February 26, 1893

Hon. Representative T. D. Rowell

Dear Sir:

I have the honor to acknowledge receipt of your letter of February 24, and, after thanking you for the courtesy and kindly interest evidenced, I beg, in compliance with your request to submit for your information, the subjoined tabulated statements hastily complied from the only reports of agricultural and mechanical colleges at my immediate command. These will serve to show in some measure the comparative cost to students in respective institutions for a nine months' session [report by college for tuition and expenses]:

Kentucky	from $173 to $192	exclusive of uniform
Colorado	$170	without uniforms
Louisiana	$176	exclusive of uniforms and books
Pennsylvania	$177	exclusive of uniforms and books
Maryland	$180	exclusive of uniforms, $25
Vermont	from $204 to $272	exclusive of uniforms and books
Arkansas	$173	exclusive of uniforms and books
Missouri	$184	exclusive of uniforms and books
Alabama	$200	exclusive of uniforms and supplies
Ohio	from $200 to $334	plus uniforms, lab fees and books

Texas

Incidental fee, $10; medical fee, $5; trust fund (which is refunded the student, less actual damages to buildings and furniture), $5; board, $125; uniforms (contract price), $15.50, making a total of $160.50. Our books are practically free, a small fee being retained for damages. Now deduct for books and drawing instruments furnished free by us, $15, which make our charges $145.50. We deduct from our statement books, because all other colleges, except Maryland, charge for them.

Mississippi

The charges are $125, including uniform; deduct cost of uniform, estimated at $15.35, and we have the amount of $109.65; to this add cost of instruments and books, estimated at $15, which will make a total of $124.35, showing an apparent difference in favor of the Mississippi college over the Texas college of about $20. Maintenance and support in the Texas agricultural and mechanical college [*sic*] includes board, fuel, washing, electric lights, books, rent, bedsteads, mattresses, pillows, washstands, chairs, wardrobes, buckets, basins and slop cans and janitor service, all of which the college furnished free.

While the report of the Mississippi college herewith inclosed [*sic*] does not itemize the various articles included under the same heading, it appears from the steward's report that janitor service and kerosene for lights are the only items mentioned as paid for on account of board. And from the report of the secretary conveys the idea that students are charged rent on their bedsteads. When all these are taken into account, I submit that the Texas college is in no respect thrown into the shadow of the contrast. It will be observed that the Mississippi legislature appropriated for the maintenance and support of their agricultural and mechanical college [*sic*] $25,000 for each year, exclusive of the endowment fund. In addition to this they appropriated for student labor $7,784.

The legislature of Texas appropriated for our agricultural and mechanical college for the same period $20,000 only for each year. The report of Mississippi agricultural and mechanical college shows the number of officers and professors with salaries paid them by the state amounting to $28,630, but this does not embrace the entire amount of salaries paid from all other sources, as is evidenced by the secretary's report where the total disbursements for salaries is shown to be $13,443.32. The Texas agricultural and mechanical college pays for total salaries $15,000. The president of the Texas agricultural and mechanical college is also treasurer of that institution; also treasure of the experiment station and ex-officio treasurer of the Prairie View state normal school, receiving and disbursing all its moneys, paying all bills and supervising its accounts, and is under a bond of $20,000.

In addition to these duties it is made his duty by the board of directors to contract for and superintend the erection of all public buildings at the agricultural and mechanical and Prairie View state normal school, which since my incumbency, has engrossed my entire time during the three summer months' vacation, believed to be enjoyed by all other college presidents.

The report of the Mississippi college shows that R. C. King [president] discharges the duties of secretary, treasurer and purchasing agent and that the president is not required to discharge duties connected with my other institution.

In regard to the military features the Mississippi report shows that the commandant, Lieutenant John B. White of the First United States artillery, "besides the prescribed studies in his chair proper is also commandant of the cadets and directly supervises the discipline under the control of the president." He is also assistant professor of mathematics, for which he is also paid by the college., it is assumed $800, as that is one-half of the amount shown to be paid two assistant professors in the schedule of salaries. The commandant of the Texas agricultural and mechanical college, Lieutenant R. C. Morse, having substantially the same duties and exercising the same discipline, is paid by the college $530. The number of students in attendance at the Mississippi agricultural and mechanical college, including the preparatory department in 1891, was 285, of whom 116 were in the preparatory department, as shown in the report. The attendance for the same year in the college classes of the Texas agricultural and mechanical college was 331. We have no preparatory department here, but I believe should have one to meet the great demand from this class of students in our state.

L. S. Ross, President

The legislative report, of which more than two-thirds involved only the A&M College, concluded the college should as quickly as possible sever electric service from the Water, Ice, and Electric Company of Bryan, some five miles away, and establish its own campus electric service. In addition, they noted, having better service on the campus, a new power plant, and "an electric light plant . . . will afford facilities for practical training in electrical engineering." There was no reference to or concern raised about the agricultural courses or training. A second finding, surely influenced by the Grange and the *Texas Farmer*, noted that "manual labor should be required of all students in the practical operations of agriculture." The third finding was a blunt criticism of the salary paid the college steward, Bernard Sbisa, at an "extravagant" $2,000 per annum. And fourth, if they could not control the A&M College, it was recommended that the University of Texas and all its branches statewide be placed under the management of one consolidated board of directors in Austin. In the aftermath of the legislative visit to the campus, Sul Ross expressed some concern about the intentions of the "visitors" in a letter to Major Holmes:

Agricultural and Mechanical College of Texas

President's Office

College, Station   April 5, 1893

My dear Major

   I was very glad to hear from you again. Hope President [Grover] Cleveland may give your application favorable consideration. [Roger Q.] Mills writes me that the office makes him nearly vain. Everybody is Washington Crazy. *Fine about however* is fair easy. They are the people nearly crazy in hunting the places they hold & should not complain when the people are at the Bat & have their inning in some measure. Poor [Richard] Coke has had to acknowledge—as I see in the [Galveston Daily] News—that he has no influence with the President. All he will get for his friends will come through a trade with Mills.

   Well the visiting committee fooled me more than I was ever fooled by anyone in life. They spoke to the cadets in the chapel in the most laudatory terms of the college. The boys & myself reported their favorable impressions to many of the professors and yet when they got back to Austin attempted to knife the whole ever since. Senator [Samuel B.] Maxey and many others of lessor [*sic*] note have written me that vindication of the College made by myself & others was "complete and unanswerable." Still I see they will try to reply this week. If they aren't being careful they will expose their talons to a heavily _____ _____ that must leave hide enough on them to patch a bullet. Dear old M G seems to have gotten himself in quite a mess, but he openly declared his intentions to keep & provide for his kinfolks, and by his subsequent election hasn't the people condemned his offense.

   Florine has gone to Seguin for a visit to her friend Annie B., Bess is growing like a weed, she is at school here at a good private teacher, I shall send her away next year to some good school. Frank getting along at the head of a large class. He is suffering however with a bad boil on his neck, Nev goes to school and scouts around generally. Harve is looking after the farm and will go there permanently in the summer or as soon as I can build an additional house. Lizzie is in fine health but worries too much over the political attacks on me.

   Give my love to Mrs. H & May. God bless them & you. Your friend.

L. S .Ross

The Visiting Committee

President Ross wrote to his former secretary, Major Holmes, shortly after the release of the visiting committee's report, expressing surprise at the duplicity. The college, faculty, and cadets had made a "favorable impression," yet the committee "fooled me more than I was fooled by any one in life." The *Galveston Daily News* briefly reviewed the committee findings, not sure of its binding conclusions, yet noted the college "rests under a black cloud" attributed to repeated attacks "normally coming from enemies of the college." Following the detailed response by President Ross in February, the A&M board of directors submitted a point-by-point formal report to the visiting legislative committee findings in March, and the committee filed a rejoinder in late April. For more than three months, the debate over the college simmered in newspapers statewide. One upshot reported in the *Galveston Daily News* was that new student "applications concerning the college are far in excess of former years." Thus the *Dallas News* concluded "the stab at Ross" was "purely political." Irritated by their backhanded, veiled comments, Ross was himself unintimidated by the report and critics.[11]

The committee's focus on both the college's and the cadets' good showing disarmed the representatives who had predetermined that they would find fault in the college. The Corps of Cadets' bearing, image, and deportment were integral to Ross putting the college on a positive track. The activities and military procedures of the Corps were discussed at the July 1893 A&M Directors meeting, yet no action was recommended or taken to alter staffing, academic programs, or the daily routine of the Corps. Possibly the more compelling report to the board was the annual US Army Inspector General's official inspection by Maj. R. D. Vroom in May 1893, which gave the Corps of Cadets and the Ross administration an excellent rating. The military features of the college prevailed, with President Ross commending the Corps of Cadets for their "obedience, studious habits, and gentlemanly bearing."[12]

With regard to the legislative committee's observation, Ross and his administration were already addressing most of their comments and concerns. In mid-January 1893 the A&M Board had many joint meetings in Austin with the University of Texas Regents to discuss their common interests. The interaction remained congenial through the balance of the Ross administration, which clearly delineated the A&M College Board as an independent, stand-alone governing body. A longtime champion of A&M, William Cavitt of Bryan was critical of relations with Austin: "It is not intended to underrate the importance of the university at Austin, or to criticize the board of regents in their management, but simply to defend the [A&M College] board of directors." However, the underlying issue was the control of and division of revenue from the university lands—an issue that festered without resolution throughout the balance of the 1890s.[13]

The student labor wage proposal, a topic also espoused by Louis McInnis, was solely based on appropriations from the legislature to pay students. The newly updated college catalog specifically addressed student labor, noting it was the intent of the college for the students "not to be engaged in mere manual drudgery" but instead training "to be leaders." Pay, from the Student Labor Fund, for on-campus work was intended to offset up to one-third of a cadet's annual college expenses. Few, if any, changes were made to the academic curriculum, yet the criticism of the mess hall, campus medical care, and laundry was addressed. Hinted nepotism in college hiring practices proved unfounded, and by November 1893 the campus electrical generating plant was online at a cost of $9,995. One positive aspect that came from the visit was added funding to develop a sustainable water supply, bathing facilities, and a natatorium. As noted by Dethloff in the *Centennial History of A&M*, the legislative committee's report was "generally ignored by Ross and the Board."[14]

President Ross's focus on campus improvements in spite of legislative meddling was further indicated in one of his letters to UCV General Stoddard. Urged to attend UCV events in Birmingham, Alabama, Ross remained focused on swift action once appropriations were made to contract new campus buildings and deferred all duties to Stoddard and his staff.

Agricultural and Mechanical College of Texas

President's Office

College Station, Texas,   April 28, 1893

Genrl. H. B. Stoddard:

   I think the suggestions of Judge Phelps timely & valuable and well worth attention. Genrl. Cabell & his major genls doubtless expect to accomplish their ends without difficulty. I shall not be able to go to Birmingham on account of the anticipated work here from this probable appropriations for buildings which we shall need at the earliest possible moment and which I shall have to contract for as soon as the appropriation is made. If Phelps & yourself can do, I would be glad.

Yours etc
L. S. Ross, M. G. Cmdg.

In general, the A&M cadets seemed unconcerned with both the political and the personal dynamics between College Station and Austin. A lack of extracurricular activities for the cadets fostered the rise of a number of unauthorized clubs and groups on campus, such as the SOL Club ("Stay Out Late"), the TTs ("True Texans"), and the "Red Head Club," which was quick to use their own "yell," which appeared in campus publications: "Red, red, red are we; The reded [sic] headed men of A.M.C." The *Battalion* provided a feature article by Dan Cushing, cadet president of the A&M "Fat Man Club," detailing the club's unanimous election of Gov. James Hogg as an honorary member. And the governor—who was, in fact, a very large man—notified the cadets that "he accepts the honor recently conferred on him." Even President Ross's eldest socialite daughter, Florine, returned to campus to work with Prof. Charles Puryear to "manage the college dramatic club" and promote programs by the college cadet orchestra, reported to "furnish excellent music." The feature production in the spring before a packed house in the Assembly Hall by the drama club, which included both faculty and cadets, was a "stirring war drama" called *The Woven Web*. In July 1892 Sul and Elizabeth announced the marriage of Florine to chemistry professor Henry H. Harrington.[15]

Anti-Clark Repercussions

While victorious for a second term as governor, Hogg and his supporters were badly bruised during the general election and held a defiant George Clark responsible. And due to Ross's loyalty to his friend and former campaign manager, he was considered fair game. As with the one-sided A&M investigation, Hogg allowed his supporters both within and outside the legislature to open investigations that could prevent the return of Clark and any of his followers. This included an attack on the Texas General Land Office over land transactions, along with an attempt to impugn then land office clerk Lawrence S. Ross Jr., age twenty-five, who played no part in the case. *The Democrat* of McKinney, Texas, concluded that Hogg's supporters looked only for enemies to punish, thus "trying to besmirch the father—a Clark man in 1892—by attacking the son (and the A&M College) which they "have failed to do." The *Texas Farmer* agreed, noting, "[T]his criticism is more against the Clark contingent than against Gen. Ross."[16]

A disenchanted group of former staff and faculty of the A&M College continued a steady behind-the-scenes campaign to discredit the college. Central to these efforts was former professor L. L. McInnis, who served as a sort of "clearing house" for correspondences and advice for former staff members, as well as a continued writing campaign to legislative members and the newspapers to convey their views on the status of the college. Former college physician John D. Read, who had taken a position at Austin College in Sherman, Texas, was one of the harshest critics of operations at A&M. Read, who contemplated a lawsuit against the board of the college for wrongful dismissal, said he would move forward "if I can find a lawyer to take the case." He actively wrote several legislative members on the subject, with little or no result. Reassuring McInnis of his support, he related a story from the parent of one of his Austin College students, Sen. Reed N. Weisiger of Victoria, Texas, who agreed that the "the whole business was rotten" at A&M. In fact, Senator Weisiger stated on the floor of the Senate that "he had as soon give his boy a pony, a six shooter, a bottle of whiskey, and a deck of cards and start him out to get an education as to send him to the 'A&MC.'"[17]

The regimented yet independent attitude of the college and its president was far removed from the committee's relaxed visits to Hempstead, Huntsville, Galveston, or the University. Ross's grit, along with a very supportive board, endeared him to the cadets, former students, and parents, as was demonstrated in the overwhelming attendance by family, former students, and patrons of the college at the four-day-long commencement ceremonies in early June 1893. Ross's demeanor and impact was best noted decades later during the seventy-fifth anniversary of the college: "In the days of the Texas frontier, each man is expected to 'win his spurs' to stand solely on his own merits as a man"—an ethos that was ingrained in the development of generations of Texas Aggie citizen-soldiers and leaders.[18]

The 1893 legislative visit was the last of such meddling from Austin during the remainder of the Ross administration. All future actions by the Texas Legislature were generally supportive, in spite of ongoing efforts to limit the college's funding. In fact, for the balance of the Ross administration, the legislature did not do much, beyond naming Senate and House representatives to attend the annual June commencement ceremonies at the college. And as soon as legislative appropriations were approved, Ross wasted no time in calling for sealed construction bid proposals, as documented in the *Galveston Daily News*—representing the largest number of capital improvements on campus since the opening of the college two decades prior.

To Contractors—

Sealed proposals for the erection of a brick dynamo room, one brick laundry and ice factory, one foundation for a stand pipe and several smaller foundations will be received by the undersigned until 12 m. Saturday, July 15 [1893].

Plans and specifications can be seen at this office.

L. S. Ross, President
Agricultural and Mechanical College, College Station, Tex.[19]

A&M's Role in Experiment and Extension Services

The provision of quality services to the farmers, ranchers, and producers was an implied mandate of the Morrill Land Grant Act of 1862, and more attention was given to the development and spread of best practices in agriculture with the formation of the "experiment station" network of offices and demonstration plots across Texas. Thus the A&M College was tasked to establish such a "station" and facilities to gain community support among agricultural producers. This effort was viewed by President Ross and the A&M board as a critical way to link campus training and programs with agricultural constituents statewide. Ross was active in this program, as is noted in his efforts to establish an experiment station in Collin County.[20]

College Station

July 14, 1893

Hon. E. W. Kirkpatrick, McKinney, Texas:

Dear Sir:

By recent act of the legislature an appropriation was made for the establishment of additional experiment stations in the state to be known as substations. It is our duty to locate these, and think that your section would like to be one. We would like to be placed in correspondence with some citizen who will take interest in such matters and co-operate heartily in the furtherance of ends to be attained. It is our purpose to visit these sections of the state in which we desire to locate stations as soon as we can find parties sufficiently interested in the matter, and will at that time arrange all necessary details for the work.

Hoping that you will consider this an important matter, and assist us without unnecessary delay, we are very truly yours.

L. S. Ross

By the mid-1890s the *Galveston Daily News* was the leading newspaper in Texas and distributed statewide by the railroad to Houston, Dallas, Austin, and San Antonio. The paper carried news reports beyond just local agriculture data, politics, and railroad updates. Since the publication was also shipped from the Port of Galveston to other ports, its stories and reports were often copied, due in part to its wide variety of content, which expanded into more cosmopolitan feature sections on fashion, sports, and numerous periodic looks at events and trends from New York City, in a section titled "Gossip in Gotham"—long before Batman comics and movies. Commercial and agrarian news was published weekly in nineteen publications across Texas, on the broader dynamic of world markets, supply-demand analytics, and pricing of commodities such as cotton, sugar, corn, beef, coal, and lumber—all of which impacted farms and ranching in Texas.[21]

For this reason, the Texas A&M Agricultural Extension Service and Experiment Stations provided a paramount statewide service to assist Texas farmers and ranchers in producing more profitable and competitive crops and livestock. The markets and pricing constantly advocated and criticized by the Grange and Farmers' Alliance (largely for political purposes)—while noble in their efforts in a restricted, closed state and regional economy—did not always serve the needs and financial pressures of Texas agricultural producers, who by the mid-1890s (maybe unbeknownst to them) competed for markets on a global scale. Available money supply and competitive markets enflamed the rancorous debate over the coinage and related value of silver and gold metallic units, which had led to ramifications in the British Empire, Mexico, China, and Egypt—all competitive crop producers (with India and Egypt dumping large quantities of cotton on the international market). This, in turn, further affected Texas producers, shippers, bankers, and politicians. The

Table 4.2. The Texas A&M Corps of Cadets, 1891–1900, enrollment by class

Year	"fish"	Sophomores	Juniors	Seniors	Graduates	Total
1891–92	94	145	49	38	5	331*
1892–93	103	100	69	17	4	293
1893–94	100	100	56	34	3	292
1894–95	133	136	66	33	4	372
1895–96	126	130	64	30	3	354
1896–97	185	85	43	30	11	297
1897–98	148	113	36	24	16	337
1898–99	134	134	28	24	16	356
1899–1900	136	143	72	25	20	396

Note: The total, in most cases, represents the highest enrollment during the session. Cadets were admitted as late as the beginning of November if they passed the entrance test and new student interview with President Ross. For example, by October 12, 1891, only 295 had been admitted, with a balance of 331 total cadets by November. Anywhere from 30 to 50 applicants each year failed to meet the requirements for admission to the college.

prime objective of the Extension Service, based on market bulletins and improved methods of production, was best captured in the following editorial comment: "A diversity of crops and reduction of cotton acreage will produce results highly satisfactory to the tiller of the soil as well as to all other classes. Texas farmers should consider the situation with earnestness and act with energy".[22]

Corps of Cadets

The Ross years at Texas A&M would prove a watershed for the Corps of Cadets. The impact and influence of Ross on A&M and its traditions are without question. From the rough-and-tumble days of the early 1890s, the Ross presidency solidified the position of the college as not just an up-and-coming institution of higher learning but also, in the spirit of the mandate of the Morrill Land Grant Act of 1862, an institution that instilled "military tactics" (i.e., leadership training and patriotism), thus producing graduates who could serve as *citizen-soldiers* if called upon. In the case of the A&M Corps of Cadets, with the help of a more active, professional approach from the well-prepared commandants, Ross instilled a sense of purpose, pride, and esprit de corps that came out of both shared adversity and a promise of future greatness. The training and preparation of the Corps during the 1890s was ably represented in the service record of those who fought in the 1898–99 Spanish American War, as well as in the growing clout of former cadets working in business, engineering, and agriculture. Furthermore, the foundation of Texas A&M's rich traditions and lore would emanate from the esprit de corps and, over time, become steadfast. Not surprisingly, the cadets who attended the college during Ross's tenure as president considered themselves special—and for half a century after departing A&M, these former cadets of the 1890s referred to themselves as the "Sul Ross Group" (see table 4.2).[23]

In the enabling legislation for land-grant colleges, there was an implied obligation for the War Department to assign trained regular army officers to carry out instruction in "military tactics" and leadership training, under the oversight of the college president. For those charged with such duty, the A&M College was a full-time regular army duty assignment. The commandant was the primary lead in developing the military programs for the new cadets—all of whom arrived from civilian lifestyles with no concept of formal military protocol, regimentation, or obligations to duty. The reason for the departure of the commandant of cadets, Lt. William S. "Willie" Scott, in August of 1890 (unwittingly a victim of the internal faculty disputes over the management of the college), was common knowledge within army circles and of concern to Scott's replacement, Lt. Benjamin C. Morse, an 1884 graduate of West Point, who arrived on campus in late September. Lieutenant Scott, who continued for months to be disgruntled with his dismissal, was helpful in providing timely observations for Morse to consider in order to avoid running afoul of campus politics. Seemingly unscathed by the turmoil of his A&M College assignment during the McInnis administration, Scott went on to become a distinguished general officer in World War I.[24]

The role of the commandant was quickly enhanced following the arrival of President Ross on campus in February 1891. Beyond the commandant's role to provide instruction in military tactics was the added feature of the lieutenant's requirement to monitor discipline and oversee deportment among the cadets, in addition to his normal role as professor of military science and tactics. "Students receive the admonition and counsel of the President before being subjected to any penalty," noted Ross, who fully recognized this added contribution and ensured that the A&M board of directors would provide an additional stipend, above the base army salary, for the extra duties required on a daily basis. Duties of the commandant and staff included overseeing the day-to-day routines of the cadets, as chronicled in a feature *Battalion* article in the fall of 1893, "A Day as a Cadet":

> Trata, tarata, ring out the notes of the lively reveille in the bugle's boisterous complaint of "I can't wake 'em up!" Lights flash out and in a moment where before everything was dark and silent, all is now bustle and excitement. Cadets are heard calling to one another or waking up their roommates and in a few minutes we see them descending the stairs and coming out in front of the building to fall in for reveille roll call.
>
> A cadet at reveille is a very different being from the one we see at dress parade. In fact, he is hardly awake yet, and his sleepy appearance, together with an old hat, an overcoat instead of a blouse, and no collar or tie, go far toward transforming him. Very little talking is heard, and that is in a subdued tone. Most of them are lying down on the gallery, or, if it is a cold morning they are crowded up in one corner trying to

keep warm. The first sergeant orders "fall in!" and at last it is heard and they quickly take their places, the inevitable "lates" coming after them.

The roll call is soon over, and it is then that the cadet's daily life begins. Within the next twenty minutes he must get ready for breakfast, sweep out, pile his bunk, and thoroughly police his room and get everything in readiness for the day. Breakfast call is sounded then and the battalion is marched down to breakfast and he manages to make a hearty meal of "reg" [syrup] and "axle-grease,"[butter] "grab-all," [?] "sawdust," [sugar] "shot-gun," [pepper sauce] "winchester," [Worcestershire sauce] cush [dessert] and other things that have received appropriate names handed down along with other customs and traditions of the cadets.

It is often amusing how slang is used to express different phases of college life. To be reported is to be "rammed," to be excused is to "ride a gim," a "goose egg" is a term used for a zero, to get one is to make a "bust," to be perfect is to "knock his eye out for a hundred," to be a favorite is to "have a bird" and so on through.

The battalion is marched directly from the mess hall to morning chapel, and strangely enough they seem to dislike this more than any other duty, and hardly waiting for the amen they rush out as soon as it is over. Guard mounting is being sounded as we leave the chapel, and a few minutes later the sick call is sounded. Guard mounting is ever a beautiful ceremony. The polished arms gleaming brightly in the morning sunlight, the quick movements, the various manoeuvers, the salutes and reports of the different officers, all combine to make it interesting and impressive, even more than a dress parade, though not on so large a scale.

Study call is sounded at 8 o'clock, and from then until 4 o'clock, when release is sounded, or half past 4, when practices cease, lessons and practices come to almost unbroken succession, excepting an hour for dinner [lunch]. The time between 5 and 6 o'clock is spent at drill.

One would hardly think in looking at a squad of "fish" at the beginning of the year that their awkward movements would be so toned down that within two months their company drill would be perfect. The change in the cadets themselves is indeed wonderful. Nevertheless a rainy day is always hailed with delight, and there is nothing that is so pleasing as "recall." Supper comes about 6 o'clock and between supper and study call there is a short interim which is the most enjoyable time of the day. It affords a pleasant relaxation that fits him better for study when study call is sounded at 7:30.

Tattoo sounds at 9:45 and taps at 10 o'clock. One by one the lights go out, and the sad sweet notes of the beautiful taps come stealing softly through the still night air.[25]

Successive regular army officer commandants and their staffs assigned to the college were tasked by the president and faculty with the enforcement of discipline, from 0600 reveille to lights out at taps by 10:00, among teenagers who had no previous formal training or regimentation. The commandant endeavored to increase drill, add rifle drill, and establish target practice events, while also seeking to enhance uniform appearance. Efforts to expand and enhance organized cadet activities included forming a small band in late 1889 and early 1890, with the "College String Band." The first A&M class ring was designed by the class of '89, featuring four very small diamonds set on a gold crest of an intertwined "AMC." Following the design of a new ring in 1890, the first few classes of the early 1890s forewent the ring to instead adopt a custom-made oak walking cane with a brass plate, engraved with their name and class. The cane was considered a status symbol of the era, and the ring was redesigned in 1894. The cadets had ample leisure time and schemed to pass free time avoiding chores, drill, and periodic inspections. Popular pastimes included hikes to the Brazos River for an evening out to swim and barbeque. The most desirous way to escape from the campus was by obtaining a round-trip rail pass on the H&TC for a trip to Houston.[26]

The college H&TC railway station was the pivotal transportation hub of the campus and the most direct means by which cadets and staff could enter and depart the campus. The trek from the center of the campus to the train depot would become a thing of legends over time. Prior to 1940, most new cadets arrived at the college by train, and all had vivid first-time memories of their instant indoctrination as a new Corps of Cadets "fish" or freshman. The inaugural walk from the depot to Old Main (later the site of the Academic Building) for an entrance exam, registration, and assignment to a cadet unit was memorable for many. The first yearbook published in 1895 (and the only annual edition published while Ross was president), known as the *Olio*—which meant "medley or potpourri of events"—highlighted cadets' first experiences in A&M College life: "How well we remember our arrival at College and the first few days following . . . we alighted from the train and saw so many old cadets around us all crying 'fish, fish! Look at the fish!' . . . a nickname given to new cadets which they bear until they have been at the College a year."[27]

Agricultural and Mechanical College of Texas: "Specimen Student Entrance Examination"—1893–1897

> Add 12 3/4, 23 5/6, and 40 7/8.
> Reduce 65rd. 2 yd. 1 ft. 5 in. to inches.
> Name the rivers of Texas.
> Write a half-page account of your trip to this place.
> Name capitals of France, Russia, Spain, Virginia, Alabama, and Italy.
> Find the interest at 8% on $425 for 2 years 5 months and 18 days.
> Name the two Austins who were founders of Texas.
> Who commanded the *Alabama*?
> "He likes me better than you." Clear of ambiguity.
> What is the Nebulas Theory?
> Give the theory of tides.
> Find the greatest common divisor of 2572 and 396.
> What is meant by a centimeter?
> What hard fighters fell at the Alamo?

Source: Texas A&M Catalog, 1893–1897

Knowing that the college was on solid footing, though always mindful of political intrigue from Austin, Sul Ross planned to take more leisure time with his family. In the days prior to air conditioning, the most popular escape from the stale heat of College Station was to Galveston and the Gulf Coast, or to one of many "spring resorts." These brief trips remained popular throughout Ross's time at A&M, as detailed in the following correspondence.

Agricultural and Mechanical College of Texas

L. S. Ross, President   A. J. Rose, Pres't Board of Directors

College Station, Texas   Aug 5th 1893

My dear Major Holmes

   I was glad indeed to hear from you all again & that you were reasonably prosperous & happy. Lizzie & I took a short visit to Wootan Wells & found it too hot for comfort or health and returned as quickly as possible. Bessie & Frank took in the Drill at Austin. Bessie is still over there. Harve is on the farm below Waco and well-fixed but says he gets terribly lonesome. He has set in to make his start and if he pursues his sober habits will win in the end. Florence has remained on the campus the entire summer. She is getting along nicely as house keeper.

I had a very cheerful letter from Dr. Dorset in which he states that he is doing very well financially. I presume he is getting his old practice back again to some extent. Dorset worried me terribly at times with his cranky fool ways, but I give him credit now for his loyalty of his friends, which shows him to be a fine man. I hope he will do well.

He and Senator Evans who edits & owns the leading paper at Brenham wants me to be Governor again. Geo. Zimpleman writes me that the Governor would be practically a _____—on the same subject I gave them no encouragement however. Think [John H.] Reagan is getting ready to enter the ring and he & Culberson will make trouble in the Hogg ranks. The populist people are getting very strong here & in McLennan and they are working all over the state while the Democrats are either asleep or pulling each other's hair.

Thus they are likely to make trouble in the next caucus unless the Democrats adjust our message and settle the business interests on a permanent basis. The Devil is going to be to pay all over the country publishing & otherwise in compromise with which the Hogg & Clark now will be but as a pleasant position. I am happy in the thought that I am so situated that I can look on & keep cool.

I had a letter from Col. Black about the [deer] skins but have not received them much to my sorrow. I wrote him today and you had better do so too. Give my love to Mrs. H & May, and hoping to see you all someday, I am as ever you friend.

L. S. Ross

Creditable Management

The fall of 1893 opened a period in which the foundations of many of Texas A&M's long-standing traditions and institutions were laid—the *Battalion* (the campus newspaper), the Aggie Band, football, and more. In sharp contrast to the hostile media coverage created by the Texas Legislature in early 1893, the *Galveston Daily News* in September 1893 reported the attendance at the college to have grown by about fifty more cadets "than this time last year, with new ones coming in all the time. Many of them are new boys, 'fish,' as they are called, which leads to the conclusion that the advertising given the institution gratuitously by the erstwhile visiting committee is having the effect of bringing the boys in. The board should adopt a resolution of thanks to the legislative committee that sought to make a political sensation but succeeded with its hypercritical report in only advertising the merits of the institution." The *News* boasted, "General behavior of the boys are most creditable to the institution and its management . . . all departments are in splendid working condition." Many improvements were made throughout the college. A new "steam" laundry (with a capacity for six hundred bundles per week), the first cold storage and ice plant (with a daily production capacity of three tons), and the distribution of electric lighting (with a capacity for 750 lights of 50 watts each) were welcome improvements, according to Cadet Eugene Kerr, "a good deal better than [gas] lamp lights . . . I can see anywhere in my room and read." The *Battalion* boasted of the college's improvements: "The College viewed from a distance at night looks like a large city."[28]

But the most welcomed addition to the campus was the opening of the natatorium and adjacent bathhouses. This was viewed as a significant step to improving the overall general health and sanitation conditions on campus. The natatorium, a 25-by-50-foot indoor swimming pool, was fed by a newly drilled artesian well estimated to flow at 100,000

The A&M College faculty in 1897. President Ross is seated in the middle of the front row. Source: Cushing Archives

gallons per day. A 100-foot-tall "standpipe" and water tanks of 10 feet in diameter were able to store about 59,000 gallons of water. The water had high white sulfur content and was "pronounced by physicians to possess great medicinal virtues." The water was routinely circulated, and one observer noted its quality was like that of a "health resort." President Ross reported with pride to Major Holmes that the campus "ladies and children nearly all learned to swim with grace and ease . . . bathing in our Natatorium is splendid." One outcome of adding deep wells on campus was the report in the *Galveston Daily News* that "the water is heavily impregnated with oil." Little did they know at the time that this was the first oil well (none producing, of course) drilled in Brazos County, and it was drilled in the center of the A&M College campus in 1893. Decades later, this would be identified as the being along the Austin Chalk and Eagle Ford oil and gas formations.[29]

The waning months of '93 ended with Sul Ross's reporting to Major Holmes that at last "the political affairs are very quiet." The Ross family and a few friends used their vacation time to visit Wooten Wells Spa, a popular health resort three miles east of Bremond, where some two hundred permanent residents and more than two thousand summer guests indulged in the warm mineral waters purported to have medicinal properties. Further good news was the on-campus birth of President and Mrs. Ross's first grandchild—a boy, christened "Sul-Ross" Harrington— to daughter Florine and Prof. Henry Harrington on October 19.[30]

San Jacinto

Beginning in the fall of 1893, a dynamic series of changes impacted the image of the Corps and foretold the traditions of the future. A fledgling drum and bugle corps was transformed into a nine-member band with a paid drum major, James R. Fisk, and expanded to fourteen members by 1896. Following the death of Major Fisk, Northgate bootmaker and lover of music Joseph F. Holick took an active role as a bugler and assisted with the reorganization and training of the band, which would grow into the Fightin' Texas Aggie Band. There were no unique A&M fight songs yet—only standard army march tunes. Identification with the A&M College by former cadets was critical and led to the redesign of the Aggie ring by E. C. Jonas '94, with many of the iconic symbols—the eagle, crossed cannons, and star—carried forward in the evolution and design of the current Aggie ring.[31]

President Ross was well aware of the need to enhance the image of the A&M College, and to do so, he fostered the travel of the Corps of Cadets to communities across Texas. The activities that gained the most interest during the Ross tenure in the mid-1890s by both cadets and former cadets alike were the numerous out-of-town Corps Trips to Houston, San Antonio, Dallas, and San Jacinto on April 21 each year. The Corps trips to Houston and San Antonio, with an occasional visit to Dallas to attend the annual state fair, gained rapid recognition. While Texas in the 1890s was more than 90 percent rural, the cadets and alumni identified with the bright lights and robust nature of commerce in the large growing metropolitan areas. President Ross was well aware of this and also was aware that the Corps itself offered the best means to promote the growth

Table 4.3. A&M College of Texas faculty and staff, 1895

Lawrence S. Ross, President

R. H. Whitlock, Mech. Eng.	W. A. Banks, English and Hist.
J. H. Connell, Agr.	A. M. Soule, Agr.
H. H. Harrington, Chem.	P. S. Tilson, Chem.
C. Puryear, Math	R. H. Price, Hort and Bot.
T. C. Bittle, Lang.	H. Ness, Hort and Bot.
Lt. G. T. Bartlett, Cmdt.	D. W. Spence, Civil Eng.
Mark Francis, Vet. Med.	R. T. Bray, Mech. Eng.
F. E. Giesecke, Drawing	J. C. Nagle, Civil Eng.
J. Clayton, Agr.	C. W. Hutson, English and Hist.
J. H. Carter, Sec.	R. F. Smith, Math
E. W. Hutchinson, Bookkeeper	D. Adriance, Chem.
Bernard Sbisa, Steward	A. L. Banks, Math
C. A. Lewis, Foreman shops	W. P. Philpott, English and Hist.
J. W. Carson, Foreman farm	

Source: *Organization Lists*, Bulletin No. 23, USDA, Washington, DC: January 1895, p. 51.

and viability of the college. Trips were generally daylong affairs, with cadets and staff transported by early-morning special-chartered trains to each city. (Former students working for the various railroads were able to assist with both special rates and trains dedicated to transporting the entire Corps.) Upon arrival, there was a Corps parade down Main Street, followed by a grand picnic sponsored by a local host committee of alumni, civic leaders, and family and friends (see table 4.3).[32]

The Corps of Cadets outings that gained the most notoriety were the trips each April 21 during the 1890s to the San Jacinto Battlefield and Park, in observance of the eighteen-minute battle that won Texas its independence. Organizers were pleased to learn that cadets would attend accompanied by their renowned president and agreed, in conjunction with the Texas State Guard, to participate in a reenactment of the famed engagement—known as a *sham* or *mock battle*. Plans were for the A&M Corps of Cadets, which had grown to more than 350 cadets by 1894, to play the role of the Mexican Army, and for the State Guard of Texas to play the role of Sam Houston's Texans. However, in their enthusiasm, the cadets failed to follow the script and each time maneuvered to overrun the state guard and win the battle. Unconcerned about rewriting Texas history, they enjoyed the festivities and meals—yet were soon not invited to return. Notwithstanding, the A&M College was on a strong footing under Ross's leadership. The alumni editor in the special Christmas issue of the *Battalion* noted: "No doubt all ye old graduates will be glad to know of the excellent moral tone that pervades the Corps at the present time. Discipline has never been better." Enhanced morale and a sense of esprit de corps would become a pivotal component, fostering the image and core traditions of A&M.[32]

Agricultural and Mechanical College of Texas

President's Office

College Station, Texas   Dec. 30th 1893

Dear Major

I have just returned from short hunt & hurry to answer your kind letter. Had some luck. Got one Buck and plenty squirrels & Ducks.

Game rather scarce in this country. Harve is down and went with me. He will probably get work in Waco on his return & can look over the Farm in a general way just as well. Florine has recovered her strength rapidly & will soon be all right. Bess is having a lively time with the Young folks of Bryan & vicinity. They had a miniature [*sic*] Mask Ball on the Campus last night. Several of the cadets remained over and were reinforced by the local chaps. They claim a good time generally. Nev got up a very creditable display of fireworks which he seemed to enjoy. We thought of you Mrs. H & May, and your presence would have made the enjoyment complete.

The political affairs are very quiet in this vicinity and from the general outlook it is hard to predict results. It seems Culberson has rather the lead for Governor, and John H. [Reagan] is making some headway. What times we have fallen upon!! Much obliged indeed for your kindly expression of interest in my future prospects. Have a great many intercessions to induce me to enter the political arena. Many reasons are alleged for the demand, but none seem imperative or convincing to me.

I am getting along very smoothly here & the Young Men seemed devoted to me. I have made great improvements & people coming here hardly recognize the place.

Love to Mrs. H & May. God bless & preserve your all –

Yours truly   L. S. Ross

Getting Along Smoothly

In a year-ending letter to Major Holmes, Ross relayed with pleasure his recent short hunt with young son Harvey in the Navasota River bottom: "We got one buck and plenty of squirrels and ducks." Harve, who had tried college for a short time, opted to instead work in Waco with uncle Tom Padgett's dry goods company (sister Katie's husband) and, to Sul's delight, take care of the family farm. Young Nev was having the time of his life growing up on the campus and would soon enter the college as a freshman cadet. Ross's pride in the Corps and the cadets' respect for their president were most evident, with Ross noting, "the young men seemed devoted to me." The *Dallas Morning News* published a number of articles on the conditions at the college, expressing concerns regarding the need for new dorms, a larger mess hall to address the cadets eating in shifts, and continued improvement in agricultural courses. Milton Parker, following a visit to his son, Cecil, a cadet sergeant major, noted, "Ross takes a very deep interest in the college . . . the *esprit de corps* of the college cannot be beaten."[33]

However, politics was not far from Governor Ross's mind as he noted yet another wave of encouragement to consider public office. Yet none of the suitors, as he advised his old friend Major Holmes, were "convincing to me." The political landscape in Texas ushered in a new generation of progressive politicians triggered by followers of the Hogg administration. By late 1893 the Grange, Farmers' Alliance, and Knights of Labor had all fallen by the wayside as membership dropped due to over-promising and underdelivering to the farmers and consistently failing to please Texans.[34] The farm organizations did, however, champion expanded education for all Texans, railroad regulations, and a focus on practical solutions and problem solving encouraged by practical methods developed by the Texas Agricultural Extension Stations. In the months prior to the 1894 governor's election, the Texas Democratic Party, in the wake of lame-duck Hogg's departure, was split between four eager candidates: Congressman S. W. T. Lanham; John H. Cochran, speaker of the Texas House; John D. McCall, comptroller; and Charles A. Culberson, attorney general. In the confusion, George Clark, who was not a declared candidate, threatened to bolt the party and nominate for reelection former governor Sul Ross. Continually engaged with the political currents shifting in Texas politics, Sul Ross was on the forefront of monitoring changes and alliances, confiding in Major Holmes, "The populist people are getting very strong here & in McLennan [County] and they are working all over the state while the Democrats are either asleep or pulling each other's hair."[35]

Once again, Col. E. M. House stepped in to organize many former Hogg supporters, assure Ross and Clark of an orderly transition, and establish a grassroots campaign in the counties to back young Dallas attorney Charles Culberson. With House's finger on the pulse of Texas politics, the *Dallas Morning News* labeled him a political operative—"a Culberson man deep-in-the-wool and rock-ribbed." Thus, as Ross correctly predicted in his December 1893 letter to Major Holmes, Charles

Culberson would be the next governor of Texas. During the weeks prior to entering office, the new governor, upon the recommendation of Colonel House, offered Ross a position in mid-December 1894 as one of the three appointed commissioners on the newly established Texas Railroad Commission.[36]

My Duty Lies Here

Governor-elect Charles Culberson's appointment of Ross to the commission was a major concern in Bryan and across Brazos County for the leadership and merchants, who were fearful that Ross would accept the new governor's offer and return to Austin. Rumors circulated that if the A&M board of directors appointed longtime professor Henry H. Harrington, Ross's son-in-law, Sul would strongly consider the position on the Railroad Commission. The board had no response. In order to

One of the last pictures of Sul Ross, taken in 1897. Source: Cushing Archives

influence Ross, a community committee composed of Bryan Mayor Clifford A. Adams and County Judge V. B. Hudson traveled on New Year's Day 1895 to the campus to present a petition signed by "several hundred of the leading people" in the county, "exclaiming that it is of paramount importance that Ross remain at the head of the institution." The petition further stated:

> The prosperity that has attended your administration of this institution for several years, and the harmony that has existed during this time between the faculty, the beneficent influence of your past life with your daily example, upon the students, your great popularity and extensive acquaintance in the state, and with all parties, lead us to feel and assert that there is no other person in Texas that can so efficiently fill your position as president of the college . . . should you leave the college at this most inopportune time we have many reasons to feel the deepest anxiety for its future.[37]

The campus gathering at the president's residence was attended by cadets and college faculty. President Ross "was manifestly affected by the petition" and the outpouring from the local community, noting he had been honored to receive scores of letters from across Texas concerning his future plans, responding as follows to the Bryan–Brazos County delegation:

> Gentlemen:
>
> I cannot find the words to thank you, and through you to express to the people of Bryan my high appreciation of their confidence and esteem. When I accepted the presidency of this institution nothing so nerved me to the new duties imposed upon me as the encouragement received from a committee of Bryan people who came to welcome me, headed by your distinguished mayor. Every man considers the governorship of Texas as one of the highest marks of ambition, a royal opportunity for good or evil, an uncrowned state of kingliness; yet never did I feel in the possession of that office more honor than I have felt as the president of the Agricultural and Mechanical College. I have always realized, as my record will show, that in the proper education of our youth rests the safety of our country.
>
> When I went over to Austin at the insistence of Governor Culberson he offered me the place on the commission, not at my solicitation, but in the light of a public duty, saying that he believed that I could do the

state a greater service and be of as much benefit to the college in the new position. I asked for time for consideration and finally accepted, with the sense of this obligation upon me. I did not know in what high esteem I was held here on campus, with the faculty and cadets; abroad in the state, among the patrons and friends of the college, and did not think it would make any material difference what disposition I might make of my services. I am therefore overwhelmed by these evidences of friendship and solicitude, which make it doubtful at least where my duty lies.

Upon hearing this, Mayor Adams rose and said, extending his hand, "Governor, it is not the selfish interest of Bryan that prompts this action, but a sincere regard for the welfare of the college. We beg you to remain with us."

Tears rose to the governor's eyes, as reported by the *Galveston Daily News*, and he said "feelingly": "It would be hard to leave under such circumstances." As the visiting group applauded . . . the governor said, "It now seems that my duty lies here."[38]

CHAPTER 5

Rough, Tough, Real Stuff

That the A. and M. college has one of the most splendid fields
in the state for all out of doors sports is not to be disputed. The
air is cool and invigorating, also the ground is a trifle soft but
not to so much so to prevent good work. We have some superb
talent in that line of sport here at present. A few of the new boys
have shown themselves to be first-class players in every respect.
No degree of excellency [sic] can be attained in "interfering"
"tackling" and sprinting with the ball, without constant practice.
The "Cadets" will have a "happy" task in attaining victory.

"Football," The Battalion, December 1893

Altogether they form the most gallant and talented body of young
men to be found in the State of Texas, heaping honors upon their
favorite institution, the greatest agricultural and mechanical
college in the South.

Galveston Daily News, June 12, 1895

In addition to enhancing the image of the A&M College, securing vital
appropriations, managing the surrounding political intrigue, and reor-
ganizing academic programs to concentrate on the mandated higher-
education mission built around agricultural and mechanical (engineering) courses, Sul Ross, by his example and presence, fostered an esprit de
corps and encouraged cadets to strive for excellence. The often-critical
Galveston Daily News praised the institution as "the greatest agricultural
and mechanical college in the South." The cadets under Ross's leadership

laid the foundation for many of Texas A&M's most well-known and perpetuated traditions, as they coined and adopted slang and practices that allowed them to "inaugurate the Aggie 'spirit,'" as noted by Edward Cushing '80, referring to the founding cadets of '76–'77. In the inaugural edition of the *Battalion*, Cushing also reflected on how these A&M cadets "handed down the customs and traditions" to succeeding classes.[1]

Prior to 1893, the A&M cadets and campus fostered a Spartan environment driven by a daily routine, from reveille to taps, of classes, meal formations and drill, and daily efforts to thrive amid the growing pains of the fledgling college. Additional activities were limited to intramural sports, primarily baseball, and an occasional game with local teams from Bryan, Calvert, or Navasota. Some large draws for those from the campus and Bryan residents were periodic baseball games between the senior cadets and the faculty. A number of "club" social groups, such as the Dramatic Club, Bicycle Club, and Austin and Calliopeon Literary Societies, filled some of the idle time. There were a few holiday events, such as the early June commencement ceremonies and a spring "sports' day" and barbeque on the statewide holiday of April 21 each year. From the earliest days of A&M, a growing lexicon of slang was generated in the mess hall, particularly related to the military aspects of cadets' daily events. But prior to the arrival of Sul Ross, there were no fight songs, no mascot, no band, no football, no class ring, no yell leaders, and no college colors—except possibly "cadet gray" (see table 5.1).[2]

Additionally, by the early 1890s, the "former cadets" of the college began to form a critical mass of "ex-cadets" and "alumni" to support the college, which proved vital to expanding the image of the college statewide. From 1876 through 1891, some four hundred Texans counted themselves among the A&M Ex-Cadets Association, and while small in number, many became very active and prosperous in agriculture and ranching, industry, medical and legal professions, engineering, and political activities. Many also assumed community leadership positions, which reflected well on the public image and prestige of their alma mater. Some of the most active included former cadets Edward B. Cushing '80, Frank A. Reichardt '79, John Carson '86, Judge William Sleeper '79, Charles Rogan '79, Temple Houston '81, David Tilson '86, Frederick Giesecke '86, and Walter Wipprecht '84. Alex M. Ferguson '94, alumni editor of the *Battalion*, reminded all ex-cadets, "The reputation [of the

Table 5.1. 1890s Texas A&M campus lingo and mess hall slang

General campus lingo		Mess hall slang	
Term	*Meaning*	*Term*	*Meaning*
Bat roost	Gathright Hall	Artillery	Beans
Batt	Battalion newspaper	Baby	Mustard
Bug hunters	Ag students	Blood	Ketchup
Bull	Military officer	Bull neck	Meat
Ex	Former student	Cackle	Eggs
Fired out	Excused from duty	Cow	Milk
"fish"	Freshman cadet	Cush	Dessert
A "german"	A dance or party	Deal	Bread
Gim riders	Shirk duty	Dirt	Black pepper
Keg rolling	Beer	Dope	Coffee
Military walk	Road in front of Old Main	Grease	Butter
O.D.	Officer of the day	Gun wadding	Jelly fritters
Rams	Demerits	Reg	Syrup
'76 fellows	Members of the founding A&M class	Timber	Toothpicks
goose egg	zero	Sawdust	Sugar
bust	to get a zero	Shot	Peas
Longhorn	college annual	Sky	Water
tattoo	call to quarters	Spuds	Potatoes
Farmers	A&M sports teams	Stud	Tea
clay pit*	small campus pond	Sour	Lemons
Nat	natatorium	Wildcat	Pineapple
police up	inspection		

Note: While used by the cadets, many of the terms were imported and adopted from the military, railroad, and ranching slang of the era.

*Clay from the pit was used to make the first bricks for Old Main and Gathright Hall, and then the pit was dammed to make a recreational pond.

college] depends largely upon the Alumni and former students, and they are scattered all over Texas. Each one of these should be a center of an active influence that will do the old college good. Public opinion needs to be stirred up on this subject."[3]

And thus, during the Ross years, many of A&M's most time-honored activities, customs, lore, and traditions were initiated, helping define the unique image and "spirit" of what would be known in years to come as the "Fightin' Texas Aggies." As the college continued to grow in the 1890s, many bedrock A&M traditions were founded, including the school's football program, the Aggie Band, the class ring, the first year-book (the *Olio*), the Ross Volunteers, Corps trips, the first publication of the student newspaper (the *Battalion*), the Glee Club (forerunner of the Singing Cadets), and numerous nonacademic customs that helped form the foundation of Texas Aggie lore. The degree to which Sul Ross inspired the rise of early traditions is very evident, and he clearly fostered a positive-spirited campus environment that set the backdrop for the A&M "image." Dedicated alumni and former students also played a critical role in establishing the emerging A&M image. Reflecting on the period, archivist David Brooks Cofer, author of a series of monographs on the early history of the college, noted, "In addition to these graduates [those prior to 1890] of eminence from the College in this pioneer period, one can find in the Nineties this same type of substantial cadet at the College—a diligent student loyal to his college and to his fellows, a young man imbued with the spirit of individual accomplishment, and a practical fellow ever ready to follow the educational leadership of such administrators as Ross." And few new activities or events in the 1890s captured the attention and fervor of both current and former cadets quite like sports—particularly the game of football, which, at the time, was spreading like wildfire across college campuses nationwide.[4]

On the Gridiron: The Farmers Fight

News of the game of football arrived in Texas in the late 1880s from reports of "northern" East Coast teams being formed in the clubs and collegiate ranks at Rutgers, Wesleyan, Princeton, Harvard, and Yale. This small group of East Coast colleges gradually spread the excitement of football to Midwest colleges. The wave of Texan enthusiasm for the

Members of the Texas A&M football team in 1894.
Source: Cushing Archives

sport first took shape in special interest reports in major newspapers from Galveston, Dallas, Houston, and Austin; from there, a call to action to field teams, as noted in the *Houston Daily Post*, "introduced the tactics and methods of the northern teams" and further increased the intrigue of the fall sport. From the earliest days of US colleges, spring and summer seasons were dominated nationwide by the sole team sport of baseball. Football would not become popular in the Southwest until the mid-1890s.[5]

Indications of the earliest interest in football at the A&M College appear in early 1891, chronicled in a feature article in the *Fort Worth Star-Telegram*, titled "'Bob' Littlejohn, First A. &. M. Coach." The 1909 account by Robert G. Littlejohn '91—more a promoter of football than a coach—provides a vivid depiction of the introduction of the game to A&M while Littlejohn was a cadet. This intriguing firsthand account of the rise of college football in Texas predates any others that are currently available, and the text of the article often has been overlooked by researchers attempting to trace the roots of the birth of the gridiron at Texas A&M:

> Robert G. Littlejohn ['92] of Fort Worth brought the first football ever used at the A&M College. That was in [the spring] 1891, when he was a cadet. Since buying the pigskin and coaching the boys in the rudiments of the great college game that year, Bob has not seen them play, although they have won several Southwestern championships.
>
> But on the sidelines in Dallas this afternoon [November 1909] Bob is probably the most interested spectator at the A. &. M.—Oklahoma battle [won by the Aggies, 14–8]. He is probably too interested to cheer for the farmers but in all the excitement of the game his thoughts will hark to the day when he appeared on the campus at the state college, bearing the strange looking object he termed a football.
>
> "In 1891, Major [William L.] Bringhurst [acting president], General Sam Houston's son-in-law, called me into his office at the college and asked me if I knew what football was. I told him I did. 'Well,' said the head of the school, 'I have been reading in the papers about the northern and eastern colleges playing a new game. Why can't we start it here? It will be great exercise and great physical training for the boys.'"
>
> So Bob bought a football, took it out on the campus and told his fellow students that he would instruct them in the game. Bob was some pumpkins in those days as a baseball player and had picked up a knowledge of football around Fort Worth before going to A. & M. The cadets took to the rough and tumble game like ducks to water. In a short time they became the best players in the Southwest and when the first football wore out another was purchased.[6]

By February 1892, football at A&M had become a club sport and was referred to as such until early 1895, playing various local opponents on a random basis, with no organized season schedule. The fall of 1892 is the earliest record of football as a competitive campus sport, yet former archivist David Chapman cautions, "The original newspaper accounts are clouded with misspellings and typographical errors . . . add to this an unstructured game in its infancy, with players appearing and disappearing from squads at random, and you have fertile ground for confusion." Numerous attempts were made to schedule home games.[7]

Notwithstanding, the first A&M cadet football teams—from two or three organized groups—were intramural in nature, formed by cadet units within the Corps. The games that followed were played with a very loose set of rules and were generally scheduled between November and February. The cadets loved the contact sport. A&M's first recorded "organized" football game was played on Washington's Birthday, February 22, 1893, against the John Carson Club team. The game was attended by a large crowd of visitors and A&M was victorious by a score of twelve to four. The *Galveston Daily News* reported, "[T]he victors were so elated by their success that they seriously talked of challenging the finest teams of high kickers in the state." By the early fall of 1893, there was a formal effort to recruit twenty-six cadets to organize a "permanent" single college team, with a backup of "two sub-teams," which in essence were practice squads. From those engaged in weekly practice, the captains would field one traveling squad of a select thirteen to fifteen cadets "that shall answer the challenges from 'foreign' teams." The newly inaugurated college paper, the *Battalion*, noted the team was named "The A. &. M. C.F.B.T." (short for "college football team"), yet aside from the John Carson game, there is no record of actual formal intercollegiate football games in 1892 or 1895 (see table 5.2).[8]

By 1894, there were some ninety colleges fielding football teams across the nation. In the mid-1890s, the playing field was 110 yards long and a touchdown was worth four points, with a successful goal-after-touchdown (free kick) adding two points. The excitement on the A&M campus regarding the gridiron was captured in the January 1894 *Battalion*: "Football at the A&MC is surely the coming game judging from indications of the present. Two years ago, comparatively no interest was manifest in the 'scrappy' game at all. Only last week was the game fully introduced into this college and has met with marked approval throughout, not to say that football has no faults." Plans to schedule games in Dallas and Galveston failed to materialize, but the intent of the A&M team was clear—they were ready to play all challengers. In 1894 the *Battalion* listed the principal members of the "Football Club," with A. P. Watt as the captain, M. W. Sims Jr. as the assistant captain, and W. S. Massenber as the team's business manager.[9]

Table 5.2. A&M football, 1893–98

Year	Opponent	A&M	Opp.	Location	Coach
1893	John Carson Club	12	4	College	Unknown
1894	Texas	0	38	Austin	F. D. Perkins
1894	Galveston Ball HS	14	6	College	F. D. Perkins
1895	No organized team				
1896	Galveston Ball HS	0	0	College	A. M. Soule
1896	Austin College	22	4	College	A. M. Soule
1896	Houston HS	28	0	College	A. M. Soule
1897	Houston HS	0	10	Houston	C. W. Taylor
1897	Add–Ran (TCU)	6	30	College	C. W. Taylor
1897	Austin College	4	0	Sherman	C. W. Taylor
1898	Houston HS	51	0	College	H. W. Williams
1898	Texas	0	48	Austin	H. W. Williams
1898	Houston HS	0	6	Houston	H. W. Williams
1898	Add–Ran (TCU)	16	0	Waco	H. W. Williams
1898	Austin College	22	6	College	H. W. Williams
1898	Fort Worth Univ.	28	0	College	H. W. Williams
Record: 9–5–1					

On the evening of October 20, 1894, before a crowd of some eight hundred spectators, many more curious about the new game than knowledgeable about its rules or purpose, packed Austin's Hyde Park to witness the first major intercollegiate football game in the state of Texas. The "Farmers" or "Cadets" of A&M, a squad numbering fifteen players total, faced off against the "Varsity" team of the University of Texas. There were no bleachers, and spectators crowded around the playing field in an attempt to be close to the teams—dressed in leather helmets and light padding, competing over the possession of a strange-looking oblong ball! The A&M players were outscored that day, 38–0, yet set in motion the emergence of an entirely new level of collegiate sports and statewide interaction among colleges, alumni, and fans. With no formal athletic conference in the early days, Coach F. D. Perkins of A&M and other college and club officials informally scheduled games and defined the local rules for the balance of the 1890s. Eager to have a rematch with the Varsity, the *Galveston Daily News*, the leading paper in the state, reported an attempt by A&M to play a second game on Thanksgiving at College Station; however, no game materialized, and a substitute was sought.[10]

Efforts were made to schedule additional games in the fall of 1894, as cadets went back to the practice field to regroup and train an entirely new squad who was eager to play. Under the leadership of cadet football captain Arthur P. Watts '95, it was mentioned in A&M's first yearbook, the *Olio*, that practice was intense and the scrimmage manned by the "fish" of the class of 1898, which "furnished some of the best material for the [1894] football team." Eager to end the season on a positive note, the Farmers were able to schedule a second home game against Galveston Ball High School on Thanksgiving Day, prevailing in front of five hundred fans surrounding the campus drill field, with a winning score of 14–6.[11]

The formalities and pageantry of today's Saturday home football games did not exist. There were no bleachers, no tickets, no tailgating parties, no Fightin' Texas Aggie Band, and few reunions. Josh Sterns '99 recalled that in the mid-1890s, "it was necessary to pass the hat" to support the team:

> On the day of the game we placed boys at the entrance gates to the college grounds to solicit change from visitors who said they had come to see the game. It was before the days of autos and only those came who lived less than ten miles away. After all expenses had been taken care of, the surplus was split 60% to the winner and 40% to the loser.
>
> From the very first I took a prominent part in collecting the necessary advance funds by going room to room to get a few nickels here and there. All of the gate keepers turned their collections over to me and I paid all the bills and did not report to anyone. Some of the boys knew and others believed that I used that racket to work my way through College.[12]

For the balance of the decade, there were no official college colors, no mascot, and no stadium. Games were played on the drill field, with no yell leaders or fight song. Yells were eventually developed in 1896, inspired by campus clubs and ex-cadets, and coined by each cadet class. The following is an example of one of the first recorded yells:[13]

Cattywampus

Rah! Rah! Rah!
Hi! Ho! Ha!
A. M. C.
Boom! Cis! Bah!
College.
Hi-ki! Hi-ki!
Listen to our noise!
We're the A. &. M football boys!
College! College! is our cry!
V-I-C-T-O-R-Y !

The transition from a "club-level" campus activity to a more structured intercollegiate competitive sports program began to draw more alumni support and media coverage of games. Without the formal oversight of a conference, shifting rules, and no NCAA, concerns were raised about the rising number of injuries (and deaths) from football, generally attributed to rough play and inferior equipment. The growing popularity and impact of football on college campuses was a national issue and discussed in detail at the annual meeting the Association of American Colleges and Experiment Stations in Washington, DC, attended by college administrators of forty-six land-grant institutions. In response

The Fightin' Texas Aggie Band in the mid-1890s. Source: Cushing Archives

to a concern "that there is too much football in the college education of today," the chairman dismissed the remark, noting, "The interest in athletic field sports, such as football, in our colleges, though but incidental to the life and work of these institutions, has nevertheless an ethical, and thereby educational value, which is worthy of high regard." Notwithstanding, the *Galveston Daily News* editorial on the growing popularity of the game indicated, "The general public maintains a strong predilection for the sport through all its changes." For the balance of the late 1890s, A&M football would continue to grow, with road trips to Houston, Dallas, Austin, Sherman, Waco, Fort Worth, and San Antonio. The opportunities raised for out-of-town travel by train became very popular with the Corps of Cadets and ex-cadets.[14]

Between 1893 and 1898, the Farmers' record in five seasons (as there were no known games in 1895) was 9–5–1. Not yet bound by any formal conference or player eligibility rules, the coach of the 1896 team, Henry W. South, suited up to play tackle in a number of games, and "players" were routinely "recruited" from passing trains to play in home games as blockers after one day of "class" on campus. One popular feature of the early games was the A&M College Band, boasting nearly two dozen members. Until the fall of 1897, students and faculty served as volunteer coaches and managers for athletic activities, after which A&M's first formal football coach, C. W. Taylor, was hired. The '97 season included only three games, with the Farmers being outscored by Houston High School and TCU, yet traveling to Sherman to defeat Austin College, 4–0. Despite a game-ending dispute in the 1899 A&M–Texas game, the Farmers agreed to play the Varsity at the San Antonio Fair in late October 1900, and they were outscored 5–0. Hundreds of cadets, former cadets, and families converged on San Antonio from across the state with the assistance of railroads offering special passes and rates of four cents per mile. The event was promoted by the A&M Alumni Association, led by Edward Cushing, E. W. Kerr, and association executive secretary P. S. Tilson.[15]

Reflecting on the formative days of football at A&M, the 1911 *Longhorn* noted, "Not very many years ago all contests took place on the drill-ground, the football equipment consisted of one pair of cleated shoes which the fullback wore, and there was no enclosed field." Sam A. McMillian '09 captured the essence of the allure of the "ruff-tuff, real-stuff" gridiron as a formative tradition for many institutions: "Why the football hysteria should so suddenly dominate the enduring and worthwhile features of A. and M. activities puzzles everyone who takes the trouble to think about it."[16]

EX-Cadets Unite

Texas A&M is an institution marked by traditions, lore, and the fierce loyalty of former students and devotees, linked by their common shared experiences during their formative years at the college. The foundation for this common bond was the Corps of Cadets—years, administrations, and students would come and go, but the Corps remained a constant. The uniformed Corps, organized under a military regime and mandated by the enabling legislation of the Morrill Act of 1862, is the only such body in an institution of higher learning in the history of Texas. The cadets in gray would "extend the feelings of fraternal regard," bonds, and friendships forged on campus into one of the most powerful alumni organizations in the nation.[17]

The first gathering or reunion of the "old" cadets was on June 26, 1879, at the Bachelor's Hall in Houston. A group of a dozen former cadets organized the Association of Ex-Cadets and resolved that at every June commencement of the A&M College as many as possible would meet on campus. The primary leaders of the new association were its first president, William M. Sleeper '79, of Waco; first vice president William A. Trenckmann '78, of Wilheim; and second vice president Pinkney L. Downs '79, of Temple. Additional driving organizers included Edward B. Cushing '80, Frank A. Reichardt '79, and William H. Brown '80. During the first decade of the organization, its primary goals were to keep track of all ex-cadets, support the college, and assist fellow cadets with job placement. In 1887 the growing organization was restructured as the Alumni Association of the A&M College of Texas—with the implied membership of those who had attained a degree from the college. During the first twenty years of the college, only 333 degrees had been awarded, while more than 3,000 "ex-cadets" had attended classes. Thus, concerned that ex-cadets who did not graduate would lack representation, in 1895 Cushing called for the organization of nongraduate former students by expanding the old Ex-Cadet Association into a newly chartered organization known as the "Alpha Phi Fraternity."[18]

President Ross was very supportive of the increasing level of activity by the former A&M students, and he lent his support to former cadets as they canvassed for jobs. One example is Ross's letter of endorsement for Alva Mitchell '94, who would return to A&M to teach engineering drawing in 1902. Mitchell would go on to become a department head by 1912 and be one of A&M's most distinguished engineering professors until 1944; he coauthored the standard textbook *Technical Drawing* with fellow Aggie Dr. F. E. Giesecke—used nationwide for more than a century and running to fifteen editions. Ross's letter of recommendation is evidence of his support of the cadets:[19]

Agricultural and Mechanical College of Texas

L. S. Ross, President   A. J. Rose, Pres't of Board of Directors

College Station, Texas   April 26, 1895

   I take special pleasure in commending Mr. Alva Mitchell ['94] as a young gentleman of most excellent character & habits. While a cadet at the A. & M. C. of Texas, his deportment & diligent application made him deservedly popular with all the officers and Professors of the Institution, and enabled him to graduate with a good record in every respect. I am quite sure he will prove eminently trustworthy & efficient in any business relations he may assume.

Respectfully
L. S. Ross, President

The two new alumni organizations were generally harmonious, with both groups taking part in campus activities, lobbying in Austin, and tracking information on their members. President Ross worked with both organizations during his administration and encouraged their active participation in sponsoring academic awards and scholarships for the cadets. The organizations also became a valuable resource for locating keynote speakers for commencement and other campus functions. As two decades of ex-cadets entered the workforce and political positions across the state, they collaborated with Ross and the A&M

board of directors to improve the image of the college, while fending off detractors that attempted to undercut the budget, such as the state legislature and news media. To enhance these efforts, the Alpha Phi promoted an ex-cadets directory, known as the "Fraternity Book," expanded job placement services, and organized "Alpha Phi Chapters" around the state—the forerunners of today's Texas A&M Clubs. At the time of President Ross's death, the two ex-cadet organizations were in talks—actively participated in by the governor's son, Dr. Frank R. Ross '94, the 1897–98 president of the Alumni Association—to combine their efforts, which resulted in one unified organization in 1900 and the eventual chartering of today's Association of Former Students.[20]

One concern on campus and with the ex-cadets was an undercurrent of negative news that continued to be repeated in the media that the site of the A&M campus was an unhealthy location, resulting in a disproportionate amount of illness. There was sickness and a number of cadet and staff deaths due to influenza and cholera, but never to the degree that detractors of the college hoped would negatively reflect on the image of the college. Concerned about the negative publicity, President Ross used the June 1894 commencement, well attended by reporters from across the state, to address the rumors:

> It takes time to build up institutions of learning, and I take this opportunity, as we have visitors here from all over the state, to correct a false impression. We suffered considerably by the impression that we are a malaria district and that it is dangerous for students to come here on account of their health. This is erroneous. We have here [on campus] a population of about 400 people and it is a fact we have had but one case of serious sickness—that of a student who is now convalescent and will take part in the afternoon exercises.

The expansion of campus facilities by 1894–95, especially major improvements in the water supply, the dormitories, infirmary, and mess hall, following the visit of the legislative review committee, were significant improvements that gradually helped shift public opinion. Notwithstanding, President Ross monitored the "sick list" prepared for the commandant of cadets each day by Dr. A. C. Gillespie, MD, and due to the small size of the Corps, Ross and his staff were in routine correspondence with cadets and families.[21]

Agricultural and Mechanical College of Texas

L. S. Ross, President   A. J. Rose, Pres't Board of Directors

College Station, Texas   1/18 1894

Cadet C. B. Stewart

Stewart Mill, Tx

Dear Sir:

    Yours 15th rec'd. Sorry you are sick and trust you may soon recover and return to school.

Resp'ly   L. S. Ross by Carter

Women at A&M

By the mid-1890s, social activities on campus were significantly improved in the rather Spartan environment. The routine of class, assembly hall, drill, and farm work was enhanced by the much-welcomed presence of wives and daughters of the faculty and staff, who began to play a more active role in extracurricular activities with both the cadets and visitors to the campus. Led by Mrs. Elizabeth Ross, Johanna Sbisa, Mary Jane Hutson, and the commandant's wife, Jesse Morse, the ladies of the campus became active "sponsors" (advisors) of each of the four units in the Corps of Cadets, becoming involved in the band and cadet choir, the Ross Volunteers, club activities, event-arrangement committees, the drama club, and literary societies, as well as the editorial staff of publications such as the *Battalion* and the *Olio*. One increasingly popular pastime was a series of "hops," or dances, during the school year, which attracted wide participation by those on campus, as well as visitors from Bryan, Waco, Houston, and Austin. Prior to 1892, most campus events were limited to the annual daylong commencement ceremonies. This soon changed, with very-popular, well-attended "hops" on Thanksgiving and Christmas, as well as the popular Military and Ross Volunteer Balls, Fancy Dress Hop, and the Alumni Hop. By 1895, a four-day-long commencement celebration in early June included hops, dinners, military-drill displays, oratory and debate competitions, and a grand open house to welcome visitors and highlight the facilities and programs taught at the college.[22]

During the last quarter of the century, there were heated debates regarding the enrollment of women at the A&M College of Texas and other all-male land-grant colleges, in line with the tradition of the time, as established by private schools. Interestingly, A&M College faculty member Alexander Hogg, a professor of pure mathematics (and no known relation to 'Gov. James Hogg), gained nationwide attention in mid-1877 academic circles by proposing the establishment of a "land-grant college for women" in each state and territory, backed by public lands in each state, along the lines of the Morrill Act of 1862. Shortly after Hogg's suggestion, A&M's first president, Thomas S. Gathright, had recommended that Prairie View Normal in Hempstead consider (due to low male enrollment) allowing women to attend, based on the same requirements used at Sam Houston Normal. At first, a shortage of housing for women delayed any action at Prairie View, but when the institution faced closure after only a few months of operation because of low male enrollment, arrangements were made for female students by 1879. This in no way changed the all-male policy at the A&M College.[23]

Professor Hogg gained further national attention at the National Education Association meeting in Philadelphia during late July 1879, following an expanded presentation of his recommendations, titled, "Industrial Education, on the Equal Education of the Head, the Heart, and the Hand." He promoted his initial views to set aside a portion of the public domain for the endowment and maintenance of at least one institution of public higher education in each state. Existing women's institutions in Texas did not seem concerned in the wake of the Hogg proposal, and Hogg's statements had no impact on A&M. The question of women at A&M would not surface again until 1883, when the University of Texas was opened.[24]

Ross had long been a proponent of co-education, noting, "the cadets would be improved by the elevating influence of the good girls," yet he concluded that the overcrowded campus facilities and limited dormitory space would not allow for full admission of co-education students in the 1890s. However, he was agreeable to accommodating limited class attendance by the daughters of faculty and staff. In addition to wives and older teenage daughters participating in the cadet activities and social events, many routinely attended class during the Ross administration. During this era, there were extensive opportunities for co-educational studies at more than two dozen colleges, institutions, and universities across Texas. One of the institutions was the University of Texas, which in the initial 1881 enabling legislation was intended to be a male-only campus, along the lines of the A&M College, until the institution was changed to co-ed at the eleventh hour by Governor Roberts and Senator Terrell, based partly on the senator's college experience at the University of Missouri.[25]

The Courtesy Students

Florine Ross returned from Austin in 1892 to jointly manage the Dramatic Club with Prof. Charles Puryear. Given the void of campus extracurricular events and social organizations, Florine soon became a driving force, fostering new activities for both the cadets and staff. The first major production of the club was the stirring 1889 war drama *The Woven Web*, presented in the Assembly Hall. This bold undertaking required the Corps to furnish an orchestra, and the cast was a mix of cadets, faculty, and their spouses. The production was a success and was followed by more plays, concerts, seasonal dances, and debates. Social events in the fall of 1892 continued with the announcement by Governor and Mrs. Ross of the grand campus wedding of Florine to Prof. Henry H. Harrington—a first for A&M. Campus activities continued during the Christmas and New Year's holidays season, highlighted by the organization of two masquerade balls for the cadets organized and hosted by Misses Bessie Ross and Rita Sbisa.[26]

The local campus women of the A&M staff—termed "courtesy" or lecture students—audited classes and sponsored clubs and Cadet units. Some of the women actively involved in the A&M community in the 1890s included Bessie Ross; Rita Sbisa, daughter of campus steward Bernard Sbisa; Emma W. Fountain, whose father was a professor of English and college chaplain; and Mary Bittle, whose father, Thomas C. Bittle, was a professor of languages. These female students could earn course credit that would transfer to a degree program at another institution. The daughters of history professor Charles Hutson—Ethel and twins Sophie and Mary (unlike Bessie Ross and Rita Sbisa, who also attended Baylor in Belton, Texas)—completed some four years of course work in engineering to be conferred a "certificate of completion" in lieu of a formal A&M College diploma. The A&M College course work of the Hutson twins prepared them for professional certifications, and they soon held engineering jobs in New Orleans. Their story provides a unique perspective of the academic regimen in the late 1890s:[27]

> Prof. Helge Ness taught us enough botany for us to have many happy hours with plants and the people who love plants. Prof. David W. Spence certainly made physics an interesting subject; Prof J. C. Nagle was most thorough in his teaching of surveying and hydraulics. Prof. P. S. Tilson and Henry Harrington gave of their time to teach us chemistry, while in the drawing department, Prof. Frederick Giesecke with the help of Mr. Gibson and Prof. Mitchell saw that we knew something of both mechanical drawing and descriptive geometry. We had some book-keeping up in that department too. In Prof. R. H. Whitlock's class we learned how to handle tools and I believe I have used that skill as much as any of the things I learned in the Mechanical Engineering Department, although we studied Strength of Materials over there. Prof. A. L. Banks and Prof. Robert Smith started us off in algebra and trigonometry so well we liked all mathematics. Prof South taught English, Dr. T. C. Bittle taught French and our father, Dr. Charles W. Hutson, taught us history.[28]

After 1895, with the mention of co-education in the first A&M annual, the *Olio*, there began to be an active debate on campus and in the news media about the role of women on the A&M campus. The debate was led by the Austin and Calliopean Societies at their periodic meetings; their programs actively raised the question, "Resolved: That Co-Education is Best," with the case for each side presented by the cadets and staff. The debate became a featured event at the June 1896 commencement exercises, with senior cadet Charles C. Todd '97, the ranking cadet in the Corps of Cadets, speaking for the affirmative and cadet E. M. Overshiner '97 addressing the negative before a large gathering of college officials, cadets, family, guests, and former students. The program was entitled, "Resolved: That civilization is promoted by the education of women." Following a spirited debate, victory was awarded to Overshiner. Notwithstanding, the June 1896 debate quite possibly set in motion the first formal legal challenge to co-education at the college. Charles Todd, one of the first regular US Army officers commissioned from A&M, served a distinguished military career, retiring and returning to practice law in Bryan. In private practice, he filed the first writ of mandamus suit in Bryan's Eighty-Fifth District Court, *Mrs. W. E. Neely, et al v. President T. O. Walton and the Board of Directors of the A&M College et al*, to allow women full-time admission in the college.[29]

The debate raged on regarding co-education at the A&M College, the two-decade-old proposal by Prof. Alexander Hogg resurfaced in calls by *Texas Farm and Ranch* to establish a state-sponsored and funded industrial school for girls. The renewed interest in co-education at A&M or the establishment of a girl's institution was largely triggered by the increasingly positive news about the growth and success of the A&M College. The improved image of the college grew in spite of the fact that overcrowding continued in all the dorms, the mess hall was woefully too small, and in 1896 some 144 applicants were refused admission simply due to a lack of room. The *Galveston Daily News*, noting that A&M is "a state institution to be proud of," circulated articles highlighting the role of President Ross to annually increase more legislative funding, resulting in an annual $100,000 payroll and a total capital valuation of college property of more than $400,000—the largest valuation of any institution in Texas in the mid-1890s.[30]

An additional factor that fueled the controversy was the rise of progressive women's groups that advocated for improvements in education, in general, and female access to all institutions—especially those funded by the state of Texas. Responding to the suggestion of an independent women's college, the Texas Women's Council (later the State Council of Women of Texas) in Dallas, organized by suffrage activist Ellen Lawson Dabbs, demanded that women be admitted to the A&M College, noting, "We have an A. & M. College, I have been told that it is developing a lot a military toughs. . . . [W]e have no law of primogeniture. . . . [T]his school [should] be opened to our girls." Dabbs's energetic approach soon evolved into an effort to create an industrial school for girls "either at the A. &. M. College or *elsewhere*." The prospect of establishing a new state college soon became a priority and was positively endorsed by President

Ross, who proposed the new college be established near the A&M College. The issue was referred to the state legislature for consideration and quickly became a political football: first, because any such measure was declined due to a lack of appropriations and, second, (notwithstanding the decline in funding) because there was a scramble by communities statewide to secure a location for the new women's college. Realizing the added economic benefits, the City of Bryan hastily formed a committee, with Ross's encouragement, to promote Brazos County as the preferred site.[31]

Agricultural and Mechanical College of Texas

L. S. Ross, President   A. J. Rose, Pres't Board of Directors

College Station, Texas   Feby 23, 1894

Dear Major,

I rec'ed your kind letter & read it with much pleasure. I was just now able to get around again. Had a pretty hard attack of Rheumatism. Glad to say the family was all well. Harve is clerking for his meals from Padgett & looking after the farm also. Frank is doing splendidly. Will go from here after graduation to medical school either in N. York or Phila. Bess is at the French school in Waco. She did not like Belton. Florine & boy are well. The chap is growing fast & is fine looking.

We were all sorry to hear you were under the cloud of ill health to some extent. Hope it is only temporary. We are anxious to see May [Holmes] & when she returns to Galveston she can by all means come this way & see us. We will make her stay pleasant and I would like very much to see you and Mrs. Holmes again and trust the good food will be very kind to you both [and] spare you for many long years.

The newspaper people frequently mention my name for third term and send me marked copies. Have many persistent people write me urgently on the same, only Dick Hall dropped to see me last week and he said that everyone was talking the same way. Of course this is pleasant as it is an utter & complete endorsement of my administration—after Mr. Hogg has disrupted the party, bankrupted the treasury & played the devil generally. I have it from a mutual friend . . . [Note: The remainder of the letter is missing.]

In addition to the daily demands of the college, tending to family, friends, and politics remained a major part of Ross's routine. Sul and Lizzie were pleased with the varied paths each of their children pursued. He consulted with Major Holmes on a regular basis, in addition to politicians, admirers, and promoters, who without any approval speculated on the possibility of Ross's third term as governor. Sul corresponded with Holmes regarding the disruption of the Hogg administration, which confirmed his careful monitoring of the "simply surprising" events in Austin. In an act exemplifying Hogg's dwindling levels of support, the state legislature "absolutely refused" a five-hundred-dollar appropriation to allow his official portrait to be placed with the former Texas governors in the supreme court library. All previous portraits had been paid for by the state, "except General Ross' which he paid for himself."[32]

And Sul always found time to get away from the campus and news media to hunt and fish.

Agricultural and Mechanical College of Texas

L. S. Ross, President   A. J. Rose, Pres't Board of Directors

College Station, Texas   May 10th, 1894

Dear friend Buck,

I was glad to hear from you again. Did not know just where you were living at this time. I have not thought of becoming a candidate for any position. I could not well afford to make a canvass for the nomination even if I was ambitious to serve the people again. Without an active personal canvass success could hardly be expected.

The A&M College is in a very prosperous condition and full at the time to the extent of its capacity. I feel warranted in the belief that you would make an acceptable presiding officer should there be a vacancy at any time. With best wishes for your present and future happiness. I am as ever your friend.

L. S. Ross

Agricultural and Mechanical College of Texas

L. S. Ross, President   College Station, Texas

May 14, 1894

S. A. Cunningham

Dear Sir:

Your explanation is perfectly satisfactory. The matter gave me special concern anyway, but name was omitted. I had no difficulty however in divining the cause, and presumed you were ignorant of the facts. I sent you a sketch of my life published by the *Bryan Eagle*. I have several others entering more length into details.

As you express a wish for incidents relating to my early exploits, I have enclosed an account of the fall of Parker's Fort and subsequent recovery of Cynthia Ann Parker which I wrote out for Genl Alford, an old Confederate, also account of the recovery of a little Girl whom I named Lizzie Ross in honor of the young lady, Miss Lizzie Tinsley of Waco to whom I was then engaged and afterward married in May 1861.

This young girl was about 8 years of age and had no knowledge of her capture. I educated her and had the pleasure of seeing her develop into a beautiful and accomplished woman. She married a wealthy merchant of California had one son as fruits of the union but both died in 1886 leaving no trace of race or linage. I expected you to use such parts or all that may suit your purpose. I send you the best photo to be had here at this time.

Very Respectfully
L. S. Ross

Will you kindly return the manuscript from Genl Alford
If you do not publish that part embracing my accounts of the two battles and recovery of captives. L.S.R.

Agricultural and Mechanical College of Texas

L. S. Ross, President　　A. J. Rose, Pres't Board of Directors

College Station, Texas　　　　　　　　　　　　　August 27, 1894

Dear Major

Don't know how long since we last heard from you all, just when I last wrote but rest assured you have not been forgotten. We talk about you every day & wonder how you are getting along. I have only taken one week vacation. Went to the Big Thicket. Killed 17 deer & had plenty wild hunting & got fat & sassy. Our health has been good all around the same. The summer has been delightfully cool here with the exception of two or three days. Lizzie did not wish to go off on hunt of pleasure but preferred to remain here.

The bathing in our Natatorium—while Sulphur water—is splendid. The ladies & children nearly all learned to swim with grace and ease. The prospect for _____ _____ attend _____ of students _____ _____ _____ _____ the labor of taking in so many Texas Boys, but guess I will _____ in keeping them _____. Frank graduated with first honors & will go to New York City in Oct to take a course of Medical _____. [H]e is a fine student & has grown tall & well proportioned. Bess will go to Waco school in Sept, Nev has become very large & strong, fear he will be too _____. Florine worships her boy. He is a fine specimen and promises to become an honor to all.

Harve has gone to Washington with the visiting Knights. He is with Tom Padgett yet but has an offer of a place in the Post Office. Don't know what he will do yet, sister May & her daughter & husband are in Waco to live. I haven't seen them. Don't know how they are getting along but for Lizzy.

The political affairs of the state are to me simply surprising. The Clark people seem to have traded the offices at success for the privilege of making the platform & ensuing Hogg, but they can hardly soon see their claimed victory after the endorsement given the administration. I saw Gen. Houston demand _____ & Buck Kilgore walked the plank—thank the Lord. He got too large for his britches.

I want you to write me a long letter & tell me what you are all doing & how you all are getting along. I shall always have deep & abiding interest in such & all yours . . .

Forever friend as ever
L. S. Ross

Ross's excitement is palpable as he writes Major Holmes on August 27, 1894, on the topics of increased efforts to promote the college statewide and inform Texans about the expanded opportunities offered by the institution. The college's yearlong construction program was cause to issue a statewide call for new students in advance of the eighteenth annual session, scheduled to open on September 13, 1894. Promotional material stressed that the college "gives a thorough scientific and practical education with theoretical and practical courses in dairying, stock breeding, agriculture, horticulture, surveying, mechanical and scientific engineering, chemistry, veterinary science, drawing, English and modern languages." Ross and his expanded faculty and staff had fully implemented an "agricultural and mechanical" course program in the full spirit of the covenants of the Morrill Act, quelling detractors who attacked the college for offering only "literary" subjects.[33]

The college's progress was further evidenced by efforts to improve the "[e]xtensive editions [*sic*] to dormitory [s] . . . a new stand pipe (water tower), ice plant, laundry and electric light plant—making the College complete in every detail." A key item that caught the attention of many and arguably increased the number of incoming cadets was the heart of the promotional program, promising "No Tuition and No Charge for Text Books." However, it was noted that the expenses for the entire fall 1894 session, except for clothing (i.e., cadet uniforms), amounted to $140.00. This amount represented the cost primarily for room and board, some fees, and a small room deposit. Ross maintained his active campus schedule, in addition to serving in his role of evaluating and approving improvements, budgets, and staffing at Prairie View Normal. He was also actively involved in securing care for disabled veterans and their families. Cold and wet weather in December 1894, coupled with Ross's recurring neurological problems from his lingering wounds, resulted in another bout of illness and hospitalization—underplayed as "nothing more serious than [a] cold." The severity of Ross's sickness was evident in private correspondence, yet it was not picked up and reported by the always-inquisitive news media.

Agricultural and Mechanical College of Texas

L. S. Ross, President   A. J. Rose, Pres't Board of Directors

College Station, Texas   Dec 27, 1894

Dear Genl Stoddard

    I hope you and yours are having a Merry Christmas. I have been sick enough to go to the hospital . . . nothing more serious than cold. . . . I'm thinking over the staff appointments I have concluded to put Rutherford in Swearingen's place, the latter gentleman has never shown any appreciation of the previous appointment that I remember, and has manifested but little concern for the association. If therefore you have not already made the announcement I would like for you to give Rutherford's name the place in the list. What think you of it?

With best wishes etc
Yours truly L. S. Ross

The 1894–95 A&M College session would usher in a growing number of new faculty and students, much-needed new facilities, and a period of continued expansion of student activities and academic programs. In September, Lt. Benjamin C. Morse was assigned to an active-duty unit at the Twenty-Third Infantry and was replaced by fellow West Pont graduate Lt. George T. Bartlett as commandant and professor of military science and tactics. President Ross prevailed upon the board of directors to maintain an additional stipend for the commandant and add additional support staff. The *Dallas Morning News*, noting that cadets "have to eat in stages" due to space constraints, strongly supported A&M's legislative budget request for a new and larger mess hall to account for the growing student body, boldly concluding, "[T]he *esprit de corps* of the college cannot be beaten."[34]

    In addition to the expanded campus activities of the Austin Literary Society, glee club, student band, and YMCA, a thirteen-piece college band was established (with the assistance of George Holick) and led by Arthur Jenkins. The college added its first museum, spearheaded by professors Mark Francis and O. M. Ball. A novelty for cadets and campus visitors, Francis collected and filled an exhibit room with large prehistoric dinosaur bones found in the Brazos River basin—including mast-odon and camel fossils from the Miocene Period. The small collection included rock samples from the geology and metallurgy department, along with a wrapped Egyptian mummy purchased by Francis from an 1891 discovery at the Valley of Kings in Karnak, Egypt. The ancient artifacts provided an ongoing source of interest for visitors, students, and news media statewide. Improvements to the barren campus, dotted with post oaks and mesquite, included an expansion of the college veg-etable gardens as well as the addition of a large apple and peach orchard. A two-year program to plant nonnative trees and shrubs proved to be a waste of both time and money, as few survived. Improved drainage, sidewalks, a new potable water supply, and expanded electric service for the dorms, classrooms, and ice factory were welcome additions.[35]

Agricultural and Mechanical College of Texas

L. S. Ross, President   A. J. Rose, Pres't Board of Directors

College Station, Texas   Nov 18, 1895

Capt Stephen

My dear Sir & Comrade

    I kindly thank you & your camp for the courtesy & compliment enclosed in your invitation. It is with regret I am compelled to decline all engagements of this character at present. My obligations hold me close for some time and however much I should be party to join the old Confederates & talk to them on the theme assigned me, I cannot do so. Hence, I ask that you do me the favor to make known to our comrades the high appreciation I entertain for the honor they would do me as well as my personal esteem for each of them individually.

I am as ever truly
L. S. Ross

To The News: College Station, Tex., Dec 19, 1895

Proposals

Separate sealed bids will be received at the President's office of the A. and M. College, Tex., until 4 o'clock p.m., Friday, Dec. 20th, '95 for privilege of selling goods at the depot, also the privilege of keeping a barber shop on the campus for one year, beginning 1st day of January next. Award to be made the highest and best bidder. Right to reject any and all bids received.

L. S. Ross, Pres.   W. R. Cavitt, Local Director and Secretary

The statewide notoriety of Sul Ross also evoked vicious attacks and attempts at fraud, unbeknownst to most Texans. Ross's sons, Frank, well-known in former student ranks and the medical profession, and Lawrence Jr., also well-known in Austin, were thus susceptible to numerous fraudulent attempts. The following letter was sent out statewide by Sul in order to address the irritating efforts of an "imposter":

To The [Galveston] News: College Station, Tex., Feb 10, 1896

For: *Dallas Morning News*, 13 February 1896

It has come to my knowledge that an imposter claiming to be my son has in several instances sought loans of money from my friends in different parts of the state. He is described as a heavy-set young man of fair complexion, about 20 years of age. In some places he represented himself as Frank, and in others as Lawrence Ross [Jr.]. I request the publication of this notice for the protection of friends, and in justice to the good name of my sons.

L. S. Ross

The calm campus presence and leadership of Sul Ross provided an effective defense of the viability of the college in the face of political opponents in Austin and some farm organizations. This was reinforced by improved conditions and a growing enrollment at the school. Sul's close attention to detail and his awareness of the inner workings of the college over time would be judged by the actions of its cadets. Fortunately, former cadet graduates fostered an environment of stability and pride in the college. During the first decade and a half of A&M prior to Sul's arrival, the college endeavored to adjust to the challenges of growing pains, meager funding, and the persistent need to prove its value to the state. Sul's leadership at the school in the mid-1890s enhanced activities on campus and provided a much-needed rallying cry as social organizations and sports—primarily football—soon inspired the broad involvement of cadets, Sul's family, the faculty, and their spouses, along with the return of ex-cadets (alumni) in support of their alma mater. It was during this period that the foundation was laid for the many time-honored traditions observed today at Texas A&M.

Gig 'em!

CHAPTER 6

Legacy

Seven years ago he found this college struggling for existence, since then, through his exertions mainly, it has risen to its present grandeur and usefulness. His was the hand of encouragement extended to us when the dark shadows of failure threatened to envelop us. During that time he learned to love the institution, to love the students, as he was revered by them. During his presidency he gave them advice such as if followed would make them all men among men.

Charles C. Todd '97, Memorial Service, January 16, 1898

Through the sheer force of his personality, Ross saved A&M.

San Antonio Express, November 5, 1950

Following the 1896 Christmas season with family and friends, Sul Ross embarked on his annual early-January hunting trip with a small group headed to the Navasota River bottom. As was often the case, the newspapers ran a short blurb about the trip, including the names of the few friends who accompanied him. This was par for the course, as the press often reported on Ross's activities, travel, and presentations throughout his life. During the last quarter of the nineteenth century, few, if any, Texans were mentioned as widely in newspaper articles from across the state. Thus it was no surprise that friends and supporters constantly quizzed Ross concerning any future desire to run for elective office, and enemies watched as closely in hopes that he would not be recruited; they also paid close attention to his visits to Austin and comments to determine how the political winds blew in the state. Ross's personal letters provide a unique window into the backdrop of the issues and concerns of his time, yet following the death of his close friend and confidant, Maj. Henry Holmes, in mid-1895, Ross essentially stopped writing such candid correspondences on politics, the college, and his family. Ross's letters were and still are sought as collector's items, and thus an unknown number doubtlessly exist in private collections, beyond those cited herein.[1]

The publicity generated over the growing debate of the possibility of co-education at the A&M College would continue from late 1896 through and beyond Ross's death in early January 1898. Ross displayed no known objection to co-education at A&M, other than managing expectations

The funeral bier of President Ross in January 1898. Former Texas governors (left to right) Charles A. Culberson, Oran M. Roberts, John Ireland, and Joseph D. Sayers surround the casket. Source: Cushing Archives

of those who were rushing for a solution. He informed an audience in Waco that "he was ready to receive girls as pupils if such became the rule."[2] The facilities and funding were not yet available to properly support the new students. The college routinely turned down scores of qualified male students, boarded cadets three to a room, increased class size, and constantly requested funding to increase both housing and a new mess hall to accommodate its growth. The co-education discussion surrounding A&M soon was changed by a new effort in early 1897–98 to establish a women's industrial college along the lines of A&M. Ross fully supported this, and with the aid of local supporters and merchants in Bryan, he helped shape the debate to lobby for such a new state women's institution to be located in Brazos County.[3]

Those in favor of co-education were quick to point out: "No affirmative legislation is needed to authorize the opening of the A. and M. College to girls. The only action necessary is for the Legislature to make an appropriation necessary to erect a dormitory for girls and for maintaining the girl's Industrial department, which need not exceed $40,000. The Board of Directors of the College will do the rest."[4]

Bryan political leaders, led primarily by A&M College board members William. R. Cavitt, W. S. Howell, and H. B. Stoddard, along with local merchants and bankers, had fared very well during the tenure of Sul Ross and the precipitous growth of the college. More cadets meant the sale of more dry goods, supplies, fuel, feedstock, and tailor services; three livery stables and several blacksmiths; an opera house and restaurants; a large brickyard; and high hotel occupancy, due to an increased number visitors. The *Galveston Daily News* confirmed, "[T]he aggregate amounts [of commerce] is quite a large sum annually." Adding a new women's institution would further enhance the local Brazos County economy. As the debate moved to Austin for possible action by the state legislature, Ross took the opportunity to state his observations on education in the press, while also reminding Texans of the role and difficult path the A&M College had endured, after two decades in operation. His reflections are very timely and interesting, noting detractors "looked upon the college suspiciously. . . . [T]here was a lack of funds . . . no models for imitation . . . and yet . . . opposition gradually yielded." The following feature article penned by Sul Ross for the *Galveston Daily News* reflected his detailed grasp of the importance of education. It received wide distribution across the state and was one of several detailed articles and editorials on higher education published in 1897:[5]

February 24, 1897

College Station, Brazos County

To the News:

As there seems to be a growing interest in industrial education in our state and some desire to engraft its features upon both public and private schools, it may not be inopportune to give a brief statement of the national land grant act by virtue of which the agricultural and mechanical college was established. It has been asserted that if in the early days of the republic the opportunities for scientific and practical education had been equal to those offered for training men of the learned professions the advent of the steamboat and rail car would have occurred at an earlier date. It was the recognition of the importance of such opportunities that led in after years to the establishment of more liberal practical education.

Conspicuous among the scientific schools were the Rensselaer Polytechnic Institute at Troy, N. Y. established in 1824; the Sheffield school, an adjunct of Yale college, which had its beginnings in 1846; the Lawrence scientific school, in connection with Harvard University, in 1847; and the Chandler scientific school in connection with Dartmouth college, established in 1851.

But the earliest practical educators desired a still more comprehensive system, the ideal of which would combine the training of the hand with that of the intellect and invest labor with the rank of honor and dignity commensurate with its values in the world's economy.

In 1859, in response to numerous petitions, a bill "to promote the liberal and practical education of the industrial classes" was passed by both houses of congress. It had been drawn with great care by the Hon. Justin S. Merrill [*sic*] of Vermont, and proposed to give the several states and territories 20,000 acres of public land for each of their senators and representatives in congress for the purpose above indicated.

The bill was vetoed by President Buchanan.

In 1862 a similar bill was passed, which gave 30,000 acres of land to the states and territories for each of their members in both branches of congress. This bill received the approval of President Lincoln July 2, 1862. Its originators called it the new education bill because it proposed to extend to the industrial classes the advantage of a liberal education by new methods of instruction. While among the sciences to be taught it was declared that the leading object was to teach those relating to agriculture and the mechanical arts, the language of the act making the grant declared specifically that it was not its purpose to exclude other sciences. The design being to establish institutions of learning of the highest order as comprehensive in scope as the design was liberal. No portion of this national fund or the interest arising therefrom can be either directly or indirectly extended for the erection, preservation, purchase or repair of buildings. It was expected that the states and territories would supply these minor and varying wants and maintain the bounty of the national government intact. The realization of the desire for a thorough system of mechanical training by shop instruction and practice for students in that department was not attained until 1876. At the centennial exposition, held at Philadelphia in that year, the Russian government made an exhibit of this feature of the system inaugurated by their people, and its simplicity and adaptability to the purposes desired at once commended it to practical educators.

It has been aptly said that the American mind is slow to adopt new ideas or principles without demonstration, but when a measure is shown to be practical it is ready to reap the benefits. The founding of these colleges for the purpose of co-educating the head and the hand and elevating the life of the farmer and the mechanic was an innovation.

The friends of existing colleges looked upon it suspiciously.

The average legislature approached it warily. There was a common belief that these colleges would simply add another to the existing institutions whose purpose was to train young men for the learned professions, and not for the active business pursuits of the country. They were tolerated rather than supported and seemed to require an apology for their existence. In some instances they were threatened constantly with strangulation by a relentless opposition. In the south especially there never was a more inopportune time for so radical a venture in education. There was a general repugnance to the system because of the auspices under which it was inaugurated. The asperities naturally engendered by a great revolution and the friction attending reconstruction, together with the dubious future of the country, environed the cause with a formidable array of discouragements. The accumulations of two centuries had been swept away, property values destroyed and the labor system disorganized. Men long accustomed to comfort and opulence were wholly impoverished, and there was exorbitant taxation and scarcity of revenue. The first directors entered upon the discharge of their duties under conditions of the most discouraging character.

There was a lack of funds for buildings and other necessary purposes. They had given the new educational scheme but little thought or study and there was little in the experience of the past to guide them. The results sought were far different from those attained by existing institutions and could be reached only by different methods.

There were no models for imitation. The colleges and universities found no difficulty in procuring trained men for the learned professions, but the men whose training and inclinations fitted them for work in the new educational scheme were scarce. In most instances they had to be trained for these positions. They had to arrange the outline of instruction in harmony with and study the limitations, suggestions and scope of the law. But in spite of every adverse influence there was an outspoken declaration of loyalty to the new system that was each day rewarded with keener sympathy and a more wakeful concern as these agricultural and mechanical colleges steadily worked their way to conspicuous place in popular regard. Public apathy retreated before clearer light and broader views. Opposition gradually yielded as men became enlightened on the subject.

We regard the university as the crowning glory of the state, and hope to see it encouraged by a liberal policy. The people are deeply interested in its prosperity, and nothing should interpose to hinder or retard its progress. The medical department [Galveston] is deserving of the most generous treatment. Its success in affording the young men of the state ample facilities for the study of medical science vindicates its claims upon the public. And the Prairie View state normal school is making steady and substantial progress as a branch of the university to afford the colored youth an opportunity for professional training. All are an indispensable part of the educational machinery and have a great work to perform. The board of directors of the agricultural and mechanical college took the initiative last year by inviting a meeting and conference with the regents to provide measures to bring the institutions into harmonious working relations and to maintain a spirit of friendly co-operation. It has been the policy of the directors not only to give no occasion for antagonism, but to refrain from perpetuating those which may have existed; the only differences which we propose to foster with either state or denominational schools are those generous rivalries which spring from earnest endeavor to further to the utmost the success of this college in those peculiar elements of power and qualities of attraction belonging to its appropriate sphere.

It is performing a service along practical lines undertaken by no other institution in the state. There is no other of equal advantages where Texas boys may be educated for less money, the cost being but little above home expenses. The broad range of its instructions and practice enables its graduates to at once become wage earners.

It frequently develops aptitudes in the students for certain lines of employment, the existence of which neither themselves nor their most intimate friends were conscious. Its influence is tending to divert a large proportion of the young men of the state from the already over-crowded learned professions to the adoption of industrial pursuits.

Men skilled in these employments are always in demand. Those endowed with talent in these lines should have ample facilities for their development. No state can be truly or permanently great in the highest and best sense of the word so long as it depends upon other states to supply these advantages. Next to the ties of kinship there is no attachment of more lasting or binding force which students feel for schoolmates. It is a sorrowful and portentous thing for the parents to deprive them of this most important element of success in social, political and business life by sending them abroad to be educated among strangers with whom they may never have intercourse or converse.

In this age of contest and rivalry in every department and business, our state should hold the place to which her geographical position, her vast resources and her rapidly increasing population justly entitle her by enabling her sons to rank with the best minds of the country.

Her own sons should be depended upon to lead and direct her great and growing interests and not be remanded to drudgery and unskilled labor because of a lack of opportunities. Upon the success of this college depend in a large measure not only the extent and degree to which agricultural knowledge shall be disseminated among the farmers of the state, but also the degree of progress which shall be made in all the arts of life. Largely over half of our voting and taxpaying population belongs to the industrial classes. They stand as a foundation for the success of all and are entitled to the fullest instruction upon the everyday problems of farm, garden, dairy and mechanical pursuits.

Chemistry is a prominent feature on account of its close relation to agriculture and the manufacturing interests of the country. There is a constant demand from the people for analyses of soils, oils, water and fertilizers. In its veterinary work and original researches and instruction in the anatomy, physiology and pathology of animals more than ordinary interest has been attracted at home and abroad, and yet its laboratory facilities and apparatus are of the most inadequate character. The college has been in existence more than twenty years without a building for the use of the agricultural features, including illustration matter, apparatus, books, records and a greater seating capacity for the large number of students under its instruction. Is it a matter of surprise that no greater number of its students have graduated from its halls to a life upon the farm? Does not this neglect, coupled with the knowledge that public honors and preferments [*sic*] lie through professional channels, serve to educate the youth far away from the farm? The greatest financial successes in agriculture are being attained in special lines of work in which a small capital brings comparatively large returns.

Our farmers are accomplishing much by the bounty of nature, but in this age of sharp competition more than ever do they need that intelligence which will enable them to do more work with less effort by systematizing their labor and economizing their time and strength by making every blow effective. Excluding these advantages resulting to the individual citizen, it is urged that in these days of frequent, violent disturbances, when commerce is blocked and the regular healthy flow of business among the industries of the country is interrupted over wide areas, we need men of trained intellects and skilled hands, state pride and patriotism, who, having been educated in sympathy with labor and invested with an intelligent comprehension of what its rights are can safely be trusted to determine where such rights end and those of capital begin.

We can submit abundant evidence that the agricultural and me-chanical college is turning out men of practical ability as well as theory in the higher agricultural and mechanical pursuits. Wherever found, they illustrate the value of the training they have received and are honoring the state that gave them birth and the institution that educated them. If a grief-stricken people emerging from a war that brought bankruptcy and imposed exorbitant taxes believed that sound public policy demanded large appropriations to found it, should their representatives in these times of comparative prosperity and light taxation hesitate to contribute to its necessary growth and expansion to meet the wants of the rising generation.

Its support rests upon the high grounds of patriotism and duty.

L. S. Ross

As the debate over education in Texas continued, Ross and all Texans were informed of Gov. Richard Coke's death in Waco on May 14, 1897. A very close personal friend of the Ross family, Coke received a state funeral and burial in Oakwood Cemetery in Waco. Pallbearers car-rying the casket included Governor Culberson and former governors Hubbard, Ross, and Hogg. As Coke was being interred, a massive storm with heavy thunder, sounding like a "furious cannonading," greeted the mourners at the graveside. Just as the casket was being lowered, a violent bolt of bright lighting hit a nearby tree, sending a shock wave through the crowd. Former Gov. Richard B. Hubbard was knocked to his knees, and former senator John H. Reagan, attorney general M. M. Crane, and Sul Ross all were riveted by the sudden commotion. As some in the gathering fainted, one observer noted that the horses hitched to the carriages seemed paralyzed, while other teams of horses broke and ran in the heavy downpour of rain. Fortunately, neither Sul Ross nor any of the bystanders were seriously injured.[6]

The Culberson Alliance

By late 1896, A&M board Chairman A. J. Rose and Sul Ross had neutralized many of the unfounded attacks in Austin and improved the image of the A&M College in the minds of Texans. Politically, the two men used their expertise and leadership to the advantage of the college—mustering former students and the agricultural community to contribute to the success of the institution. Faculty and administrative unrest during the mid-1890s at the university in Austin soon made Ross the leading proponent of improved funding and facilities for the state's institutions of higher learning. This high-profile role came about due to his close relationship with incoming governor Charles Culberson. Ross continued his outreach to the University of Texas, attending the June 1896 commencement in Austin and orchestrating a joint meeting of the college and university boards in his first-floor office in Old Main on June 30, 1896—"for the purpose of jointly considering the future welfare of the two institutions . . . and advance the educational interest of all Texans." Rumored plans to consolidate the two boards into one were quickly dismissed.[7]

In the fall of 1896, the forthcoming elections dominated discussions across the state of Texas. Ross received numerous invitations to speak at gatherings of the "Bryan and Sewall Clubs," in support of presidential candidate William Jennings Bryan and his running mate Arthur Sewall. Texas voters were interested in his views on the candidates, public education, and issues of the day. His written response to the Waco club is in reply to a request to speak a week prior to the general election and was published in newspapers statewide:

Hon. Seth P. Mills, President

College Station, Texas, October 26—I have the honor to acknowledge receipt of your communications advising me that the Bryan and Sewall Club of Waco had, by a complimentary resolution, invited me to become their quest, etc. While I can not consistently, with my obligations as president of this State institution, accept your invitations to deliver a political address, I beg you to assure the club, in whose behalf you act, of my profound sense of their courtesy and kindness. I believe our public schools should be common to all without distinction of creed or party, and free from influence or party and free influence or direction of a denominational or partisan character. To inject politics into the system would constitute a kind of political sacrilege, against which every patriot should feel called upon to solemnly protest. It is our objective to teach the youth of the State to become moral, thinking people, capable of forming opinions for themselves and acting for themselves, and in effect to perform the duties which may pertain to them as individual citizens. While cultivating and developing a sentiment of intense patriotism and feeling of attachment to our country, its history and its institutions, we remind them that it is according to the genius of our institutions that political differences should never engender personal animosities. The right to private judgement and free speech is a right so sacred and belongs so sacredly to all that we are bound to recognize it and respect it in our opponents if we would preserve it for ourselves. The great American principal [*sic*] of toleration lies at the foundation of our civil as well as religious liberty and that principal [*sic*] is obeyed in its true spirit only by those who have not merely to tolerate an opponent, but to honor and respect an honest and manly adversary. Nevertheless, in response to the many inquiries from friends of every political affiliation, I regards [*sic*] it as my right and duty to avow, in direct and unequivocal terms, that while not in full accord with their National and State platforms, and not indorsing [*sic*] all the sentiments expressed by the candidates, I shall cast my vote for Bryan and Sewall and the Culberson administration.

Very respectfully,
L. S. Ross

By the fall of 1896, Ross was at the height of his administration of the A&M College of Texas. Far removed from the college's often tense relationship with former governor Hogg and his Austin staff and political supporters, Governor Culberson was a fast ally of President Ross, and this alliance proved beneficial to the college. Working jointly with the Ross, the governor appointed Archibald J. Rose as the commissioner of agriculture, and for the first time in six years, there was a significant change in the composition of the college board of directors. William Cavitt concluded his membership after thirteen years on the board but remained a special advisor. Following much speculation and little surprise once proposed, the governor appointed the first former student of the A&M College to the board, Houston businessman Frank A. Reichardt '79, on December 23, 1896. In addition to being a close personal friend of Sul Ross, he was commander of the Houston Rifles,

During late January 1898, the A&M cadets and faculty held a memorial service in the campus Assembly Hall; this is a view of the stage. President Ross was interned at Oakwood Cemetery in Waco on January 4, 1898. Source: Author's collection

a local militia group authorized by the governor, which was on call in the event of any assignment by the chief executive. And shortly after the Reichardt appointment, the second A&M former student to be added to the board, Judge Charles Rogan '80, of Brownwood, was confirmed. After an interim appointment as chairman of the board in January 1897, Frank Reichardt, who would begin a nine-year membership on the board, was named the permanent chairman in July. The newly confirmed 1896–97 A&M Board of five members also included new appointees Jefferson Johnson, from Austin; Frank P. Holland, from Dallas; and George C. Pendleton, from Belton.[8]

Following the fanfare of the co-education debate and Sul Ross's February 1897 *News* article, the Texas Legislature scheduled its annual campus visits to Huntsville, Galveston, Hempstead, and College Station. There were few comments in the newspapers statewide, as the visitors clearly stated in their final report that "we found all the institutions in excellent condition." The visit to A&M gained the most praise (and made no mention of co-education in the final report) and, more importantly, included a unanimous committee recommendation for a biannual legislative appropriation of $120,000, to include a special earmark of $30,000 for a new mess hall.[9] Official Texas Legislative praise for the A&M College focused almost completely on the leadership of its president:

> Texas and her farmers' sons are certainly to be congratulated upon having at the head of the Agricultural and Mechanical College such a man as Governor Ross. Jefferson devoted the years left after retiring from the Presidency to building the University of Virginia and urging a system of public schools for Virginia. Lee, upon the dispersion of his veterans, became a college president and devoted his remaining days to the higher education of the youth of Virginia and the South.
>
> How fitting it is that one so much loved in Texas as Governor Ross, after filling the position of highest political honor and responsibility that lies within the gift of our people, should upon his retirement gather around him the young men of Texas and consecrate his life to their education. No one can visit the college without being impressed with the simple, yet noble, character of the president, and its healthful and elevating effect upon the young men by whom he is surrounded. Governor Ross had undoubtedly found this place of the greatest usefulness, and his labors will extend their gracious influences throughout Texas for generations after he has been gathered to his fathers.[10]

Prairie View

While the A&M College continued its upward trend, the historically black Prairie View campus also grew and expanded. Dating from his days as governor, Ross championed increased opportunities for African Americans. He routinely met with black leaders both at Prairie View and at his home on the A&M campus. He personally oversaw Prairie View campus contracts and building programs, and he was active in briefing pro-education Austin legislators on progress at Prairie View. Ross's support of Prairie View extended to the A&M board of directors, who were actively represented at Prairie View by board member William R. Cavitt of Bryan. Prof. E. L. Blackshear, principal and chief administrative officer of PV, received the following inquiry from the *Dallas Morning News* on June 27, 1897: "In what way is General Ross connected with your school?" He responded:

> The Prairie View State Normal is a branch of the Agricultural and Mechanical College of Texas, of which Gen. Ross is president. He is also the treasurer of both institutions. It affords me pleasure to be here in the home of Gen. Ross to testify to the nobility of his character and to his genuine interest in the education of not only a white youth, but of the colored youth as well. Gov. Ross recently paid a visit (s) to Prairie View, and in a short talk to the young men, fraught with wisdom, urged them to cultivate true manhood and to prepare themselves for the high duties of citizenship. The Negroes of Texas have never forgotten him as the champion of the colored deaf, dumb, and blind institute at Austin, nor have they forgotten that he first in a message urged the establishment for negroes of a branch university or college as provided for in the state constitution . . . we shall remember with gratitude his unselfish interest in the improvement of all classes of people in Texas.[11]

Splendid Condition

Sul Ross continued to make a major impact on both Texas A&M and Prairie View. The *Austin Daily Statesman* touted praise for Ross from the A&M board: "The members of the board of directors congratulated President Ross and the faculty upon the splendid condition of the A&M College, the experiment station, and also Prairie View Normal."[12]

The expansion of the A&M College student body and facilities would continue throughout the years. Soon the campus would need to address a number of concerns related to the growth of the college staff and their families, numbering more than fifty in 1896. Some of the faculty and staff had allowed their livestock to graze at random on campus, which proved detrimental to efforts to plant shrubs, grass, gardens, and young trees. To address the grazing problem, Ross persuaded the board to approve a "loose stock provision" that prohibited any private grazing of stock without the written approval of the president. Violators would be fined fifty cents for each head of loose stock. At last, the college's growth had surpassed its ability to be self-sufficient in a number of respects. A special notice was issued in the papers statewide for increased contracting and services—a sure sign of the institution's success. These notices were further proof to the legislature and citizens across the state that there was a high demand for enrollment in the college. In addition, A&M graduates were making an impact on the growing Texas economy. In the agricultural sector, the total value of farm production had nearly doubled statewide over the decade of the 1890s to more than $209 million (see table 6.1). While at one time the cadets themselves cut wood and hauled water, the growth of the college necessitated the securing of contracts for expanded services and supplies—for example, J. H. Suber was contracted for 3,000 cords of wood at $1.60 per cord and local merchant W. C. Boyett was contracted to supply meat at $3.90 per 100 pounds of grass-fed beef.[13]

Table 6.1. Vital Texas statistics and trends, 1870–1900

Year	Avg. farm size (acres)	Avg. value of farm	Total value of farm products	Cattle price per head*
1870	301.0	$1,322	$49,185,170	$19.45
1880	208.4	$1,479	$65,204,329	$16.10
1890	225.3	$2,420	$111,699,430	$16.60
1900	357.2	$2,733	$209,346,434	$22.15

* Price is based on a three-year average.
Source: US Census, 1900, Vol. IV and Supplement for Texas, p. 667; US Census, 1870–1910: Statistics of Agriculture; USDA Yearbook, 1910, p. 630.

The high demand for enrollment was noted both in the fall of 1896 and the fall of 1897, with the publication of a notice issued by the president's office that the college could "receive no more students."

NO MORE STUDENTS

Demagogic Legislators Can Now Rise Up and Do Some Explaining

Bryan, Tex., Sept. 8.—(Special) 1897

Three hundred and ten students are already at the Agricultural and Mechanical College and President Ross authorizes your correspondent to announce the following:

The public is advised that the Agricultural and Mechanical College can receive no more students at present. We will make an effort to provide for those who have been promised places.

L. S. Ross, President

The *News* concluded that if the "people of Texas knew of the great work of the college, sufficient pressure [would be brought] to bear in the legislature to secure appropriations for buildings." The *Galveston Daily News* also made note that there were "339 matriculations," but owing to the overcrowding conditions of the dormitories, some "were sent home until there is room for them." Notwithstanding the crowded dorms, the improvement under Ross was very apparent to the staff, cadets, and visitors—with a new steam laundry, an ice plant, an electric light plant, a natatorium, an expanded library, a museum, and a new extensive mess hall under construction. Meanwhile, tuition expenses to attend for nine months remained at the rate of $140.00 per cadet.

In the fall of 1897, the A&M Campus was in the best shape of the institution's history. "Florist" and college groundskeeper George Eberspacher had been given a free hand to enhance the campus foliage. Abandoning some three years of attempts with nonnative trees and shrubs, the campus adopted post oaks and yaupon shrubs, native to the region. Campus and individual faculty gardens were allowed to expand, along with the installation of improved walkways and cinder-covered streets. Weather conditions were mild, and the overall health of the cadets and staff was considered the best it had been in years. The opening of the natatorium and bathhouse, along with an improved water supply, were considered largely responsible for this improvement. However, these campus improvements would soon be challenged by an epidemic threat in the fall.[14]

Very pleased with the deportment and military training of the Corps of Cadets under Lt. George T. Bartlett, President Ross petitioned the War Department to extend the commandant's duty assignment on campus. The extension was granted until April 1898. Bartlett went on to a very successful career and was promoted to major general in 1918, in command of all World War I operations in England.

Agricultural and Mechanical College of Texas

L. S. Ross, President   A. J. Rose, Pres't Board of Directors

College Station, Texas   Dec. 1897

Hon. J. [Joseph] D. Sayers, M. C.

Washington, D.C.

Dear Sir:—

Geo. T. Bartlett, 1st Lieut. 3rd Artillery, was assigned to duty as Military Instructor at the college by special order 179 A. G. O. August 1st 1894, and has demonstrated such a high degree of zeal and efficiency that I exceedingly regret his term of service will expire at the end of this session. I write to ask you, as a special favor, that you endeavor to secure from the War Department a continuation of his detail for at least one year.

His services have proved so efficient and valuable to the College that Col. Lawton, Inspector General of the Department of the Southwest, on his last visit, reported to the Adjutant General's Department that he found the discipline excellent and that the College was the best equipped and conducted institution of its character in the Southwest. Much of this credit is due to the efficiency of Lieut. Bartlett as Commandant, and hence I regard the possibility of his early retirement as a misfortune.

Please say to the Secretary of War, Gen. Alger, that I would esteem it a positive service to the country to have Lieut. Bartlett retained, and I would hold his favorable action in grateful remembrance. If necessary, the Board of Directors, the Governor of the State and State administration will doubtless join me in this request.

Possibly Mr. Hawley can render some assistance, and I dare say

would be pleased to join you in presenting this request to the Hon.
Secretary of War.

I am quite sure that my old friend, Gen. Stanley, would esteem it a
pleasure to aid you, if in your judgement his services are important.

I regret to trouble you with this matter, in view of your arduous
duties, but plead by way of apology the great interest of the institution
which I have the honor to represent as President.

Very respectfully,
L. S. Ross

The Scare

The *Bryan Daily Eagle,* which routinely included a full page of "international" news, began to report on an epidemic of "smallpox" in Cuba
and the Caribbean Islands in April 1897. The report used the word
"smallpox" without full confirmation of the true nature of the illness.
Many took note of the headlines when dozens of deaths were reported
in New Orleans, Mobile, and Pensacola due to the "fever's ravages," and
concerns only increased with reports of more new cases of illness. The
epidemic and deaths in New Orleans were traced to be the direct result
of newly infected passengers arrivals at the port, causing many in Texas
to quickly demand the prohibition of foreign ships docking in Galveston
and Houston.[15]

Rumors spread across the South that the epidemic—"the scare"—
could enter other Gulf of Mexico ports and, in fact, could be a combination of yellow fever, dengue, black tongue, malaria, or similar ailments,
and until a "case of black vomit was discovered, did [the doctors] suspect
for an instant the disease prevailing was that of yellow fever." While a
clear conclusive diagnosis was not immediately found or confirmed,
scores of people and animals began to die along the Gulf Coast of Texas,
and the illness was moving inland. In late September, Galveston ordered
a city-wide quarantine and limited disembarkations at the port. Concerned with the spread of the unidentified epidemic to the A&M College,
on October 2, 1897, local officials ordered, "Hereafter no trains will be
allowed to stop in the Brazos County for any purpose. Trains would
not use the side tracks to slow down and must not stop at the stations

[at College and Bryan]. . . . [I]f this is violated they will not allow them to enter the county. Effective at once." All railroad employees were laid off and the stations closed. Mayor C. A. Adams of Bryan issued a notice to citizens to promptly "clean up their premises and use disinfectants liberally." While no visitors were allowed on campus, a number of cadets did become sick, and Cadet Will Allison, of Sonora, "died of congestion." The *Galveston Daily News* praised the college for its swift action, and noted the timely steps taken to address the potential epidemic. By late October, the threat had passed and regular train schedules resumed, yet there was no clear conclusion of the cause and origins of the deadly epidemic. An almost identical crisis scenario erupted on the Texas A&M campus in October 1918 during the influenza pandemic, resulting in more than fifty deaths.[16]

Dr. Frank Ritchie Ross '95

One of the unwritten goals of Sul Ross in accepting the presidency of the A&M College of Texas was the possibility that his children could continue their education by attending the college. Three of his sons attend classes, and two, Frank '95 and Neville '02, graduated as members of the Corps of Cadets .

Frank attended A&M at age fifteen and was an accomplished student leader and excelled in his academic courses. Due to a great interest in science he was awarded the honor of the best veterinarian studies cadet. He was a baritone in the Glee Club, the secretary-treasurer of the Dramatic Club, and the president of the Calliopean Literary Society, a scholarly debate organization. As a cadet he enlisted in the Sixth Infantry Regiment, Texas Volunteer Guard.

In the Corps of Cadets leadership he was the third ranking cadet and cadet quartermaster as a junior, member of the Ross Volunteers, and as a senior the number two ranked cadet and adjutant on Corps Staff. Frank regained his eye sight and graduated with honors in June 1895. He first attended the University of Virginia and then enrolled in the Tulane Medical School and postgraduate studies in Vienna, Austria. Upon graduation he returned to Waco and Houston to practice medicine.

In an address to the Corps of Cadets at the June 1896 commencement Dr. Ross stressed the need to be honorable in all endeavors and to be a leader upon graduation: "You must assert yourself and be a man if you desire to become a factor and not a mere figurehead in the everyday pursuit of life."

At the time of his father's death in January 1898, Frank was the president of the Texas A&M Alumni Association and attended the May 1919 installation of his father's statue. Younger brother Neville was a freshman cadet in 1897–98 and graduated in 1902.

Heretofore unreported were Sul Ross's efforts to enhance not just the stability of the college but also the development of the faculty, to enhance the college's image in academic circles. One of the first catalysts for faculty improvement was the establishment of the Agricultural Experiment Station at A&M, which required research on and publication of practical applications for agriculture and industry across the state. Nationwide accolades for the experiment station appeared in the *Southern Mercury*: "We can submit abundant evidence that the Agricultural and Mechanical College is turning out men of practical ability as well as theory in the higher agricultural and mechanical pursuits." These activities also helped build a link with private-sector research and advancements in emerging areas of technology. President Ross's statewide editorial in July discussed "new educational schemes" and contained the outright statement that "the people of Texas are deeply interested in its prosperity, and nothing should interpose or retard its progress"—comments not often heard in the state. He further made the college an active member of the Texas Academy of Science, supporting faculty participation at its annual gathering. With the college at its peak of success, Ross provided the keynote address for the 1897 annual academy meeting held on campus—twelve days before his death—in his last public presentation:[17]

An Address to the Texas Academy of Science

December 22, 1897

A&M College of Texas—Assembly Hall

By Governor L. S. Ross

President of the Agricultural and Mechanical College of Texas

Mr. President and Gentlemen:

The people of Texas have always been noted for a boundless hospitality, where the guest is made to feel that he is at home, and to admire the easy freedom and graceful dignity of a host who banished all formality in the nobleness of his welcome and the simplicity and generosity of his entertainment.

We trust that there shall be no exception to the general rule, and in making welcome so may representatives of an organization which has to do with the arts and sciences and other allied interests of our State, it will be a source of no small pride to me personally if I shall be able to contribute in [a] humble way to the success of your meeting. I am keenly alive to the importance of your work, because upon its action depends, in a large measure, not only the extent and degree to which scientific knowledge and research shall be fostered and disseminated among the people, but also the degree which shall be made in all the arts—the future development of our untold natural resources, the productiveness of our domain, and the position and power of our State. Only questions pertaining to the existence, integrity, and honor of our commonwealth take higher rank. I believe with Franklin, that the world owes more to great inventors than to all its warriors and statesmen, and that the prizes of the future will be found upon the highway of scientific education. It derogates nothing from the value of your aims, but rather heightens their claim to popular regard to admit that inventions evolved from the brains of unlettered men laid the foundations of our material prosperity, and have been among the most potent factors of the nation's wonderful growth.

The statesmen of the revolutionary period who formulated the self-evident truths upon which is based and framed the Constitution, intended to lay down and define the powers and duties of a mighty government in all its details, had been educated in the colleges and universities of that time. But those of whom I speak had not been favored with corresponding educational advantages, and I believe that if in the early days of the republic the opportunities for scientific and practical education had been equal to those afforded for training men for the learned professions, the advent of the steamboat and rail car would have occurred at an earlier date. It was the recognition of the importance of such opportunities that led in after years to the establishment of scientific schools, and the earth has been made to give forth her treasures, and the forest has yielded its choicest woods to show what art and science can do in their victory over inanimate nature.

Hereafter intelligence more than ever is to be counted as a factor of success. Thoughtful men are beginning to appreciate its importance to the pressing problems of the future where the possibilities of our State defy prophecy. It needs such work as yours to make these possibilities a living reality. It is practical and material, and will help our State to realize her greatness, and to impress her individuality upon the history of the times.

It is like threshing over old straw to say that among the important subjects that engrossed the attention of the inventor of early days was steam—its properties, adaptations, and possibilities as an agency for moving machinery; and it has been said that the birth of the Republic and that of the steam engine were contemporaneous events. We are informed that the first condensing engine built in this country was constructed by John Fitch, a native of Connecticut, in 1787, with the assistance of a common blacksmith. This successful experiment by Mr. Fitch, who had been favored with only the slightest opportunities for an education, made him the world's pioneer in steam navigation. After perfecting his engine and using it to propel a boat on the Delaware River, he was forced by adverse fortune to abandon his plans for bringing his invention into practical use—not, however, before predicting that some better equipped and more fortunate man, inspired by the success already attained, would acquire fame and fame and fortune from his invention, and that the time would come when large rivers would be navigated by steam, and that ships would be propelled across the Atlantic by the same agency. This man, as you know, soon appeared in the person of Robert Fulton, who transferred steam navigation from the stage of experience to that of a successful agency to promote the convenience and welfare of the growing Republic. It was not until he had acquired reputation as an inventor that he sought in Paris the scientific training which has given him immortality of fame.

Early in the present century, Oliver Evans, a native of Delaware, having previously invented an engine on the high pressure principle, demonstrated that it could be used for the propulsion of land carriages, and claimed that the time would come when transportation would be carried on over land on railways of iron by the agency of steam, and though his opportunity for early education had been of limited character, he may be justly regarded as the pioneer of our present system of railroad transportation, which has filled our solitary and waste places with people, and furnished them as agency for distribution and consumption not easily overestimated.

When a child, it fell to my lot to sit at night before the log fire of our frontier cabin, and with deft but tired fingers pick from the cotton seed the lint which was to be carded, spun, and woven into clothing for the family, and I have lived to see it taken from the farmer's wagon, and while manipulated almost entirely by machinery, pass into a compact and perfect commercial package or bale. The invention of the cotton gin not only more than doubled the value of every acre of cotton-producing land in the South, but it brought into more conspicuous prominence that ancient plant which sprang from the centuries numbering back to the deluge, but not until the seventeenth century, when first introduced into the South, did it find a soil and climate best adapted to it, and a people with both the skill and intelligence necessary to give it the most successful cultivation, until its yield has become an element of the largest manufacturing interest in the world, a currency within itself, and the greatest boon to human industry.

A hundred years ago agriculture was in little better condition all over the world than it was a thousand years before. It is almost within the limit of my memory that the use of iron for manufacturing of farm implements was unknown. They were made of wood, and our present superb equipment of farm machinery existed nowhere. The advance made in all its branches has been prodigious, due largely to the creation of mechanical appliances by American inventive genius. In recounting a few of the indicative trophies which scientists have brought from their experiences of every province of knowledge, it may be added that as unimportant as it may have appeared at the time, nevertheless, the discovery of the uses of either in surgery disarmed sickness of half its pain, and death of half its terrors. And scientific research for the mitigation of sorrow and misfortune of those afflicted with physical infirmities gave eyes to the fingers of the blind, and taught the deaf and dumb articulate speech.

It occurs to me that surely it must defy the power of human measurement to graduate the depth and intensity of the pulse-stirring anticipations which thrill every nerve and amount to the brain of the happy scientist when, as if by magic alchemy, he succeeds in transmitting the visions of the enthusiast into some living reality.

I congratulate you that your time and talents are devoted to the study of those things which will shed light upon the everyday problems of life, and better the condition of your fellows.

We hope this occasion may prove to be one pleasant in the remembrance, and that when you separate, it may be with renewed and a united determination to put increase effort in extending the scope and usefulness of the Academy of Science.

On the Navasota River

The college completed its most successful year to date following the culmination of the Academy of Science meeting and final exams for the cadets. Mild weather and a pleasant Christmas season was a welcome relief. The college had escaped any bad publicity during the smallpox epi-

demic that swept the state in October. And the year-end break ensured
the likelihood of no new political upheavals from Austin. As had been
tradition, Sul Ross enjoyed time with his family, and on the Tuesday after
Christmas, Sul; Nev, who had just finished his first semester as a "fish"
in the Corps of Cadets; and a few friends took their buggies and hunting
dogs southeast of campus to the Navasota River bottom to hunt deer.
They faced a week of driving rain and dropping temperatures, which was
normal for the season. A product of frontier Texas, Ross greatly enjoyed
the outdoor excursions and sleeping under the stars.[18]

On Thursday, December 30, Sul Ross fell ill shortly after breakfast. It
is difficult to discern exactly what happened next, and today there are a
number of secondary accounts of the event, yet it seems that Sul ingested
some partially uncooked sausage and undercooked biscuits. This possibly triggered a bout of bad indigestion, which coincided with Ross's
reoccurring bouts with poor health, partly due to the severe arrow and
gunshot wounds he suffered in his youth. Not wanting to spoil the hunt
for others, he drove back to campus alone, arriving in the early evening.
He is reported to have received medical treatment, yet he remained
fairly congested on Friday and Saturday, with signs of improvement on
Sunday morning. By Sunday evening, he was again in pain and his condition rapidly deteriorated. Family members already had been notified

The stage for the dedication of the Sul Ross statue in front of the Academic
Building, on May 19, 1919. Source: Cushing Archives

of Lizzie's concerns, and by noon on Monday, January 3, there was little doubt his condition was serious. Dr. Fountain asked how the governor felt, and in his last words, Sul calmly said, "I feel altogether like a new man." Surrounded by Lizzie and his family, he "pressed [the] hands of his wife and children" and died peacefully at 6:35 p.m. He was fifty-nine years old. There was no autopsy and no recorded death certificate, yet evidence strongly indicates the death of the old warrior, statesman, and educator was caused by a possible severe case of influenza and congestive heart failure. Word of his death spread fast across Texas and the South.[19]

As arrangements were being made to return the body for burial in Waco, the commandant, Lt. George T. Bartlett, took immediate charge of the situation. Bartlett gathered faculty and staff leaders for consultations, in addition to contacting Chairman of the Board Frank Reichardt, the governor's office, and the H&TC Railroad for possible assistance. He assigned Cadet Joseph E. Abrahams of New Braunfels in his dress uniform to stand guard over the body of Governor Ross in the president's residence. Mrs. Ross and daughter Betty went to the home of son-in-law Dr. Henry Harrington. Alone in the darkened home, Abrahams recalled, "I walked up and down the hallway, passing now and then to look at our president." The following morning at 9:00 a.m., the body lay in state in the Assembly Hall, located at the south end of Military Walk, and was viewed by hundreds of cadets, staff, and residents from the surrounding country. This solemn gathering was followed by a brief memorial eulogy conducted by Dr. T. C. Bittle. At noon, a special train provided by the H&TC Railroad was dispatched from Houston and waited at the college depot to board the family, A&M staff, board members, and the Corps of Cadets, under the charge of Senior Captain Gus Newton '98, of Milano, for the somber ninety-mile journey to Waco.[20]

The train, draped in flags, was met by several hundred people in Waco, as "the veterans and spectators stood in line with bowed heads as the train drew up." Sul Ross was escorted by a military honor guard of the Corps and a local contingent of Confederate and Union veterans to the residence of his brother-in-law, Tom Padgitt. The following morning, the governor lay in state in the city auditorium during the day and was viewed by thousands. A service followed, with a procession to Oakwood Cemetery, led by Gov. Charles Culberson, accompanied by former governors Oran M. Roberts, John Ireland, and Joseph D. Sayers; a delegation of Masons;

and the honor guard of cadets, along with an endless line of carriages, buggies, and horsemen. At the graveside, Harry H. Tracy '98 played taps and the Ross Volunteers firing squad of twenty-one cadets fired three volleys. More than eight thousand people were at the cemetery. On Sunday, January 16, a special public memorial service to honor Governor Ross was held in the campus Assembly Hall, with presentations by alumni, faculty, and a representative of the Corps of Cadets.[21]

The End of an Era

Sul Ross's very nature seemed to attract attention, as his life closely paralleled the growth and development of Texas from the open, untamed frontier to the dawn of the twentieth century. His death marked the end of an era. Ross's character was strongly enhanced and influenced by his environment and the early rugged training given him by his father, Shapley Prince Ross. That Lil' Sul—as he was fondly called—was a fighter and leader throughout his life was no accident. His record on the Texas frontier as a Ranger was commended before he turned twenty years of age. Ross's record in the West is only eclipsed by his distinctive service and leadership during the Civil War. As Bill Minutaglio has noted, Ross cast a long, wide shadow on Texas public life and politics, "saluted as a hardworking visionary and a conqueror of Texas demons. . . Directly and indirectly, every politician after him would have to weigh 'how Texan' they wanted to be. . . ." [22]

The outpouring of respect and homage that followed his passing was no surprise to Texans of the era. Articles about Sul and his family were part of a new rise in celebrity journalism that, for more than four decades, maintained a steady flow of stories and biographical sketches in the media. Sul's frontier father, Shapley, helped set the stage for the public's introduction to the "boy captain," who experienced years of high-profile friendships and antagonisms. The media in the 1890s played an increasing role in the emerging new social order and heightened the visibility of business and political icons, lionizing these key personalities and their activities. Some examples of other individuals who gained fame and public recognition via the rise of "celebrity journalism" in the late 1890s include Teddy Roosevelt, Winston Churchill, Alfred Thayer Mahan, Mark Twain, and William Jennings Bryan.[23]

More than any other leader of his day, Ross bridged post–Civil War Texas with the goals and aspirations expressed by his lifelong friend Gov. Richard Coke, to settle, develop, and educate a new generation of young Texans. His resilience and initiative, won through conflict and action, placed him at a unique juncture in the state's history. Biographer Benner concluded, "Ross can be considered an illustrious example of an American *citizen-soldier* who serves his state and country when needed and then returns to civilian life once the crisis is passed." In the months after Ross's death, the *Battalion* reported that eighty-nine former members of the Corps of Cadets from the 1890s served in the Spanish American War in Cuba and the Philippines. An appeal to selfless service was instilled in the college's cadets of the 1890s and would follow with generations of Texas Aggies answering the call to duty. The *Austin Daily Statesman*, which had reported on Ross's life and career for more than three decades, hailed the man "affectionately called Sul Ross" as "noble. . . . [H]e knew no fear."[24]

Interestingly, Ross's term as governor was one of the calmest periods in Texas's transition from the post-Reconstruction era into the twentieth century. A fiscal conservative, his leadership was greatly appreciated by the citizens of Texas, and his foes fretted about how they would overcome his stature and popularity. While many analysts have commented that Ross's term in Austin was not as progressive or dynamic as they would have liked, the fact is, from the time he left office until shortly before his death, Texans harkened back to the calm and staid days of the popular governor—repeatedly urging him to stand for a third term. Though often tempted to return to the active political arena, once Ross was committed to the presidency of the A&M College, he stayed the course to fend off agitators, utilizing his personal gravitas to aid the Corps of Cadets and build a solid foundation for the institution's growth and prestige.

For the first time in the college's history, the struggling institution had a seasoned chief executive who championed both the enhancement of higher education and the need for the regimented training offered in the ranks of the Corps of Cadets. The Corps underwent major changes and significant growth during the 1890s. Ross's emphasis on education and the college's reputation led to major improvements in the institution's faculty, curriculum, and facilities. Enhancements in cadet discipline and image were augmented by higher levels of funding from the Texas

Legislature and citizens' increased acceptance and understanding of the role of the college statewide.

Ross was the first administrator of Texas A&M to understand the importance of the institution's former ex-cadets. The A&M alumni and ex-cadets would prove critical to assisting with the promotion of their alma mater. Ross welcomed on-campus gatherings of former students during commencement ceremonies. In presentations to both cadets and former students, Ross challenged the A&M cadets and graduates to excel in their "chosen profession" as a key outward indication of the value of their education. Thus the esprit de corps of their campus days transformed them into active ambassadors of the college. The introduction of the Aggie class rings in the early 1890s would prove a vital linkage among all that attended the institution. In Ross's honor, a marble tablet was placed in the wall of the Assembly Hall along Military Walk:[25]

> Erected by the Faculty of the Agricultural and Mechanical College in memory of Lawrence Sullivan Ross, President 1890–1898. He brought the maturity of experience as a Soldier, as Legislator and Governor, to the service of the youth of the state. Died Jan. 3rd 1898, aged 59 years.
>   Come up, Higher.

There was a strong bond among those who attended A&M while Sul Ross was president, referred to as the "Sul Ross Group." In early 1900, the Sul Ross Group was recognized as a distinct body of ex-cadets within the Association of Former Students. Annual reunions and gatherings followed for decades. As the years passed and class sizes grew, in the early 1950s, the association recast the Sul Ross Group as comprising those former students who had been out of college for at least fifty-five years.

There were a number of proposals to name a Texas county for Sul, but after several attempts, the state legislature chose to erect a statue on the A&M campus and name a college in West Texas in his honor. Ross was recognized for his statesmanship, championship of education at all levels, demand for law and order, and public service to all citizens of the state of Texas. Although there were immediate calls for a suitable permanent memorial on the A&M campus, the Sul Ross statue was erected following a resolution and appropriation of five thousand dollars by the Thirty-Fifth Texas Legislature, with the inscription of "Lawrence Sullivan Ross, 1838–1898, Soldier, Statesman, and Knightly Gentleman,

Brigadier General C.S.A., Governor of Texas, President of the A&M College," as crafted in the November 1917 legislation. The design was created and sculpted by Pompeo Coppini of San Antonio. Significantly, the statue depicts Ross in civilian clothing, placing its visual emphasis on his non-military accomplishments. It was placed in front of the Academic Building and unveiled on May 4, 1919. The Ross family was represented by Dr. and Mrs. (Florine) H. H. Harrington and their son, Ross; Dr. and Mrs. Frank R. Ross '95; Capt. Robert S. Ross; and Miss Mary Ross. In 1917 the State of Texas named Sul Ross Normal College in Alpine, Texas, in the late governor's honor, with the named changed to Sul Ross University in 1969.[26]

Ross created an environment that fostered the traditions and esprit de corps of what was to become one of the nation's leading universities. Raised on the open frontier of Texas, Sul Ross utilized his wit and life lessons learned to set the A&M College on a solid footing. He fostered a sense of excellence that shaped a generation of students, both past and present, engendering a legacy of lifelong dedication to selfless service. This environment of shared experiences, time-honored traditions, and loyal alumni has proven pivotal to the unique image and success of the institution.

There are few honors greater than those conveyed by a son to his father. The impact of Sul Ross's loss on his family is eloquently captured in the words of Dr. Frank Ross '95, as written to his mother shortly after the funeral in Waco:

> Our loss is indeed a great and irreparable one and as each day passes I realize more forcibly this sad truth. Yet we must bear our burden with resignation and strive to live the life of nobleness and purity that Papa lived. He would not have you grieve and if he could but speak he would urge you to guide and direct your children through life, to teach them all that is good, noble and pure of which he was the personification, so that when finished the journey of life we may all meet him and be with him through all eternity. Your children love you and they will consider it a happy privilege to labor to make you comfortable and happy for all your remaining days on earth. You have the power to do a great deal of good in life and it is your duty to realize and work to that purpose.
>
> Papa has left us a noble heritage and the sweet memory of his faithfulness to fellow man, of good deeds well and dutifully performed. The

Soldier, Statesman, and Knightly Gentleman—the Sul Ross statue, dedicated in May 1919. Source: Author's collection

beautiful precepts he taught his family and all mankind, his kindness of heart, his modesty and his characteristically will be a happy inspiration to us in striving to emulate him.[27]

Sul Ross

A hero's gone. We are wrapped in gloom,
  sadness fills the soul,
O'er all our lovely commonwealth,
  bells of sorrow toll.

They mourn the loss of a soldier true,
  Who never knew to fear.
Who loved his State with devotion rare,
  Holding life so dear.

By Academus' shady groves,
  He shapes the future State,
Leading the Youth to nobler things,
  Teaching to be great.

Edward L. Blackshear, Principal, Prairie View Normal College, *Houston Post*, January 9, 1898

Soldier—Statesman—Knightly Gentleman

Notes

Chapter 1

1. Note the term "Indian" is used here and throughout the manuscript to reflect the parlance of frontier Texas. L. L. Foster, *First Annual Report of the Agricultural Bureau of the Department of Agriculture, Insurance, Statistics, and History, 1887–88*, Austin: State Printing Office, 1889, pp. 3–17.

2. Elizabeth "Bessie" Ross Clarke, "Life of S. P. Ross and Sul Ross," unpublished manuscript by the daughter of Lawrence Sullivan Ross, in Ross Biographical Papers, Texas A&M University Archives, Cushing; original in the L. S. Ross Papers, Texas Collection, Baylor University, Waco, pp. 1–35; Judith Ann Benner, *Sul Ross: Soldier, Statesman, Educator*, College Station: Texas A&M University Press, 1983, pp. 3–21; Richard W. Clement, *Books on the Frontier*, Washington, DC: Library of Congress, 2003. See also Myrtle Whiteside, "The Life of Lawrence Sullivan Ross," MA thesis, University of Texas, 1938, and Lester T. Porter, *A Centennial Commemoration of Lawrence Sullivan Ross*, College Station: Association of Former Students, 1993.

3. Capt. S. P. Ross, Commanding Company, Texas Mounted Volunteers, "Waco Village Station, February 1, 1848, Order No. 2," Waco Village Papers, The Texas Collection, Baylor University, Waco Texas; S. P. Ross, Proprietor, "Waco Village Ferry," *The South-Western* American (Austin), August 30, 1850; John S. Ford, *Rip Ford's Texas*, Austin: University of Texas Press, 1963, pp. 439–56; "Captain Shapley P. Ross," *Frontier Times*, August 1928, pp. 417–19; W. M. Sleeper and A. D. Sanford, *Waco Bar and Incidents of Waco History*, Waco: n.p., 1941, pp. 13–14; Lavonia J. Barnes, *Early Homes of Waco and the People Who Lived in Them*, Waco: Texian Press, 1970, pp. ix–xiv. See also A. J. Sowell, *Early Settlers and Indian Fighters of Southwest Texas*, Austin: Ben C. Jones & Co. Printers, 1900 (reprint State House Press, 1986), pp. 331–96. Note: Shapley Ross's interest in education is further emphasized by his efforts with a group from McLennan County to, with the approval of the Texas Legislature, open the Waco Male and Female Academy; see the *Texas State Gazette,* January 11, 1851.

4. "Ex Gov Payne in Waco," *Richmond Daily Dispatch*, July 28, 1853; Interview in "Coke in Retirement," *Galveston Daily News*, October 27, 1894; R. Henderson Shuffler, *Son, Remember . . .* , College Station: n.p., 1951; Coke Scrapbook and Photographic File, Richard Coke Papers, Texas Collection, Baylor; George S. Perry, *The Story of Texas A and M*, New York: McGraw-Hill, 1951, pp. 56–57. Note: In addition to General Houston's encouragement to go to Texas, Coke recalled that former Lt. Governor Henderson and a Waco merchant named William C. "Billy" Walker, an early settler in Waco along with Shapley Ross, also strongly recommended Waco: "It is the center of a rich country that would be densely populated some day [*sic*]." See also Norman Kittrell, *Governors Who Have Been and Other Public Men of Texas*, Houston: Dealy-Adey Elkin, 1921, p. 61, and Dede W. Casad, "The Lives and Legacies of Two Texas Governors: Richard Coke and Lawrence Sullivan Ross," PhD diss., University of Texas at Dallas, December 2001.

5. Letter from Robert S. Neighbors to Charles E. Mix, September 10, 1855, *Annual Report of the Commissioner of Indian Affairs*, 1855, Washington, DC: 1856, pp. 177–79; "Belknap, Capt. Ross of the Agency," *Dallas Daily Herald*, July 24, 1858; David La Vere, *The Texas Indians*, College Station: Texas A&M University Press, 2004, p. 197; W. W. Newcomb, *The Indians of Texas*, Austin: University of Texas Press, 1961, pp. 334–35, 357; Benner, *Sul Ross*, pp. 22–61; Robert F. Pace and Donald S. Frazier, *Frontier Texas: History of a Borderland to 1880*, Abilene: State House Press, 2005, pp. 52–57.

6. "A. and M. College," *Galveston Daily News*, June 5, 1894; Raymond L. Dillard, "A History of the Ross Family and Its Most Distinguished Member Lawrence Sullivan Ross," MA thesis, Baylor University, 1931; T. J. Stiles, *Custer's Trails*, New York: Alfred A. Knopf, 2015, p. 12; James Findlay, "Agency, Denominations, and the Western Colleges, 1830–1860," in Roger Geiger, ed., *The American College in the Nineteenth Century*, Nashville: Vanderbilt University Press, 2000, pp. 115–26; Carrie J. Crouch, *A History of Young County*, Austin: n.p., 1956, p. 87. Note: Nationwide in 1858–60, there were an estimated two hundred colleges, averaging less than one hundred students each. Sul Ross apparently remained in periodic contact with his alma mater—for instance, sending his daughter Bessie to attend the June 1897 reunion to meet "many of his friends there." See Dr. Frank R. Ross to Major T. P. Weakley, n.d., *Confederate Veteran*, vol. 6, 1898, p. 129.

7. Letter from Shapley P. Ross to Robert S. Neighbors, September 6, 1858, *Annual Report of the Commissioner of Indian Affairs*, No. 70, 1858, pp. 181–83; "Major Van Dorn's Expedition," *Dallas Daily Herald*, September 29, 1858; "Another Atrocity Committed upon the Reserve Indians," *Dallas Weekly Herald*, May 18, 1859; Clara L. Koch, "The Federal Indian Policy in Texas, 1845–1860," *Southwestern Historical Quarterly* (hereafter *SWHQ*), October 1925, pp. 99–104.

See also George Klos, "'Our People Could Not Distinguish One Tribe from Another': The 1859 Expulsion of the Reserve Indians from Texas," *SWHQ*, April 1994, p. 604.

8. Major Van Dorn's Report, September 26, 1858, US Congress, House, *Annual Report of the Secretary of War*, 35 Cong., 2nd sess., H. Exec. Doc. 2, pt. 2, pp. 267–70; "Van Dorn," *Dallas Herald*, October 10, 1858; "For the Gazette San Saba," *Texas State Gazette*, November 13, 1858; Charles M. Robinson, *Men Who Wear the Star*, New York: The Modern Library, 2001, pp. 117–18.

9. L. S. Ross, "The Parker Captives," *Galveston Daily News*, June 4, 1875; Clark, "Life of Sul Ross," pp. 51–54.

10. "Ex-Governor Ross," *Galveston Daily News*, February 26, 1894; Benner, *Sul Ross*, pp. 29–32; Campbell, *Gone to Texas*, pp. 203–4.

11. "Ex-Governor Ross," *Galveston Daily News*, February 26, 1894; "Ex-Gov. Ross Dead," *Caldwell News-Chronicle*, January 7, 1898.

12. Zachariah E. Coombes, *The Diary of a Frontiersman 1858–1859*, Newcastle, TX: private print, 1962, pp. 1–84. See also Jim Dillard, *Zachariah Ellis Coombes: Frontier Teacher on the Brazos Indian Reservation*, Fort Worth: n.p., 2016.

13. L. S. Ross, "The Parker Captives," *Galveston Daily News*, June 4, 1875. Note: On the same day the Ross article appeared in the *News*, there was a front-page headline article about Gov. Richard Coke holding the first A&M College board meeting and construction inspection at the new campus.

14. Elizabeth Ross Clarke, "Life of Sul Ross," Ross Family Papers, Texas Collection, Baylor University, Waco (hereafter cited Clarke Ross Family Papers), pp. 50–56.

15. L. S. Ross to Sam Houston, September 18, 1860, Governors' Papers, Sam Houston, Texas State Archives, Austin; "Citizens of Palo Pinto County," *New Orleans Daily Crescent*, November 3, 1860; "The Frontier Troubles," *Houston Weekly Telegraph*, December 25, 1860; Clarke Ross Family Papers, pp. 56–61.

16. "The Parker Captives," *Galveston Daily News*, January 4, 1875, and June 3, 1875; Mamie Folsom Wynne, "History Centers about Cynthia Ann Parker's Home," *Frontier Times*, April 1929, pp. 258–60; Clarke Ross Family Papers, p. 61; *Dallas Herald*, January 2, 1861. Note: For a picture of Cynthia Ann Parker (ca. 1825–ca. 1871), see Campbell, *Gone to Texas*, p. 205.

17. "Remarkable Life Story of Quanah Parker," *Frontier Times*, October 1923, pp. 28–30; J. W. Wilbarger, *Indian Depredations in Texas*, Austin: Hastings Printing House, 1889, pp. 326–47; Jo Ella Powell Exley, *Frontier Blood: The Saga of the Parker Family*, College Station: Texas A&M University Press, 2001, pp. 149–65; Robinson, *Men Who Wear the Star*, pp. 118–20. See also J. B. Pulley, "Historical Reminiscences," *San Antonio Daily Express*, November 22, 1908, and Margaret S. Hacker, *Cynthia Ann Parker: The Life and Legend*, El Paso: Texas Western Press,

1990, and Paul Carlson, *Myth, Memory and Massacre: The Pease River Capture of Cynthia Ann Parker*, Lubbock: Texas Tech University Press, 2010.

18. L. S. Ross to Victor M. Rose, October 5, 1880, Ross Family Papers, Baylor; L. S. Ross to Susan Parker St. John, transcript, 1894, Joseph Taulman Papers, Briscoe Center, Austin; James T. DeShields, *Cynthia Ann Parker: The Story of Her Capture*, 1886, reprint, Dallas: Chama Press, 1991, pp. 42–44; Paul H. Carlson and Tom Crum, "The 'Battle' at Pease River and the Question of Reliable Sources in the Recapture of Cynthia Ann Parker," *SWHQ*, July 2009, pp. 32–52.

19. L. S. Ross to Victor M. Rose, October 5, 1880, Ross Family Papers, Baylor; "L. S. Ross to General Sam Houston," *Weekly Civilian and Gazette* (Galveston), January 15, 1861; "Camp Barton," *Dallas Herald*, September 11, 1861; S. C. Gwynne, *Empire of the Summer Moon*, New York: Scribner, 2010, p. 174; J. Frank Dobie, *Cow People*, Austin: University of Texas Press, 1968, pp. 287–88; Charles Goodnight to Hon. L. S. Ross, June 18, 1887, Governor L. S. Ross Papers, Austin, Texas State Archives, nos. 301–124. Note: Texas panhandle rancher Charlie Goodnight, who at one time owned some 1.3 million acres in Texas, had been with Sul Ross as a scout fighting Comanche raiders when Parker was captured. Some two decades after Ross's death, when Goodnight was eighty-three-years-old in 1919, he expressed the view that Ross used his notoriety for "vote seeking" along the road to the governorship of Texas. Goodnight's opinion of Ross was also based on a decades-old dispute over the cost of leased grazing lands, "illegal enclosure," and public lands opening to settlers (which Goodnight wanted only as open range land) in the sparse Texas Panhandle. These issues were soon settled but not without great political cost to Goodnight and the Panhandle Stockmen's Association. See also Robert C. Cotner, *James Stephen Hogg*, Austin: University of Texas Press, 1959, pp. 106–14; J. Evetts Haley, *Charles Goodnight: Cowman & Plainsman*, Norman: University of Oklahoma Press, 1949, pp. 359–92; Octavia F. Rogan, *Land Commissioner Charles Rogan*, Austin: San Felipe Press, 1968, pp. 5–8; William T. Hagen, *Charles Goodnight: Father of the Texas Panhandle*, Norman: University of Oklahoma Press, 2011.

20. *Dallas Herald*, August 14, 1861, September 11, 1861, and February 5, 1862; 1860 McLennan County, Texas, US Census, 1860; Marquis James, *The Raven: A Biography of Sam Houston*, Indianapolis: The Bobbs-Merrill Company, 1919, pp. 404–12; Harold B. Simpson, *Hood's Texas Brigade: Lee's Grenadier Guard*, Waco: Texian Press, 1970, p. 32; Pearl C. Jackson, ed., "Elizabeth Dorothy Tinsley," *Texas Governor Wives*, Austin: E. L. Steck. 1915, pp. 103–7; Benner, *Sul Ross*, pp. 62–64. See also Glen Sample Ely, "Gone from Texas and Trading with the Enemy: New Perspectives on Civil War West Texas," *SWHQ*, April 2007. Later accounts of the military action at Keetsville offer a different tally than that presented by Colonel Stone. See, for example, the records of the National Park Service (available at https://www.nps.gov/civilwar/missouri.htm) and the *White River*

Valley Historical Quarterly, V 5, #1 (available at https://thelibrary.org/lochist/periodicals/wrv/V5/N1/f73b.html).

21. US War Department, *The War of the Rebellion: A Compilation of the Official Records of the Union and Confederate Armies*, Ser. 1, Vol. VIII, p. 302 (hereafter O.R.); John Adams, "Lawrence S. Ross: 1861–1865," unpublished manuscript, College Station, April 1972. Note: This is the first documented use of the accolade of "knight" or "knightly" in reference to Sul Ross. This term was in wide use in the South prior to the war and viewed as a traditional term and recognition of "noble manhood," chivalry, valor, and honor. See also Eugene D. Genovese, "Chivalric Tradition in the Old South," *Sewanee Review*, spring 2000, pp. 188–205, and "The Death of Ex-Governor L. S. Ross," *Austin Daily Statesman*, January 5, 1898.

22. L. S. Ross to Dr. D. A. Tinsley (father-in-law), March 13, 1862, and L. S. Ross to Lizzie Ross, March 13, 1862, August 10, 25, 27, 1862, and August 29, 1863, Ross Family Papers, Baylor.

23. O.R., Ser. 1, Vol. X, Pt. 2, pp. 548–51, and Vol. XXXII, Pt. 1, p. 368, 382–91; Ross to Lizzie Ross, June 14, 1862, and July 20, 1862, Ross Papers, Baylor; Homer Kerr, ed., *Fighting with Ross' Texas Calvary Brigade, C. S. A.*, Hillsboro: Hill Jr. College Press, 1976; Marcus J. Wright, *Texans in the War, 1861–1865*, Hillsboro: Hill Jr. College Press, pp. 15, 191–92, plate no. 67; Benner, *Sul Ross*, pp. 96–114; Sid S. Johnson, *Texans Who Wore the Gray*, Waco: Eakin Press, n.d., pp. 94–95.

24. Kerr, *Fighting with Ross' Texas Calvary*, 1976, pp. 186–98; Victor M. Rose, *Ross' Texas Brigade*, Louisville: The Courier-Journal Book and Job Room, 1881, pp. 114–20, and Shelly Morrison, ed., *Personal Civil War Letters of General Lawrence Sullivan Ross*, Austin: S. and R. Morrison, 1994, pp. 67–69; Ralph A. Wooster and Robert Wooster, eds., *Lone Star Blue and Gray*, Denton: Texas State Historical Association, 2015, pp. 1–6. Note: In addition to Ross, thirty-six other Texans served as general officers in the Confederate Army, of which ten died during the war.

25. For an excellent overview of Texas during the war, see Jesus F. de la Teja, ed., *Lone Star Unionism, Dissent, and Resistance: Other Side of Civil War Texas*, Norman: University of Oklahoma Press, 2016, and Wooster and Wooster, eds., *Lone Star Blue and Gray*, 2015.

26. "General and Governor Ross of Texas," *Confederate Veteran*, June 1894, p. 169; L. S. Ross to My Dear Wife, January 12, 1865, L. S. Ross Family Papers, Texas Collection, Baylor University; O.R., Vol. XLIX, Pt. 2, pp. 1150–51, 1277; Kerr, ed. *Fighting with Ross' Texas Cavalry*, pp. 201–7; Benner, *Sul Ross*, pp. 111–16.

27. NARA, Case Files of Application for former Confederates, Presidential Pardon, 1865–67, Roll 64, Group I, L. S. Ross, McLennan Co., Texas, filed DoJ, December 18, 1894; Texas Adjutant General Papers, Reconstruction, Special Pardons, R-Misc., Texas State Archives, Austin; Benner, *Sul Ross*, pp. 116–17.

28. Acie Sooner, "Texas after the Civil War," *Frontier Times*, April 1927, pp. 36–40.

29. *Galveston Daily News*, June 22, 1881; *Annual Report of the Commissioner of Indian Affairs, 1875*, Washington, DC, 1875, pp. 96, 178; Jack D. Welsh, *Medical Histories of Confederate Generals*, Kent, Ohio: Kent State University Press, 1955, pp. 188–89; J. Frank Dobie, *Out of the Old Rock*, p. 116; "Abundant Variety," *National Life-Stock Journal*, July 1883, pp. 200–201; Jesse Dorsett, "Blacks in Reconstruction Texas, 1865–1877," PhD diss., TCU, pp. 111–16; Edward King, *Texas: 1874*, Houston: Cordovan Press, 1974, p. 129; US Department of Agriculture, "Proceedings of the Interstate Convention of Cattlemen," March 11–13, 1890, Washington, DC: US Government Printing Office, 1890, p. 14; Joseph G. McCoy, *Cattle Trade of the West and Southwest*, Kansas City: Ramsey, Millett & Hudson, 1984, pp. 424–27; "Texas Beeves," *The Daily Phoenix* (Columbia, SC), November 4, 1965; "Arrivals at the Principal Hotels," *New Orleans Times-Picayune*, October 9, 1866; Woodward, *Origins of the New South*, p. 178; Edward E. Dale, *Cow Country*, Norman: University of Oklahoma Press, 1964, pp. 30–31. Note: For cattle prices per head between 1867 to 1900, see *U. S. D. A. Yearbook, 1910*, Washington, DC: US Government Printing Office, 1911, p. 630. Furthermore, the 1875 report of the Commissioner of Indian Affairs reported between 56 and 119 Tonkaway tribe members in Texas; the 1878 annual report made no mention of Natives in Texas. Richard Parker, *Historical Recollections of Robertson County, Texas*. Salado: Anson Jones Press, 1955, 49–51, notes demand and shortage of agricultural labor were impacted by three items: (1) mechanization of agriculture, (2) the movement of African American workers to urban areas, and (3) the rapid influx of Mexican labor to take the place of departing African American tenants. Parker also notes that in 1975, cattle sold at fifteen to eighteen dollars per head, and the beef retail price in Houston was four cents per pound. Also of note, in Worchester, there is an interesting mention of Capt. Shapley Ross: "In 1854 Capt. Shapley Ross of Central Texas bought five hundred steers from his neighbors for thirteen dollars a head and sold them in Missouri for twenty-seven dollars." Don Worchester, *The Texas Longhorns*, College Station: Texas A&M University Press, 1987, p. 41.

30. W. C. Holden, "Law and Lawlessness of the Texas Frontier, 1875–1900," *SWHQ*, October 1940, pp. 142–46; Alwyn Barr, *Reconstruction to Reform: Texas Politics, 1876–1906*, Austin: University of Texas Press, 1971, p. 122; Ezell, *The South Since 1865*, p. 122; Williams, *Beyond Redemption*, pp. 12, 18, 79; *Galveston Daily News*, July 25, 1873; "Masonic," *Waco Daily Examiner*, January 16, 1874. See also William B. Bizzell (President of Texas A&M, 1914–25), "Farm Tenantry in the United States," *Texas Agricultural Experiment Station Bulletin*, no. 278, April 1921, and Roger N. Conger, "Fencing in McLennan County, Texas." *SWHQ*, October 1955, pp. 215–17; *Galveston Daily News*, July 25, 1875. Note: In 1880,

Texas had 64,468 tenant family farms, 37.6 percent of all farms in the state, with the percentage of farms increasing to 41.9 percent in 1890 and 49.7 percent in 1900. For white violence against other whites, see C. Vann Woodward, *Origins of the New South, 1877–1913: A History of the South*, Baton Rouge, LSU Press, 1951, p. 159.

31. "Chivalrous Ross," *Waco Daily Examiner*, April 21, 1874; "During the Fire," *Waco Daily Examiner*, August 29, 1974; "Two Desperadoes Named William A. Posey," *Galveston Daily News*, March 24, 1874; "The Texas Frontier and Rangers," *Galveston Daily News*, June 5, 1875; "[Ross'] Stolen Horse Captured," *Austin American Statesman*, June 27, 1875; King, *Texas: 1874*, p. 74; "Campaign Thunder," *Austin American Statesman*, March 15, 1886; n.a., *Bella Starr: Bandit Queen or the Female Jesse James*, New York: Richard K. Fox, 1889; Dorsett, "Blacks in Reconstruction Texas, 1865–1877," pp. 168–75; Sammy Tise, *Texas County Sheriffs*, Hallettsville: Oakland Printing, 1989, p. 365; Woodward, *Origins of the New South*, p. 159. Note: Attacks on stagecoaches and army supply trains, bank robberies, and murders continued in Texas through the early 1880s. See W. C. Holden, "Law and Lawlessness on the Texas Frontier, 1875–1890," *SWHQ*, October 1940, pp. 142–46, and Kathryn T. Carter, *Stagecoach Inns of Texas*, Waco: Texian Press, 1972, notes there were more than thirty stagecoach lines across Texas, with the line most important to the future A&M College in the early 1870s running from Houston via railroad to Hempstead to Waco via Anderson, Piedmont Springs, Boonville, Wheelock, Alto Springs, and Marlin, then Waco; Thomas T. Smith, *The U. S. Army & the Texas Frontier Economy 1845–1900*, College Station: Texas A&M University Press, 1999, pp. 158–60; James B. Gillett, *Six Years with the Texas Rangers*, Chicago: The Lakeside Press, 1943, pp. 258–59; "A Convention of Sheriffs," *Dallas Daily Herald*, August 18, 1874. Note: Sheriff Ross drafted and offered a resolution on mob lawlessness: "Resolved, that we deprecate the spirit of mob law and lawlessness and crime that is so rife in various sections of the state, and that we pledge ourselves officially and individually to use all the powers and influence that we possess to enforce the laws and make the honored, respected and obeyed; and that we will, to the best of our ability, discountenance and prevent the exercise of mob law, and to protect our citizens to the extent of our legal power, in the enjoyment of life, liberty and property. And to this end we earnestly invoke the aid and active co-operation of all the good citizens of the state." This was seconded and approved by the sheriffs assembled.

32. Inaugural Address of Governor Coke, January 15, 1874, *Collections of the Archives & History Department of the Texas State Library: Governor's Messages*, Austin: Texas State Library, 1916. See also Shirley, *Temple Houston*, p. 160.

33. "Gen. Sul Ross," *Weekly Democratic Statesman* (Austin), July 29, 1875; *Waco Weekly Examiner and Patron*, July 30, 1875; Seth S. McKay, *Making the Texas Constitution of 1876*, Philadelphia: University of Pennsylvania Press,

1924, pp. 74–77; L. S. Ross to Lizzie Ross, October 9, 1875, Ross Papers, Baylor; *Journal of the Constitutional Convention, 1875*, pp. 3–4, 8, 15, 35, 228, 339, 404, 802–7, 811–13; Fred Gantt Jr., *The Chief Executive in Texas*, Austin: University of Texas Press, 1964, 32–36; Geiger, ed., *The American College*, p. 163; Woodward, *Origins of the New South*, p. 66, and quote from the *Houston Daily Telegraph*, quoted in S. D. Myers Jr., "Mysticism, Realism, and the Texas Constitution of 1876," *Southwestern Political and Social Science Quarterly*, vol. IX, 1928, p. 180. Note: Peter F. Ross (1836–1909) was elected McLennan County sheriff after L. S. Ross, serving from February 15, 1876, to November 2, 1880.

34. Letters John G. James, President to George Pfeuffer, January 10, 1883, and H. H. Dinwiddle, Chairman of the Faculty to Pfeuffer, May 10, 1885, George P. Pfeuffer Papers, Cushing Library, Texas A&M; Texas Constitution of 1876, Article VII, Sec. 13, App. G; Dethloff, *Centennial History of Texas A&M*, vol. 1, pp. 14–20, 63–66, 88–92. See also "Gauging the University," *Galveston Daily News*, March 8, 1885; "Kleberg's University Bill," *Galveston Daily News*, March 6, 1885; and H. H. Dinwiddle, "The Value of Industrial Education," *Galveston Daily News*, March 23, 1885; and Bill Page, ed., "Gathright Papers," Cushing Library.

35. "The Gubernatorial Contest," *Galveston Daily News*, February 15, 1878; "Gen. L. S. Ross of Waco," *Brenham Weekly Banner*, January 9, 1880; "The State Capitol," *Galveston Daily News*, January 26, 1881; L. S. Ross to Victor M. Rose, April 21, 1881, Ross Family Papers, Baylor; Patsy M. Spaw, *The Texas Senate: Civil War to the Eve of Reform, 1861–1889*, vol. II, College Station: Texas A&M University Press, 1999, pp. 280–81, 293; Charles K. Chamberlain, "Alexander Watkins Terrell, Citizen, Statesman," PhD diss., University of Texas, August 1956, pp. 170–79.

36. Edward E. Dale, *Range Cattle Industry—1865–1925*, Norman: University of Oklahoma Press, 1930, pp. 102–18.

37. L. S. Ross to Victor M. Rose, February 15, 1880, Rose Papers, Briscoe Center, Austin; *Waco Daily Examiner*, February 1, 1883; *Austin Daily Statesman*, February 8 and 13, 1881; "General L. S. Ross and the Daily and Weekly Examiner," *Dallas Weekly Herald*, December 8, 1881, and February 16, 1882; W. C. Nunn, ed., *Ten More Texans in Gray*, Hillsboro: Hill Jr. College Press, 1980, 128. See also Pearl C. Jackson, *Texas Governors' Wives*, Austin: E. L. Steck, 1915, pp. 102–7.

38. "Campaign Thunder," *Galveston Daily News*, March 15, 1886; Benner, *Sul Ross*, pp. 148–53.

39. Benner, *Sul Ross*, pp. 135, 148–53, 235; "Gen. L. S. Ross," n.p., n.d., Florine Ross Papers, Cushing Library, Texas A&M University, clippings file; "General Ross," *Austin Weekly Statesman*, April 1, 1886; W. R. Poage, *Politics—Texas Style*, Waco: Texian Press, 1974, pp. 62–63. Note: Ross was possibly influenced by

Richard Coke, who, as one author noted, "was a Jeffersonian Democrat of the strictest kind."

40. "The Inaugural Ball," *Austin Daily Statesman*, December 12, 1886; "An Incident of the Ball," *Galveston Daily News*, January 21, 1887; Benner, *Sul Ross*, pp. 148–58; Rosalind Langton, "The Life of Colonel R. T. Milner," *SWHQ*, April 1941, p. 439. Note: there are numerous versions of the inauguration incident involving Captain Shapley Ross; see also Bessie Ross Clark, "S. P. Ross and L. S. Ross," pp. 84–86.

41. Dudley G. Wooten, ed., *A Comprehensive History of Texas, 1685–1897*, vol. II., 1898, reprint, Austin: THSA, 1986, pp. 266–75; Gantt, *The Chief Executive in Texas*, p. 262; Campbell, *Gone to Texas*, pp. 320–21.

42. "Gov. L. S. Ross's Inaugural," *Galveston Daily News*, January 19, 1887. See also "The Governor's Message [to the Texas Senate and House]," *Galveston Daily News*, January 21, 1887. Note: Ross's inaugural address was published in German, Bohemian, and Spanish, as well as English.

43. L. S. Ross, Gubernatorial Address to Joint Session, January 18, 1886, *Journal of the House of Representatives of the Twentieth Legislature*, Austin: State Printers, 1887, p. 66; "The State Land Board," *Galveston Daily News*, June 9, 1887; Cotner, *James Stephen Hogg*, pp. 106–8; Alwyn Barr, *Reconstruction to Reform: Texas Politics, 1876–1906*, Austin: University of Texas Press, 1971, pp. 83–84.

44. *Galveston Daily News*, February 4, 25, 1886; Haley, *Charles Goodnight*, pp. 359–92; Cotner, *James Stephen Hogg*, 106–12; Williams, *Beyond Redemption*, pp. 11–12, 90–92, 107–8; Billy Jones, *The Search for Maturity: The Saga of Texas, 1867–1900*, Austin: Steck-Vaughn Company, 1965, p. 100. See also "The Farmers' Alliance," *Dallas Morning News*, August 8 and 19, 1886; Henry D. McCallum, "Barbed Wire in Texas," *TSHQ*, October 1957, pp. 207–19.

45. Edward E. Dale, *The Range Cattle Industry: Ranching on the Great Plains from 1865–1925*, Norman: University of Oklahoma Press, 1969, 102–21; Marion Clawson, *The Western Range Livestock Industry*, New York: McGraw-Hill, 1950, pp. 88–96; Barr, *Reconstruction to Reform*, pp. 95–98; "The State Grange," *Galveston Daily News*, January 10, 1878; *Annual Report of the Agricultural & Mechanical College of Texas*, 1889, p. v.; Proceedings of the 4th Annual Sess., Texas State Grange, 1878, pp. 24, 51; James M. Bender, *History of the Original Texas State Grange*, n.p.: ca. 1960, p. 15. Note: On average, prior to 1900, Texas produced one bale of cotton (between 450 to 500 pounds) per acre.

46. Joseph Nimmo, "The Range and Ranch Cattle Business of the United States," Washington, DC: House Ex Doc. 7, Part III, 48th Cong, 2nd sess., 1885; *The Cattle Industry of Texas and Adjacent Territory*, St. Louis: Woodward & Tiernan Printing Co., 1895, pp. 45–59; H. L. Bentley, "Cattle Ranges of the Southwest," *U.S.D.A. Farmers' Bulletin*, no. 72, 1898, pp. 1–31; Mary W. Clarke, *A Century of Cow Business*, Fort Worth: Texas and Southwestern Cattle Raisers

Association, 1976, pp. 35–42; William W. Savage, *The Cherokee Strip Live Stock Association*, Columbia: University of Missouri Press, 1973, pp. 34–39. See also Walter P. Webb, *The Great Plains*, pp. 298–99, 309, 317, and J. Evetts Haley, *The XIT Ranch of Texas*, Norman: University of Oklahoma Press, 1967, pp. 87–88; Chamberlain, "Alexander Watkins Terrell," pp. 258–59. Note: Barbed-wire fencing was introduced in 1873, and by 1880, more than 86,900 tons of barbed wire had been sold for use on the Great Plains. In the fall of 1886, the XIT Ranch in the Texas Panhandle installed 781.25 miles of barbed-wire fence. Senator A. W. Terrell championed strong legislation to "for the punishment of those guilty of committing offenses," noting there were nine reasons for fence cutting:

* The coming of poor people into Texas faster that they could be assimilated.
* The rapidity that laws had been adopted, which favored a class and had enabled the stockmen to grow rich on the lands of other people.
* The construction of vast pastures, which had thrown reckless herdmen out of employment.
* The absence of proper road laws.
* The enclosing of public and private lands by out of state corporations.
* Large herds, whose owners owned no land, which were driven from place to place to consume grass.
* Fencing up water holes, fraudently [*sic*] leased as dry sections of land.
* Enclosing the school lands and private property to the exclusion of owners and others.

47. S. Hogg to L. S. Ross, September 10, 1889, J. S. Hogg Papers, Briscoe Library; S. G. Reed, *A History of Texas Railroads*, Houston: St. Clair Publishing Co., 1941, pp. 545–57; T. R. Fehrenbach, *Lone Star: A History of Texas and the Texans*, New York: Wings Books, p. 615; Barr, *Reconstruction to Reform*, pp. 114–19; Clawson, *The Western Range Livestock Industry*, pp. 79–93. See also Edward Everett Dale, *The Range Cattle Industry*, Norman: University of Oklahoma Press, 1930, and Williams, *Beyond Redemption*, p. 167.

48. "Ross Proclamation," *Fort Worth Gazette*, June 22, 1887; "Gov. Ross Means Business," *New York Times*, October 28, 1887; "The Little Cavalryman: His Utter Condemnation of Mob Law of Every Character," *Austin Daily Statesman*, March 7, 1888; "Ross and Wharton County," *Austin Daily Statesman*, March 23, 1888.

49. L. S. Ross, "His Utter Condemnation of Mob Law of Every Character," *Austin Daily Statesman*, March 7, 1888; "Mr. Kleberg and Captain R. King," *Austin Weekly Statesman*, October 31, 1889.

50. *Austin Weekly Statesman*, May 10, 1888; "Prohibition Is Political," *Galveston Daily News*, June 7, 1887; "Republican Identity with the Prohibition Movement," *Galveston Daily News*, July 26, 1887; "Be Ye Temperate in All Things," *Galveston Daily News*, July 27, 1887; "Fighting for Prohibition," *New York Times*, August 2, 1887.

51. "L. S. Ross for Governor," *Austin Daily Statesman*, August 26, 1880; "A Big Demonstration," *New York Times*, July 27, 1887; "What Texas Will Vote For," *New York Times*, August 4, 1887; Seth S. McKay, *Seven Decades of the Texas Constitution of 1876*, Lubbock: Texas Tech College Press, 1942, pp. 190–91; Williams, *Beyond Redemption*, pp. 29, 165; Benner, *Sul Ross*, pp. 144, 151, 164–65; Barr, *Reconstruction to Reform*, pp. 88–92; Chamberlain, "Alexander Watkins Terrell," pp. 170–79.

52. Wooten, ed., *A Comprehensive History of Texas*, vol. II, 269–71; Benner, *Sul Ross*, pp. 152–58, 166–68; Campbell, *Gone to Texas*, p. 321; Jerry Thompson, *Tejano Tiger*, Fort Worth: TCU Press, 2017, pp. 318–20; Shirley, *Temple Houston*, pp. 17–18, 150–59.

53. L. S. Ross to Grover Cleveland, August 9, 1887, and Grover Cleveland to L. S. Ross, September 7, 1887, Presidential Papers of Grover Cleveland, microfilm, Evans Library, Texas A&M; "The Green County Suit," *Galveston Daily News*, March 8, 1896; L. S. Ross to Lizzie Ross, n.d., from Washington, DC, 1890, Ross Papers, Briscoe Center; "Deposition of S. P. Ross," *Evidence Pertaining to the Boundary between the United States and Texas*, Austin, 1886, pp. 37–39. See also Rowland T. Berhoff, "Southern Attitudes toward Immigration, 1865–1914," *Journal of Southern History*, August 1951, pp. 328–60; Williams, *Beyond Redemption*, 11–12, 107, and Barbara J. Rozek, *Gone to Texas*, College Station: Texas A&M University Press, 2003, pp. 113–17, 122–23. Note: As early as 1871, Texas organized a bureau of immigration agents to promote the state. Though the Texas constitution provided no funding for such recruitment, it is unknown how it was financed. Also, Ross, on behalf of the Texas Veterans Association, discussed with both Presidents Harrison and Cleveland (who issued an executive order) the return of captured Confederate colors to Texas, yet the return had been opposed and blocked by the Association of the Grand Old Army of the Republic in mid-1887. This was never resolved. See *Austin Daily Statesman*, June 14, 15, 17, 22, 1887.

54. R. H. Jayne, *The White Mustang: A Tale of the Lone Star State*, New York: American Publishers Corp., 1889, p. 106. See also John A. Adams Jr., *Conflict and Commerce on the Rio Grande*, College Station: Texas A&M University Press, 2008, pp. 61, 72, 84–85; "Information for Immigrants," *Burke's Texas Almanac—1883*, Houston: J. Burke, 1883, pp. 27–31, 79, 93–112. Note: Volumes on the West were not limited to just eastern American publishers, but also very popular in London; see, for example, Mary Jaques, *Texan Ranch Life*, London:

Horace Cox, Windsor House, 1894 (reprinted by Texas A&M University Press, 1989).

55. "The Lone Star Look towards the East," *Austin American Statesman*, June 5, 1890; "Well Written: Gov. Ross Speech to Cleveland," *Austin American Statesman*, June 11, 1890; "An Impractical Scheme: What Gov. Ross of Texas Says about the Suggested Boycott," *New York Times*, July 29, 1890.

56. *Austin Statesman*, May 25, 1890; "We had the pleasure," *Dallas Herald*, October 8, 1870. Note: Prior to 1900, Sul Ross was the most traveled Texas governor, traversing the southern states in the 1850s and 1860s, with a two-month visit to California in August to September 1870 and a visit to the East Coast in mid-1890.

Chapter 2

1. J. S. Hogg to L. S. Ross, September 10, 1889, James S. Hogg Papers, Briscoe Library, Austin; Robert L. Peterson, "Jay Gould and the Railroad Commission of Texas," *TSHQ*, January 1955, pp. 422–32; Wooten, ed. *A Comprehensive History of Texas*, vol. II, pp. 273–81; Barr, *Reconstruction to Reform*, pp. 104–5, 197–98; W. R. Poage, *Politics—Texas Style*, Waco: Texian Press, 1974, pp. 62–65; Bob Alexander, *Rawhide Ranger, Ira Aten Enforcing Law on the Texas Frontier*, Denton: University of North Texas Press, 2011, pp. 132–33. Note: Gubernatorial votes in 1888 were tallied as Ross with 250,338 and Martin with 98,447. See also "Texas Anti-Trust," Gammel, ed., *The Laws of Texas*, vol. IX, pp. 1169–70.

2. Message of Governor E. J. Davis, 12th Leg., 1st Sess., *Journal of the Senate*, January 10, 1871, pp. 26–29; "The Agricultural College Bill," *Houston Daily Union*, June 24, 1871; "The State Agricultural College Again," *Houston Daily Union*, June 28, 1871; "Agricultural and Mechanical College of Texas," *Galveston Daily News*, July 23, 1871; "The Agricultural and Mechanical College," *Austin Tri-Weekly Statesman*, September 2, 1871; "From Bryan," *Galveston Daily News*, June 3, 1875, and "Texas Agricultural and Mechanical College," *Galveston Daily News*, June 4, 1875; Dethloff, *Centennial History of Texas A&M*, vol. I, pp. 27–36. Note: Even prior to the passage of the 1862 Morrill Land Grant Act, a similar name known in Texas was used under the organization label of the "Dallas County Agricultural and Mechanical Association," forerunner of the Dallas State Fair, *Dallas Herald*, September 11, 1861. Nomenclature and land-grant institution name designations (between 1846 and 1876) were often inconsistent and changed periodically; for example, "A&M" was often substituted with "state" or "institute"—or not at all. See Geiger, ed., *The American College in the Nineteenth Century*, pp. 162–63, and T. A. Fuller, "Twenty Years of A. & M. College Existence," *Battalion*, January 1897, pp. 7–13.

3. Governor's messages, Coke to Ross, 1874–1890, p. 138; "Texas Agricultural

and Mechanical College," *Galveston Daily News*, June 3, 4, 1875, and September 13, 1876; "The Agriculture College," *New York Times*, June 9, 1875; *Daily Banner* (Brenham), October 6, 1876; Wooten, ed., *A Comprehensive History of* Texas, vol. II, pp. 279–83, 459–62; Dethloff, *Centennial History of Texas A&M*, vol. I, p. 28. See also Joint Committee of the Senate and House, *Journal of the Senate of Texas*, 22nd Leg., Extra sess., Austin: Henry Hutchings, April 2, 1892, pp. 109–19.

4. Texas Constitution of 1876, Article VII, Sec. 13.; Sul Ross, Gubernatorial Address, Joint Session, January 18, 1886, Journal of the House of Representatives of the Twentieth Legislature, Austin, January 11, 1887, pp. 66–67; H. P. N. Gammel, ed. *Laws of Texas*, Austin: Gammel Book Company, 1898, vol. IX, pp. 800, 862, 927, 927, 948, 1169; "The Amount of Warrants," *Austin Daily Statesman*, September 30, 1894; Wooten, ed. *A Comprehensive History of Texas*, vol. II, pp. 310–11; Williams, *Beyond Redemption*, p. 156.

5. Thomas L. Miller, "Texas Land Grants to Confederate Veterans and Widows," *SWHQ*, July 1965, pp. 59–65; O. M. Roberts, "Sul Ross," in *A Comprehensive History of Texas, 1865–1897*, ed. Dudley G. Wooten, Dallas: William G. Scorff, 1898, pp. 270–79. See also Amy S. Kirchenbauer, "The Texas Confederate House for Men, 1884–1870," MA thesis, University of North Texas, August 2011.

6. "American," *San Antonio Herald*, August 30, 1875, and September 14, 1875; "Correction—Peace and Quiet—Faithful Officers," *Galveston Daily News*, May 10, 1876; C. L. Sonnichsen, *Ten Texas Feuds*, Albuquerque: University of New Mexico Press, 1857, pp. 5, 87–107. See also Webb, *Texas Rangers*, pp. 325–28; and David Johnson, *The Mason County "Hoo Doo" War, 1874–1902*, Denton: University of North Texas Press, 2006.

7. Prof. Louis L. McInnis to L. S. Ross, April 28, 1890, McInnis Papers, Cushing; *Galveston Daily News*, April 30, 190. Note: The cadets also collected and donated $71.25 for a monument to the defenders of the Alamo in San Antonio; *San Antonio Daily Light*, May 11, 1889.

8. "The Death of Ex-Governor L. S. Ross," *Austin Statesman*, January 5, 1898; Ross memo, "Education of the Colored Race," Austin, 1889; C. L. Sonnichson, *I'll Die before I'll Run*, New York: Harper & Brothers, 1951, pp. 213–20; "The Lynching at Forsyth," *Dallas Morning News*, March 7, 1888, and "Out of Place in Organized Society," *Dallas Morning News*, March 9, 1888; Benner, *Sul Ross*, p. 175. See also Patrick G. Williams, *Beyond Redemption: Texas Democrats after Reconstruction*, College Station: Texas A&M Press, 2007, pp. 78–80, 172–73. On Ross's opposition to poll taxes, see *Journal of the Constitutional Convention of the State of Texas: Begun and Held at the City of Austin, September 6th, 1875*, n.p., Galveston, 1875, pp. 307–10.

9. Hubert S. Jenning, "Stirring Days at A. and M.," *Southwest Review*, autumn 1946, pp. 341–44.

10. E. L. Blackshear, "Gives His Views of the Conditions of the Negro's Con-

dition in Texas and the South," *American Statesman*, April 30, 1890; Bureau of the Census, "Negro Population 1790–1915," Washington, DC: US Government Printing Office, 1918, p. 143.

11. Ross Family Papers, Baylor. Note: Only Sam Houston served three terms as the ranking Texas executive—twice as president of Texas and once as governor.

12. *Annual Report of the Agricultural and Mechanical College of Texas*, 1888, pp. 3–10; Clarence Ousley, *History of the Agricultural and Mechanical College of Texas*, College Station: Bulletin, December 1, 1935, p. 58; Charles W. Crawford, *One Hundred Years of Engineering at Texas A&M 1876–1976*, College Station: privately published, 1976, p. 10. See also Spratt, *The Road to Spindletop*, pp. 158–65.

13. Scrapbook, A. J Rose Papers, Briscoe History Center, Austin; Robert A. Calvert, "A. J. Rose and the Granger Concept of Reform," *Agricultural History*, January 1977, pp. 181–96; C. N. Ousley, ed., *Texas Farm and Ranch*, to L. L. McInnis, July 10, 1888, in Cofer, *Early History*, p. 188; Roscoe C. Martin, "The Grange as a Political Factor in Texas," *Political and Social Science Quarterly*, March 1926, pp. 363–83; Spratt, *The Road to Spindletop*, pp. 151–209. See also Ralph A. Smith, "The Grange in Texas, 1873–1900," *SWHQ*, April 1939, pp. 297–315, and Ralph A. Smith, "'Macuneism,' or the Farmers of Texas in Business," *Journal of Southern History*, May 1947, p. 243; Hardaway Hunt Dinwiddie, "State Grange," *Texas State Journal*, vol. 2, 1884, p. 309; C. J. Bradley, "Lawrence S. 'Sul' Ross," MA thesis, Midwestern State University, 2012, pp. 102–4.

14. Minutes of the Board of Directors of A&M, January 24–5, vol. I, pp. 44–47; Joint Committee Visit to A&M College, *Journal of the Senate of Texas*, 21st Leg., Reg. sess., January 8, 1888, pp. 541–42; *Journal of the House of Representatives of Texas*, 21st Leg., Extra sess., April 19, 1888, pp. 45–46; *Annual Report of the Agricultural and Mechanical College of Texas*, 1887, pp. 22–25; Dethloff, *Centennial History of Texas A&M*, vol. I, pp. 136–46; Cofer, ed., *First Five Administrators of Texas A. & M., 1876–1890*, pp. 40–47. See also J. J. Lane, *History of the University of Texas*, Austin: Henry Hutchings State Printer, 1891, pp. 140–50.

15. Lucius Holman to Mrs. P. G. Weeks, October 10, 1888, Holman Papers, Cushing Archives. See also G. A. Rodgers to Prof. L. L. McInnis, June 29, 1888, in David Brooks Cofer, *Early History of Texas A. and M. College through Letters and Papers*, College Station: Association of Former Students, 1952, pp. 71–72; *Dallas Morning News*, September 11 and 27, 1890; *Galveston Daily News*, September 25, 1890.

16. McInnis Papers, Cushing Archives; *Bryan Eagle*, March 5, 1896; "State Capital: Governor Ross Has Gone to Bryan," *Austin Weekly Statesman*, June 12, 1890. See also David Brooks Cofer, *First Five Administrations of Texas A. & M. College*, College Station: Association of Former Students, 1952, pp. 40–47; Ralph Smith, "The Farmer's Alliance in Texas, 1875–1900: A Revolt against Bourbon

and Bourgeois Democracy," *SWHQ*, January 1945, pp. 346–69. Note: T. M. Scott became a trustee of Add-Ran Christian University in Thorp Spring, Texas, the forerunner of Texas Christian University.

17. *Annual Report of the Agricultural and Mechanical College of Texas*, 1889, pp. iii–iv; Dethloff, *Centennial History of Texas A&M*, vol. 1, p. 148–53; "A. J. Rose—Salado," Brown, *Indian Wars and Pioneers of Texas*, 1880, pp. 695–96. Note: In addition to serving on numerous political and agricultural organizations activities, Rose also served for more than two decades on school and college boards, including Salado College, Salado Public Schools, and Baylor Female College. He was also chairman of the A&M College board of directors, which included a leadership role at Prairie View Normal.

18. A. J. Rose to L. L. McInnis, February 29, 1890, McInnis Papers; Minutes of the Board of Directors, June 7–18, 1890, vol. I, p. 88; Jenning, "Stirring Days at A. and M.," *Southwest Review*, pp. 342–43.

19. Benner, *Sul Ross*, pp. 116, 198–204.

20. Texas A&M Board of Directors Minutes, June 7–10, 1890, pp. 89–90; "The Agricultural College," *Galveston Daily News*, June 10, 1890.

21. Texas A&M Board of Directors Minutes, July 1, 1890, p. 92; "William Lorraine Bringhurst," Cofer, ed., *Second Five Administrations of Texas A. & M College*, College Station: Texas A&M University Press, 1954, pp. 48–60; Dethloff, *Centennial History of Texas A&M*, vol. I, pp. 151–3.

22. "Called to a College," *Galveston Daily News*, July 6, 1890.

23. Benner, *Sul Ross*, pp. 198–203; "Indorsing Ross," *Galveston Daily News*, July 6, 1890; *Bryan Eagle*, July 3, 1890; *Austin Daily Statesman*, July 6, 1890.

24. "In a New Field of Service," *Galveston Daily News*, July 12, 1890; *Dallas Morning News*, March 25, 1892; Benner, *Sul Ross*, pp. 198–203.

25. L. S. Ross to Major Holmes, June 21, 1891.

26. Texas A&M Board of Directors Minutes, I, p. 94; College Station, *College Journal*, vol. III, February 1892, p. 20; *Austin Statesman*, September 25, 1887; Gammel, *Laws of Texas*, vol. IX, p. 937. Note: President Ross's salary was paid with $3,000 from the A&M College fund and $500 from the Extension Service funding; he received no additional pay for his duties related to Prairie View.

27. Marilyn M. Sibley, *George W. Brackenridge*, Austin; University of Texas Press, 1974, p. 171; Frank E. Vandiver, "John William Mallet and the University of Texas," *SWHQ*, April 1950, pp. 422–42; Lane, *History of the University*, pp. 153, 268–70.

28. "Called to a College," *Galveston Daily News*, July 6, 1890; "The Farmers' Alliance," *Galveston Daily News*, July 2, 1890; Martin, "The Grange as a Political Factors in Texas," *Political and Social Science Quarterly*, March 26, 1926, pp. 367–68.

29. Benner, *Sul Ross*, p. 201, n. 11.

30. L. S. Ross to President Rose and Members of the Board of Directors, August 8, 1890, Minutes of the Board. Note: In neither the appointment letter by the board, nor in Ross's response, is there a mention of other duties such as the Agricultural Extension Service or Prairie View.

31. Cofer, *First Five Administrators*, pp. 40–47; Dethloff, *Centennial History of Texas A&M University*, vol. 1, pp. 58–64.

32. Minutes of the Association of Former Students of the Texas A&M University, June 8, 1891, vol. I, pp. 1–3, and June 6, 1892, vol. I, p. 2; Cofer, *Fragments of Early History*, p. 24. See also John A. Adams Jr., *We Are the Aggies*, College Station: Texas A&M University Press, 1979, pp. 22–28, and Lane Stephenson, "E. B. Cushing: A&M's Savior in Dark Hour," *Texas Aggie*, March 2016, pp. 40–41.

33. E. B. Cushing to L. L. McInnis, July 12, 1890, March 27, 1891, and April 2, 1891, McInnis Papers. Note: "The State Capitol," *Galveston Daily News*, January 9, 1877, reported the enrollment for the first session in the fall of 1876 was thirty-two students.

34. L. L. McInnis to A. J Rose, August 8, 1890, and September 8, 1890; A. J. Rose to L. L. McInnis, October 28, 1890, McInnis Papers. Note: Days after Sul's letter of acceptance, the college placed a notice in a national publication, "State Agricultural and Mechanical College," *Southern Mercury*, August 14, 1890.

35. *Report of the Agricultural and Mechanical College of Texas*, 1891, p. 8; "Texas—Views of the H&TC Railway," *Frank Leslie's Illustrated Newspaper*, November 8, 1890, p. 251; Dethloff, *Centennial History*, vol. I, pp. 158–60.

36. "Governor Hogg," *Austin Statesman*, September 27, 1891; Cotner, *Hogg*, pp. 189–209, 277, 292; Maury Klien, *The Life and Legend of Jay Gould*, Baltimore: John Hopkins University Press, 1986, pp. 305, 428, 444; Williams, *Beyond Redemption*, pp. 94, 168; June R. Welch, *The Texas Governors*, Dallas: G. L. A. Press, 1977, p. 94.

37. "Appealing for Aid," *Austin Weekly Statesmen*, July 25, 1889; Benner, *Sul Ross*, pp. 195–97; Spratt, *The Road to Spindletop*, pp. 213–21; "Bryan and Sewall Club," *Houston Daily Post*, October 29, 1898. See also Richard Coke to Dr. D. R. Wallace, August 24, 1890, seen in "An 1890 Richard Coke Letter," *SWHQ*, January 1962, p. 69.

38. Barr, *Reconstruction to Reform*, p. 117; "Complimentary German," *Austin Weekly Statesman*, January 14, 1891.

39. L. S. Ross to Major Holmes, February 2, 1891, Ross Papers. See also Ratchford Papers, Cushing Archives. Note: Frank '95 and Nev '02, who remained with their father as other family members departed, graduated with honors from the A&M College.

40. Dethloff, *Centennial History*, vol. I, p. 99.

41. J. J. Lane, *History of the University of Texas: Based on Facts and Records*, Austin: Henry Hutchings State Printer, 1891, pp. 67–69, 141. Note: For a detailed

source of documents relating to both the A&M College and the University of Texas in their formative years, see Benedict, "A Source Book Relating to the History of the University of Texas," *University of Texas Bulletin*, no. 1757, October 10, 1917.

42. Roselind Langston, "The Life of Colonel R. T. Milner," *SWHQ*, April 1941, p. 38; Lane, *History of the University of Texas*, pp. 139–44, 276–82, 291. Note: Governor Roberts, also called "The Old Alcalde," is considered a founder of the University of Texas.

43. Lane, *History of the University of Texas*, pp. 150–53; Nell I. Painter, *Exodusters: Black Migration to Kansas after Reconstruction*, New York: Alfred A. Knopf, 1977, pp. 137, 147, 200–201; Lawrence D. Rice, *The Negro in Texas 1824–1900*, Baton Rouge: Louisiana State University Press, 1971, pp. 13–14, 226–30. See also Fredrick Douglas, "The Negro Exodus from the Gulf States," ca. 1879, Library of Congress, Manuscript Division, www.loc.gov/resource/mfd.

44. Lane, *History of the University of Texas*, pp. 140–51; "An Ungenerous Act," *Galveston Daily News*, August 14, 1883.

45. J. D. Read to L. L. McInnis, July 24, 1891; A. C. Brietz, "To Whom It May Concern," June 3, 1891, and E. B. Cushing to L. L. McInnis, May 4, 1891, McInnis Paper, Cushing.

46. L. S. Ross to Major Holmes, February 13, 1891, and March 9, 1891; J. D. Read to L. L. McInnis, March 19, 1892, and April 2, 1892; W. M. Imboden to L. L. McInnis, May 9, 1893.

47. McInnis Papers, Cushing Archives.

48. Charles W. Crawford, *One Hundred Years of Engineering at Texas A&M 1976–1976*, College Station: privately published, 1976, p. 25; Dethloff, *Centennial History*, vol. I, pp. 158–60; Paul D. Casey, *The History of the A&M College Trouble*, Waco: J. S. Hill, 1908.

Chapter 3

1. J. Frank Dobie and Mody C. Boatright, *Straight Texas: A Texas Folk-Lore Society Book*, Austin: The Steck Company, 1937, p. 13.

2. Ross to President Rose and Members A&M College Board of Directors, August 8, 1890; John Adams *Keepers of the Spirit*, College Station: Texas A&M University Press, 2001, pp. 38–57; Ernest Langford, *Here We'll Build the College*, College Station: Texas A&M Archives, 1963, p. 16; Benner, *Sul Ross*, pp. 222–25.

3. Langford, *Here We'll Build the College*, pp. 1–6; "A. & M. College," *Leslie's Illustrated Newspaper*, November 8, 1890; College Station, *Olio*, 1895, p. 49.

4. "A. and M. College," *The Texas Health Journal*, vol. 4, no. 8, p. 218; Dethloff, *Centennial History of Texas A&M*, I, pp. 100–25; Cofer, *Second Five Administrators*, pp. 25–47; Langford, *Here We'll Build the College*, pp. 1–14.

5. Bike Club Minutes, August 1897, Bicycle Club Collection, Cushing; Jennings, "Stirring Days at A. and M.," *Southwest Review*, 1946, p. 341.

6. Dethloff, Centennial History of Texas A&M, vol. I, pp. 160–61; Minutes of the A&M Board of Directors, February 18, 1892, vol. I, p. 125.

7. Ross to Gov. Hogg, May 13, 1891, and Ross to Major Holmes, June 21, 1891, Ross Papers.

8. Langford, *Here We'll Build the College*, pp. 43–46; Ross to Holmes, June 21, 1891, Ross Papers.

9. Campbell, *Gone to Texas*, pp. 313–20.

10. Williams, *Beyond Redemption*, pp. 174–78; Barr, *Texas Politics*, pp. 38–70; Buenger, *The Path to a Modern South*, pp. xvi–xxv, 5–6.

11. Grange and Farmer's Alliance, A. J. Rose Papers, Briscoe; Spratt, *The Road to Spindletop*, pp. 111–18

12. Gantt, *The Chief Executives in Texas*, pp. 263–67; Cotner, *Hogg*, pp. 260–73.

13. "The Commission and Railroad Grants," *Galveston Daily News*, February 5, 1893; "Has the State Been Swindled," *Dallas Morning News*, August 18, 1891; Gammel, *Laws of Texas*, vol. X, p. 57; Campbell, *Gone to Texas*, p. 323; Woodward, *Origins of the New South, 1877–1913*, pp. 147–55; Spratt, *The Road to Spindletop*, pp. 19–36; James R. Norvell, "The Railroad Commission of Texas: Its Origin and History," *SWHQ*, April 1965, pp. 465–80; M. M. Crane, "Recollections of the Establishment of the Texas Railroad Commission," *SWHQ*, April 1947, pp. 478–86.

14. Charles Seymour, *Intimate Papers of Colonel House*, Boston: Houghton Mifflin, 1926, vol. 1., pp. 27–29; Gantt, *The Chief Executives in Texas*, p. 263; H. Y. Benedict, ed., "History of the University of Texas," *University of Texas Bulletin*, October 10, 1917, pp. 297–312; Cotner, *Hogg*, pp. 268–69. See also "The Populist Party State Platform," *Dallas Morning News*, August 18, 1891.

15. Clark, *A Glance Backward*, pp. 88–91; Cotner, *Hogg*, pp. 266–93; Seymour, *Intimate Papers of Colonel House*, pp. 29–38; Barr, *Reconstruction to Reform*, pp. 131–42; Bailey, "Life of Stephen Hogg," p. 463–64, 480; Woodward, *Origins of the New South*, pp. 261–63; Campbell, *Gone to Texas*, pp. 331–33; Rupert N. Richardson, " Edward M. House and the Governors," *SWHQ*, July 1957, pp. 51–65; Jones, *The Search for Maturity*, p. 167. Note: Colonel House, once engaged with a candidate, controlled all facets of the campaign, winning every race; he would not allow a candidate (as was custom) to make any "patronage commitments"—noting his rule was "to keep 'em guessing was to keep 'em working."

16. Rupert N. Richardson, *Colonel Edward M. House: The Texas Years, 1858–1912*, Abilene: Hardin-Simmons University, 1964; Charles E. Neu, "In Search of Colonel Edward M. House: The Texas Years, 1858–1912," *SWHQ*, July 1989, pp. 25–29; David Houston, *Eight Years with Wilson's Cabinet*, New York: Doubleday, Page & Company, 1826, pp. 21–22; Gould, *Progressives and Prohibitionists*, pp.

100–106; Alexander L. and Juliette L. George, *Woodrow Wilson and Colonel House*, New York: Dover, 1956, p. 92; Adrian Anderson, "President Wilson's Politician: Albert Sidney Burleson," *SWHQ*, January 1974, pp. 339–54; Seymour, *Intimate Papers of Colonel House*, p. 37. Note: While Colonel House did not seek elected or appointive public office, Governor Culberson nominated him to the Texas Pardons Board in 1894, which he declined.

17. "Commencement Exercises of the A&M College of Texas," n.p., n.d. (ca. June 5, 1892), seen in John H. O'Bar Scrapbook, Cushing Archives; "Mr. J. Foley," *Galveston Daily News*, February 26 and 28, 1891.

18. L. S. Ross to Major Holmes, October 12, 1891, and December 20, 1891.

19. Texas A&M Catalogue, 1891–92; "Ex-Cadets of the A&M College," *Galveston Daily News*, July 24, 1891; Adams, *Keepers of the Spirit*, pp. 4–25.

20. "The Beginning of Ross Volunteers," Cofer, *Fragments of Early History*, pp. 23–27; see also *The Olio*, pp. 64–66.

21. "The Beginning of Ross Volunteers," Cofer, *Fragments of Early History*, pp. 23–27.

22. "The Beginning of Ross Volunteers," Cofer, *Fragments of Early History*, pp. 23–27; "A. & M. College," *Galveston Daily News*, June 7, 1891; "The Ross Volunteers, Again," *Bryan Daily Eagle*, October 4, 1905.

23. "An Answer to Sam Jones: One of His Friends Explains 'Turn Texas Lose,'" *Galveston Daily News*, May 28, 1892; George Clark, *A Glance backward or Some Events in the Past History of My Life*, Houston: Rein & Sons Company, 1914, pp. 11–68, 84–89; Colter, *Hogg*, pp. 202–8; Buenger, *The Path to a Modern South*, pp. 12–16; "El Gobernador," El Paso *El Ciudadano*, February 27, 1892; "Ross Is for Clark," *Waco Evening News*, February 29, 1892. Note the following letter was released statewide in English and Spanish:

College Station, February 26, 1892

Hon. G. B. Gerald:

In reply to your letter will say, I am in no sense a candidate. The expressions of partiality you notice are purely voluntary. I have not in any manner, either directly or indirectly, signified a desire for a third term. I shall support Hon. George Clark. Having been on intimate social and friendly terms with him as a neighbor since the war, I can say in all truth my faith is his wisdom, patriotism, incorruptible integrity and devotion to the highest and best interests of Texas people is utter and entire.

Very respectfully,   L. S. Ross

24. "Third Party Movement," and "The Injustice to Mr. Chilton," *Galveston Daily News*, March 27, 28, 1892; Clark, *A Glance Backward*, pp. 89–91; Gould, *Progressives and Prohibitionists*, p. 10. See also "The Populist Party State Platform," *Dallas Morning News*, August 18, 1891.

25. *Austin Statesman*, May 17, 1888; Clark, *A Glance Backward*, 89–91; H. Y. Benedict, ed. "History of the University of Texas," *University of Texas Bulletin*, Austin, October 10, 1917, pp. 236, 283–96, 303, 755–56; Lewis L. Gould, *Alexander Watkins Terrell: Civil War Soldier, Texas Lawmaker, American Diplomat*, Austin: University of Texas Press, 2005, pp. 113, 119–23. See also Alwyn Barr, "Texas Politics, 1876–1906." PhD diss., University of Texas, 1960.

26. Gould, *Terrell*, pp. 74, 85, 117, 149; Rice, *The Negro in Texas*, pp. 116, 132; Williams, *Beyond Redemption*, p. 79, 168–70; *Austin Statesman*, February 21, 1891; *Galveston Daily News*, August 9, 1891. For Ross's opposition to poll taxes, also see *Journal of the Constitutional Convention*, pp. 307–10. For more on Ross's pardons of African Americans, see note 48, below.

27. Gould, *Terrell*, pp. 121–23; Walter Moore and James Day, eds., *The Texas Almanac 1857–1873*, Waco: Texian Press, 1967, p. 515; Wooten, ed., *A Comprehensive History of Texas*, vol. II, p. 423; Interview with Bill Page '76, June 29, 2016.

28. *Galveston Daily News*, March 28, 1892; *Austin Statesmen*, March 3, 1892; *Dallas Morning News*, March 31, 1892; Gould, *Terrell*, p. 122. Note: The rejoinder by Sul Ross invokes historical and philosophical references to statesmanship drawn from Dante, Thucydides, and Machiavelli, taken from a volume of political essays published by Thomas Babington Macaulay in *Critical, Historical, and Miscellaneous Essays and Poems*, vol. I, New York: John B. Alden, 1883, p. 210. It is unknown if this volume was in the personal collection of President Ross or in the small A&M College Library on the third floor of Old Main.

29. "Another Word with You, Judge Terrell," *Austin Statesman*, August 10, 1891, and March 20, 1892; *Dallas Morning News*, March 22, 24, 1892; Gould, *Terrell*, pp. 57, 79–81, 120–23; Chamberlain, "Alexander Watkins Terrell," pp. 358–63.

30. *Galveston Daily News*, April 8, 1892. See also "A and M College," *Texas Health Journal*, 1892, p. 219.

31. *Galveston Daily News*, April 9, 1892

32. *Austin Statesman*, December 6 and 29, 1906; Gould, *Terrell*, 122, 158; Robert Calvert and Arnoldo De Leon, *The History of Texas*, pp. 222–23; Fehrenbach, *Lone Star*, pp. 619–22; Arthur D. H. Smith, *The Real Colonel House*, New York: George H. Doran Company, 1918, pp. 46–49; June R. Welch, *The Texas Governor*, Dallas: G. L. A. Press, 1977, p. 100.

33. "The Confederate Home Dedicated Yesterday," *Galveston Daily News*, March 14, 1887; "Ross Assumes Command," *Galveston Daily News*, April 21, 1892.

34. "Ross and the Veterans: The 'Little Cavalryman' Enthusiastically Re-elected," *Galveston Daily News*, April 22, 1893; "The Texas Reunion at Houston," *Confederate Veteran*, May 1893, p. 154; "Texas Camps," *Confederate Veteran*, March 1893, p. 86.

35. "The Confederate Home," *Confederate Veteran*, March 2, 1893; "Paraded with the Boys," *Confederate Veteran*, April 22, 1893, and "A. & M. College of Texas," *Confederate Veteran*, April 17, 1893.

36. "United Confederate Veterans," *Galveston Daily News*, January 4, 1892, and *Galveston Daily News*, March 6, 1893. Note: A Special Order of December 22, 1892, noted the role and mission of the UCV: "The object of this organization is to unite veterans of Texas into local associations, which shall form a part of a general federation, in which shall be cherished the ties of friendship that should exist among men who have shared common dangers and endured common sufferings and privations, to promote our social interest, to preserve a history of its members and to extend help to all our disabled and needy."

37. "United Confederate Veterans," *Galveston Daily News*, March 6, 1893, and "The Confederate Home," *Galveston Daily News*, March 2, 1893; "The Confederate Home," *Austin Daily Statesman*, September 10, 1894; "Henry Bates Stoddard," *Knight Templar*, September 2015, pp. 7–9.

38. *Galveston Daily News*, May 15, 1886; Jones, *The Search for Maturity*, p. 100; Bill Page, ed., "L. S. Ross and Hunting," Cushing Archives, February 8, 2019.

39. L. S. Ross to Major Holmes, July 22, 1892, and November 5, 1892.

40. L. S. Ross to Major Holmes, July 22, 1892.

41. "State Normal School of Texas for Colored Students," *Galveston Daily News*, October 1, 1880; George R. Woolfolk, *Prairie View: A Study in Public Conscience, 1878–1946*, New York: Pageant Press, 1962, pp. 3–25; Evans, *The Story of Texas Schools*, pp. 92–93, 104, 109; Dethloff, *Texas A&M Centennial History*, vol. 1, p. 48. See also Jared Stallones, "Struggle for the Soul of a Normal School," *Journal of the Midwest History of Education Society*, vol. 23, 1996, pp. 102–6.

42. Wooten, ed., *A Comprehensive History of Texas*, vol. II, pp. 462–63; Department of Commerce, Bureau of the Census, "Negro Population 1790–1915," Washington, DC: US Government Printing Office, 1915, p. 143.

43. "Industrial Training," *Dallas Morning News*, December 17, 1894; Lane, *History of the University of Texas*, p. 56, 70–73; Gould, *Alexander W. Terrell*, p. 57; letter, William J. Swain, Comptroller to Governor L. S. Ross, Austin, March 28, 1888, *Journal of the House of Representatives*, 20th Leg., Extra sess., Austin, April 16, 1888, pp. 26–27.

44. E. L. Blackshear, "Gives His Views of the Condition of Negro's in Texas and the South," *Austin Statesman*, April 30, 1890; "A Visiting Colored Editor," *Dallas Morning News*, December 5, 1894.

45. Governor Ross, "Education of the Colored Race," Austin, n.d., ca. 1890; "Needs of the Negro," *Galveston Daily News*, October 5, 14; "The Negro Problem Is Settling Itself," *Austin Daily Statesman*, December 8, 1897; "The Colored University," *Dallas Morning News*, January 30, 1892.

46. "The Colored University," *Galveston Daily News*, January 2, 1892; Clark, *A Glance Backward*, p. 91. Note: The continued politicization of higher education is further demonstrated by the fact that it has been suggested that Col. Edward House add a plank to the 1896 Democratic platform, calling for an appropriation of 50,000 acres of land to endow a "university for African Americans." See Rupert N. Richardson, "Edward M. House and the Governors," *SWHQ*, July 1957, p. 64, and Winkler, ed., *Platforms of the Political Parties in Texas*, p. 388.

47. Blackshear quote seen in Rice, *The Negro in Texas, 1874–1900*, p. 193, and Jesse Dorsett, "Blacks in Reconstruction Texas, 1865–1877," PhD diss., Texas Christian University, August 1981, p. 119; Evans, *The Story of Texas Schools*, p. 304.

48. "Religious Matters," *Galveston Daily News*, August 27, 1894; for notes on pardons, see Bill Page, "L. S. Ross Working Notes," May 1, 2015, College Station, sample of pardons seen in *Dallas Morning News*, February 11, 1887; *Austin Daily Statesman*, August 23, 1887, December 28, 1887, May 21, 1889, and May 13, 1890; *Dallas Morning News*, August 3, 1887; on mob violence, see L. S. Ross to Judge Long of Panola County, *Fort Worth Gazette*, March 9, 1888, and executive letter from L. S. Ross to Sheriff of Angelina County, January 5, 1890, *Austin Statesman*; Benner, *Sul Ross*, pp. 172–73, 177–81. Note: With regard to the Ku Klux Klan, W. D. Wood in 1906 stated he "has no knowledge that the Klan of which General Nathan Forest was chief, included Texas in its organization . . . and did not exercise any official jurisdiction over Texas." There were racial incidents in Centerville and Millican, Texas, in 1868–69 that could well have been, as Charles W. Ramsdell notes in *Reconstruction in Texas*, "imitative and local" Klan-inspired responses to localized unrest, but there was no known sustained organized Klan effort. A less publicly known group was the Knights of the White Camellia in deep East Texas, which was in decline by 1869 and, according to Christopher Long, by 1870 ceased to exist as an organization. See "Knights of the White Camellia," *The New Handbook of Texas*, vol. 3, p. 1147. Rice in *The Negro in Texas*, p. 124, notes that the Klan was defunct by the early 1870s. Long notes the "organizations in general ceased to exist after Congress passed the Ku Klux Klan Act in 1871." See "Ku Klux Klan," *Handbook of Texas*, pp. 1165–66. In my review of more than a dozen leading newspapers of Texas from 1880 to 1900, there is no mention of Klan activities in Texas. To be sure, there were numerous incidents ascribed to what Rice called "that ghostly body," including the suppression of black voters, mob violence, and horrific lynchings, which were nearly always instigated by a single local incident. Such incidents were publicly denounced by Gov. Sul Ross repeatedly in writing from the executive desk and

in newspapers. There is no mention of the Klan in Cotner, *James Stephen Hogg: A Biography* (1959). The first organized Klan activates in Texas started around 1920. See Walter Buenger, "Memory and the 1920s Ku Klux Klan in Texas," in Cantrell and Turner, eds., *Lone Star Pasts* (2007); Gould, *Progressives and Prohibitionist*, 280–81, 288; Steen, *Twentieth Century Texas* (1942), pp. 299–302; and Buenger, *The Path to a Modern South*, pp. 195–96, 202–9, 256. See also W. D. Wood, "The Ku Klux Klan," *SWHQ*, April 1906, pp. 262–68; and Charles W. Ramsdell, *Reconstruction in Texas*, Gloucester, MA: Peter Smith, 1964, p. 233; and James Smallwood, "When the Klan Rode: White Terror in Reconstruction Texas," *Journal of the West*, October 1986, pp. 4–16

49. "A Splendid Oration," *Houston Daily Post*, April 22, 1893; "Minister Terrell Sworn," *Galveston Daily News*, May 5, 1893; Wooten, ed., *A Comprehensive History of Texas*, vol. II, pp. 296–309; Gould, *Terrell*, pp. 128–35.

Chapter 4

1. Rose Scrapbook, A. J. Rose Papers, Briscoe Library, Austin. See also Ralph Smith, "The Farmer's Alliance in Texas, 1875–1900: A Revolt against Bourbon and Bourgeois Democracy," *SWHQ*, January 1945, pp. 346–69.

2. A. C. True, "The Work of the Office of Experiment Stations," Proceedings of the Eighth Annual Association of American Agricultural Colleges and Experiment Stations, Washington, DC: November 13–15, 1894, pp. 39–42; Irvin May, "The Origins and Development of the Texas Agricultural Experiment Station, 1888–1892," *Panhandle-Plains Historical Review*, January 1976, pp. 55–79; R. L. Hunt, *A History of Farmer Movements in the Southwest, 1873–1925*, College Station: 1934, pp. 12–14; Geiger, *The American College in the Nineteenth Century*, pp. 149, 154; Gammel, *Laws of Texas*, vol. IX, p. 910; "For Industrial Education," *Galveston Daily News*, February 27, 1897; Dethloff, *Centennial History*, vol. I, p. 219. See also Henry Dethloff, "Mark Francis and Veterinary Medicine in Texas, 1880–1936," *Journal of the West*, January 1988, pp. 40–46, and Alfred C. True, *A History of Agricultural Education in the United States, 1785–1925*, Washington, DC: US Government Printing Office, 1929, pp. 23–94.

3. "The State Press: The Brazos Pilot," *Galveston Daily News*, March 4, 1893. See also "The AM College Problem," *Galveston Daily News*, June 28, 1993; "Amalgamation of the University and the A. & M. College," *Bryan Enterprise*, ca. 1883, seen in L. L. McInnis Scrapbook, Cushing Library.

4. "Strangers in Town," *New Orleans Times-Picayune*, February 14, 1893; "Public Domain: An Attack Likely," *Galveston Daily News*, February 22, 1893; "The Attack Opened," *Galveston Daily News*, February 25, 1893; "After the A. and M.," *Galveston Daily News*, March 5, 1893; "Texans Abroad," *Dallas Morning News*, February 27, 1893.

5. US Department of Agriculture, *Report of the Secretary of Agriculture—1893*, Washington, DC: US Government Printing Office, 1894, pp. 450–64. Texas Agricultural Experiment Station, *Bulletin*, College Station: A&M College, 1890–93, "Cattle Interests," bul. no. 10, pp. 5–31; "Screw Worm," bul. no. 12, pp. 21–24; "Feeding Hogs," bul. no. 21, pp. 195–208; "Alfalfa Root Rot," bul. no. 22, pp. 211–15; "The Cattle Tick," bul. no. 24, pp. 237–56; "Cost of Cotton Production," bul. no. 26, pp. 291–308; George T. Jester, "Cotton Growth in Texas," *Galveston Daily News*, January 5, 1888. See also Robert L. Haney, *Milestones: Marking Ten Decades of Research*, College Station: Texas Agricultural Experiment Station, 1989, pp. 1–6.

6. Report of the Joint Committee of State Institutions of Learning, *Texas House Journal*, 23rd Leg., March 4, 1893, pp. 526–30.

7. Report of the Joint Committee of State Institutions of Learning, *Texas House Journal*, 23rd Leg., March 4, 1893, pp. 528–30. See also "College at Bryan," *Dallas Morning News*, December 16, 1894, and "The A. and M. College," *Dallas Morning News*, December 5, 1895.

8. "After Gen. Ross," *Galveston Daily News*, March 5, 1893; "A&M College," *Galveston Daily News*, March 27, 1893. Note the following costs of A&M College housing in 1893–94: president's home, $4,500; five brick residences, $15,000; six frame cottages, $10,000; shop foreman's residence, $1,000; and landscape manger's cottage, $500. Interview with Bill Page, July 22, 2016. And despite the addition of new campus dwellings, the new housing was insufficient, with two families sharing the same residence.

9. "Ross Replies to Critics," *Galveston Daily News*, March 1, 1893. Note: Each year, a notice of expenses at the A&M College of Texas was printed "for the entire session except clothing, $140.00 and no tuition and no charge for text books," *The Olio*, 1895, p. 141.

10. Ross to Holmes, April 5, 1893; "After Gen. Ross," and "After the A. and M.," *Galveston Daily News*, March 5, 1893; "Reply of the Directors," *Galveston Daily News*, March 25, 1893; "The Legislative Committee Replies to the Directors," *Galveston Daily News*, April 30, 1893; "A. & M. College of Texas," *Galveston Daily News*, May 22, 1893.

11. Minutes of the Board of Directors, July 1893; "Major Vroom's Report [May 3, 1893]," *Battalion*, October 15, 1893.

12. "The A. and M. Affairs," *Galveston Daily News*, March 15, 1893.

13. "That A. and M. Report," *Galveston Daily News*, March 19, 1893, and "Reply of the Directors," *Galveston Daily News*, March 25, 1893; Dethloff, *Centennial History*, vol. I, pp. 164–67; "Student Labor," *A&M Catalog, 1897–98*, p. 29. Note: Student labor could be paid at the maximum rate of 12.2 cents per hour.

14. "College Station," *Dallas Morning News*, March 7, 1892; "College Station Society," *Galveston Daily News*, March 7, 1892; "Ladies of the A. and M. College,"

Galveston Daily News, March 14, 1892; "The Fat Man Club," *Battalion*, October 15, 1893; "A. and M. College," *Galveston Daily News*, October 6, 1893; *The Olio*, 1895, p. 113. See also Bill Page, ed., "Bands, Orchestras and Similar Groups at the A and M College of Texas, 1876–1899," Cushing Archives, March 20, 2018.

15. "What Does It Mean?" *McKinney Democrat*, March 30, 1893; "Twenty-Third Legislature," *Austin Weekly Statesman*, May 11, 1893.

16. John D. Read to L. L. McInnis, March 15, 1893, McInnis Papers; *Catalogue of Texas A&M, 1891–92*, pp. 68–72.

17. Program, "Commencement Exercises of the A&M College of Texas, 4,5,6, Jun 1893," John H. O'Bar Scrapbook, Cushing. Note: Prior to the organization of a college band, the 23rd Infantry Band, USA, stationed in San Antonio, provided music for Corps of Cadets parade and commencement events.

18. "To Contractors," *Galveston Daily News*, July 9, 1893.

19. "Experiment Station: Collin County on the Move," *McKinney Democrat*, July 20, 1893; Ousley, *History of the Agricultural and Mechanical College of Texas*, pp. 60–62.

20. Wooten, ed., *A Comprehensive History of Texas*, vol. II, p. 423.

21. "Farming in Texas," *Galveston Daily News*, November 2, 1894; "Standard of Value: What a Ratio of Sixteen to One Means," *Galveston Daily News*, October 22, 1894; "Fall of Cotton," *Galveston Daily News*, November 10, 1894; "Gossip of Gotham," *Galveston Daily News*, November 18, 1894; Editorial, "Overproduction and Prices of Farm Products, *Galveston Daily News*, October 20, 1894; "Grange and Alliance," *Galveston Daily News*, May 31, 1893; U. S. D. A., *Report of the Secretary of Agriculture, 1893*, pp. 450–64; Henry C. Dethloff, "Marck Francis and Veterinary Medicine in Texas, 1880–1936," *Journal of the West*, January 1988, pp. 42–43. See also Ralph Smith, "The Farmers' Alliance in Texas, 1875–1900," *SWHQ*, January 1945, pp. 346–69, and Jester, "Cotton Growth in Texas," *Galveston Daily News*, January 5, 1888.

22. Adams, *Keepers of the Spirit*, pp. 38–57.

23. Adams, *Keepers of the Spirit*, pp. 38–57; Dethloff, Centennial History, vol. I, pp. 141, 149–52, 284. Note: On November 11, 1919, Gen. William Scott returned to the A&M Campus as the keynote speaker for the grand campus convocation commemorating the first anniversary of Armistice Day.

24. "A Day as a Cadet," *Battalion*, fall 1893. See also "The A&M College," *Galveston Daily News*, October 24, 1897.

25. "The Texas Colleges," *Galveston Daily News*, November 19, 1894. Note: From 1883 to February 1893, the daily routine was marked by the "drum" calls of veteran Maj. James R. Fisk. Following his death, Joseph Holick became the official "college bugler." As an accomplished musician, the Northgate boot maker organized a "string band of nine pieces" forerunner to the Fightin' Texas Aggie Band. See "A. & M. College," *Galveston Daily News*, September 25, 1893, and "Major James R. Fisk," *Galveston Daily News*, February 25, 1893.

26. *The Olio*, 1895.

27. "The A. and M. College," *Galveston Daily News*, September 11 and 14, 1893, and "Editorial," *Galveston Daily News*, September 16, 1893; "How They Commenced the Fall and Winter Term," *Galveston Daily News*, September 18, 1893; Eugene W. Kerr to Mrs. O. J. Kerr, October 29, 1893, Bernard Sbisa Papers, Cushing Library.

28. "Improvements at A. and M. C." *Battalion*, October 1, 1893.

29. L. S. Ross to Major Holmes, December 30, 1893, Ross Papers; B. M. Walker, "Henry Hill Harrington," *Journal of Mississippi History*, July 1940, pp. 156–58; "Wooten Wells, Tex.," *Austin Daily Statesman*, August 4, 1893; Janet M. Valenza, *The Waters in Texas*, Austin: University of Texas Press, 2000, pp. 105–8, 208–9.

30. *The Olio*, 1895, p. 97; *Galveston Daily News*, February 25 and 27, 1893; "Czech Shoemaker Formed Famed Texas Aggie Band," *Battalion*, February 16, 1866; Adams, *Keepers of the Spirit*, p. 25.

31. *The Olio*, 1895, pp. 130–31; "San Jacinto Day Celebrated," clipping in "Scrapbook—Programs and Social Events, 1894–1917," Cushing Archives.

32. *Battalion*, December 1893.

33. "The A. and M. College," *Dallas Morning News*, December 5, 1894; "College at Bryan," December 1893, December 16, 1894; *Texas A&M Catalog, 1894–95*, p. 13.

34. "Consolidation of the Grange and the Alliance Effected," *Galveston Daily News*, May 29, 1893; "The Farmers Alliance," *Galveston Daily News*, July 2, 1890; "Gov. Hogg as a Populist," *Galveston Daily News*, September 16, 1893; "Talking about Texas," *Galveston Daily News*, September 14, 1893.

35. L. S. Ross to Major Holmes, August 5, 1893, and December 30, 1893; Seymour, *Intimate Papers of Coronel House*, pp. 30–36. See also "The Papers of the State," *Waco Evening News*, March 7, 1894, and "The Slick Clarkies," *Texas Farmer*, May 13, 1893.

36. "On the Eve of Battle," *Austin Daily Statesman*, August 14, 1894; and "Culberson," *Austin Daily Statesman*, August 17, 1894; "As to Texas' Vote," *Dallas Morning Times*, November 7, 1894; "Railway Commission," *Dallas Morning Times*, November 9, 1894, and May 22, 1894; *Austin Statesman*, May 14, 1894; "Culberson's Appointments," *Dallas Morning News*, December 17, 1894; Arthur D. Smith, *The Real Colonel House*, New York: George H. Doran Co., 1918, pp. 47–54; Cotner, *Hogg*, pp. 394–400, 413–17; Woodward, *Origins of the New South*, p. 289; Buenger, *The Path to a Modern South*, p. 28; Barr, *Reconstruction to Reform*, pp. 154–58. See also Arthur S. Link, "The Progressive Movement in the South, 1870–1914," *North Carolina History Review*, April 1946, p. 177. Note: With the possible addition of Ross to the commission, governor-elect Culberson would replace L. L. Foster and retain the appointments of sitting commissioners former US senator John H. Reagan and former lieutenant governor Leonidas

Jefferson Storey. Foster was rumored in 1895 to be appointed to follow Ross as president of A&M, a position he would eventually fill, by the appointment of the A&M College Board, in July 1898 following the death of Sul Ross.

37. "Gov. Ross' Appointment," *Dallas Morning News*, December 17, 1894; J. D. Read to L. L. McInnis, January 29, 1895, in Cofer, *Second Five Administrations*, p. 66; "Referring to the Appointment of Gov. Ross" (with comments from the *Austin Statesman* and *Galveston Tribune*), *Dallas Morning News*, December 21, 1894; C. C. Todd, "Valedictory Address," *Battalion*, June 1897, p. 10.

38. "Want Ross Where He Is," *Dallas Morning News*, December 21, 1894; "Gov. Ross' New Year," *Galveston Daily News*, January 2, 1895, and "The Commission-ership," *Galveston Daily News*, January 4, 1895; "An Open Letter from Colonel George P. Finlay to General Ross," *Galveston Daily News*, January 2, 1895; Cofer, *Second Five Administrations*, pp. 70–77. Note: Colonel Finlay, reflecting the tone of letters and telegrams received by Sul, was passionate in his appeal for Governor Ross to stay at A&M: "My dear general, pardon me, but you are the ideal, and many a mother's prayer ascends daily to the great white throne beseeching for her daring boy the example and sheltering care of one whose walk of life has been that of a good, true man." An A&M Board meeting was called by A. J. Rose for Thursday, January 3, 1895, "to consider the matter of naming a successor for Governor Ross," yet it was hastily canceled. To fill the open seat on the Railroad Commission, L. L. Foster (future president of Texas A&M) was reappointed by Governor Culberson.

Chapter 5

1. "A Day as a Cadet," *Battalion*, December 1893; Judge Charles Rogan to P. L. Downs, June 14, 1924, Cofer, *Early History*, pp. 105–6; Joe E. Abraham '00 to D. B. Cofer, April 24, 1952, *Early History*, pp. 122–23; Sterns, "College Anecdotes," Cofer, *Fragments of Early History*, pp. 90–94; Adams, "History of the Association of Former Students, 1876–1976," PhD diss., Texas A&M University, 1977, p. 22.

2. "A. and M. College of Texas," *Galveston Daily News*, April 24, 1893; Adams, *Keepers of the Spirit*, pp. 10–37; "W. A Trenckman,'78 Relates History of Early A. & M. Days," *Texas Aggie*, March 1995, p. 24, and "Early Days of A&M Recalled by Judge Rogan," *Texas Aggie*, November 24, 1924, pp. 1–2; "Professors at the Bat," *Galveston Daily News*, April 18, 1892; *Rules and Regulations of the Agricultural and Mechanical College of Texas, 1876*, pp. 1–28; Ousley, *History of the A&M College*, pp. 45–46. See also Dethloff, *Centennial History*, vol. I, pp. 85–95, and Perry, *The Story of Texas A. and M.*, pp. 23–25, 52–72.

3. Interview with Carl Wipprecht '18, Rusk, Texas, May 28, 1975, and with Ida Wipprecht Kernodle, Bryan, January 6, 1976; F. E. Giesecke to D. B. Cofer,

December 14, 1951, F. E. Giesecke Papers, Cushing Archives; May W. Cole Diary, June 26, 1883, Cushing Archives. See also Adams, *We Are the Aggies*, pp. 15–28.

4. *Texas A&M Catalogue 1895–96*, pp. 74, 77–78, 85; E. S. Woodhead '98 to Editor of the *Texas Aggie*, November 7, 1950; Cofer, *Early History*, pp. 115–16; Adams, *We Are the Aggies*, pp. 39–51; Cofer, *Second Five Administrators*, p. 47.

5. "Intercollegiate Football: News Rules Adopted for the Better Government of the Game," *New York Times*, October 28, 1887; "Gone Football Mad," *Galveston Daily News*, October 28, 1894; John S. Watterson, *College Football: History, Spectacle, Controversy*, Baltimore: John Hopkins University Press, 2000, pp. 1–17, 32–53; Ezell, *The South Since 1865*, p. 337; "Original 'fish' Guyler Relates Old Experiences," *Texas Aggie*, May 20, 1924, p. 3. Note: R. W. Guyler, class of 1879, confirms that during the early years, all sports were "club" sports played within the Corps of Cadets and sometimes with teams from Bryan or Navasota.

6. "'Bob' Littlejohn First A&M Coach," *Fort Worth Star Telegram*, November 17, 1909; "Fame of Local Players," *Galveston Daily News*, May 31, 1891; Texas A&M Former Student Directory, 1938, p. 112. Note the A&M College Farmers won the game 14–8 and the following week defeated Texas, 5–0, to give first-year coach Charlie B. Moran a 7–0–1 season record in 1909. During Moran's first three seasons at A&M, he compiled a record of 29–3–1, amassing a total of 567 points scored versus 55 by the opposition. He completed his six-year career at A&M with a record of 38–8–4. See also *Directory of Former Students*, College Station, Texas, September 1949, p. 260.

7. Interview with David Chapman, June 3, 2014.

8. "The A. and M. College," *Galveston Daily News*, February 27, 1893; "Football," *Battalion*, November 1, 1893; Billy Matthews, "Football," *Battalion*, December 1893, p. 13.

9. "John Carson," *Galveston Daily News*, February 27, 1893; "A. and M. College," *Galveston Daily News*, January 29, 1894; "Football Club," *Battalion*, October 15, 1893, and November 1, 1893; "Football Club," *Battalion*, December 1894.

10. "Football Today," *Austin American Statesman*, October 20, 1894; Wilbur Evans and H. B. Elroy, *The Twelfth Man: A Story of Texas A&M Football*, Huntsville: Strode Publishers, 1974, pp. 23–27; Cofer, *Fragments of Early History*, pp. 91–93.

11. "Footfall: First Games of the Season at Hyde Park," *Austin American Statesman*, October 18, 1894; *The Olio*, 1895, pp. 114–15; "Galveston—A. and M. Game," *Dallas Morning News*, November 30, 1894. Note: Arthur Watt '95 was a veteran of WWI and retired with the rank of colonel.

12. Josh Sterns '99, "College Anecdotes"; Cofer, *Fragments of Early History*, p. 93.

13. "Visiting College Station," *Galveston Daily News*, November 29, 1894; "Was Football Day," *Galveston Daily News*, November 30, 1894; "As to Football,"

Galveston Daily News, December 4, 1894; "The College Yell," *Battalion*, October 1896, and *Battalion*, December 1897, p. 33; J. E. Stubbs, "Report of the Section on College Work," Proceedings of the 10th Annual Convention of the Association of American Agricultural Colleges and Experiment Stations, Washington, DC, November 10–12, 1896, p. 17.

14. "Sporting Topics," *Galveston Daily News*, November 4, 1894; "College Yell," *Battalion*, October 1896; "Hi-Ki!," *Battalion*, December 1897; "A Word as to Football," *Galveston Daily News*, October 26, 1897.

15. "Football Trip," *Battalion*, December 1897, p. 30; Sam M. McMillian '09, "Reminiscences," Cofer, *Fragments of Early History*, p. 88

16. "A&MC Gridiron," *Battalion*, November 1897; *Longhorn*, 1911. Note: Rivalry football games by the mid-1890 were scheduled nationwide, many on Thanksgiving. These games were so important. The first-ever indoor football game, featuring Michigan versus Chicago University, was played in the Chicago Coliseum, where the wood floors were removed and replaced by "clay and then rolled" flat. "Indoor Football," *Galveston Daily News*, November 25, 1986.

17. Adams, *We Are the Aggies*, pp. 8–13; Sam A. McMillian '09 to David B. Cofer, January 22, 1953, seen in Cofer, *Fragments of Early History*, p. 88.

18. Edward B. Cushing to All-Ex-Cadets, July 1, 1880, and "Annual Reunion of the Association of Ex-Cadets Programme," June 26, 1883, seen in Frederick E. Giesecke Papers, Cushing Archives; Cofer, *Early History*, pp. 84–99, 130–31; *The Texas Aggie*, December 15, 1926; Adams, *We Are the Aggies*, pp. 14–48. See also *Catalogue of the A and M College, 1891–2*, pp. 59–63, with a roster of A&M ex-cadets from 1878 to 1891.

19. L. S. Ross letter, April 26, 1895, Mitchell Papers, and L. S. Ross letter, April 12, 1897, TAMU Archivist Collection, in Cushing Archives. The second letter of introduction was for A. J. Burleson '97:

I take special pleasure in commending Mr. A. J. Burleson, a citizen of Texas to my friends in Mexico, as a gentlemen of estimable character and reputable standing in the community in which he resides. He visits Mexico on a mission of business and pleasure, and will duly appreciate such kindly courtesies as may be extended him. Any consideration shown him will be likewise held in grateful remembrance by the writer hereof.

Very respectfully L. S. Ross

20. L. S. Ross letter, April 26, 1895, Mitchell Papers.

21. Constitution of the Alumni Association of the A. and M. College of

Texas, 1888, and Giesecke to D. B. Cofer, December 11, 1951, Giesecke Papers; Interview with Ida Wipprecht Kernodle, January 6, 1976; Minutes of the A&M Board of Directors, June 30, 1896; *Battalion*, January and June 1897; Adams, "History of the Association of Former Students," PhD diss., pp. 43–67.

22. "A. and M. College," *Galveston Daily News*, June 6, 1894; Sample "Sick List," A&M College, A. C. Gillespie, MD, Surgeons Office, October 19, 1897, and November 27, 1897, "Scrapbook: Programs and Social Events," Cushing Archives. See also "Cadets Call the Committee Down on the Charges against the Surgeon," *Galveston Daily News*, March 19, 1893; "A. & M. College of Texas," *Galveston Daily News*, May 15, 1893; and "A. & M. College of Texas," *Galveston Daily News*, May 29, 1893, noted "out of an average [campus] population of 350 there have been but five deaths within the past ten years, a minimum rate of mortality that can be surpassed by no other place in the state."

23. "Scrapbook: Programs and Social Events, 1894–1917," Cushing Library; "A. & M. College," *Galveston Daily News*, March 14, 1892, and May 6, 1895; "A. and M. Exercises," *Galveston Daily News*, June 10, 1895, and "Commencement Days," *Galveston Daily News*, June 11, 1895. See also Perry, *The Story of Texas A. and M.*, pp. 75–77, and "Jesse Cable Morse Papers," compiled by Bill Page, June 16, 2016. See also for an overview of women at Texas A&M, Heidi Ann Knippa, "Salvation of a University: The Admission of Women to Texas A&M," MA thesis, University of Texas, Austin, May 1995, and Tommy DeFrank's five-part series on "The History of Coeducation at Texas A&M," *Battalion*, February 15–21, 1966.

24. "Higher Female Education," *Galveston Daily News*, September 17, 1877; "The A. and M. College," *Galveston Daily News*, June 28, 1878; "Higher Education," *Columbus* [Georgia] *Daily Enquirer-Sun*, March 13, 1878; Barbara Solomon, *In the Company of Educated Women: A History of Women and Higher Education in America*, New Haven: Yale University Press, 1985, p. 44. See also *National* [*New England*] *Journal of Education*, May 29, 1879, p. 345. See also Charles F. Smith, "Southern Colleges and Schools," *Atlantic Monthly*, October 1884, pp. 542–57.

25. "Methods of Education Discussed," *New York Times*, August 1, 1879; "National Educators in Congress," *National Journal of Education*, August 14, 1879, pp. 66–67; "State Press," *Galveston Daily News*, September 28, 1883; Smith, "Southern Colleges and Schools," *Atlantic Monthly*, October 1884, p. 544.

26. "College Station Society," *Galveston Daily News*, May 7, 1892; Wedding announcement, Florine Ross and H. H. Harrington, August 10, 1892, H. H. Harrington Papers, Cushing Archives; "Bryan," *Houston Daily Post*, December 31, 1893; Crawford, *One Hundred Years of Engineering at Texas A&M*, pp. 28–29.

27. *Bryan Daily Eagle*, April 2, 1897; Gould, *Terrell*, pp. 79–81; "Waco Female College," *Galveston Daily News*, March 6, 1893; "The A. and M. Commencement," *Galveston Daily News*, June 7, 1892; Benedict, *Source Book*, p. 248; "Intended for

All," College Station, Cushing Library, 2002, pp. 5–12; Sophie Hutson Rollins to Mrs. J. H. Binney, January 29, 1951, seen in Cofer, *Early History*, pp. 118–20. Note: Institutes in Texas for co-education in the 1890s included Sacred Heart Academy, Texas Medical School, Ursuline Convent, and St. Mary's University in Galveston; Waco Female College and Baylor in Waco; Add-Ran University in Thorp Springs (later converted to TCU in Fort Worth); St. Edwards University, St. Mary's Academy, and the University of Texas in Austin; North Texas Female College and Austin College in Sherman; Southwestern University in Georgetown; Sam Houston Normal College in Huntsville; Prairie View Normal in Hempstead; Mary Nash College and Oak Cliff College in Dallas; Trinity University in Tehuacana; Grayson College in Whitewright; Texas Presbyterian University in Taylor, Williams County; Alexander Institute in Jacksonville; Weatherford College in Weatherford; Coronel Institute in San Marcos; and Thomas Arnold Institute in Salado.

28. Sophie Hutson Rollins to J. H. Binney, June 29, 1951, seen in Cofer, *Early History*, p. 118–20; "Texas A. and M. College," *Galveston Daily News*, December 3 and 4, 1893; "Is to Be a Household Engineer," *Houston Daily Post*, September 21, 1913; Bernard Sbisa Papers, Cushing; Crawford, *Engineering at Texas A&M*, pp. 28–30; Dethloff, *Centennial History*, vol. I, pp. 173–75. Note: The brothers of Bessie, Rita, and the Hutson girls all attended the A&M College.

29. *The Olio*, 1895, pp. 8–9, 12, 81; "A. and M. College," *Galveston Daily News*, February 17, 1896; "Commencement Exercises," *Battalion*, June 1896, p. 61; *Longhorn*, 1903, pp. 9–10; "Colonel C. C. Todd Assumes Duties as Commandant at A. and M," *Bryan Eagle*, January 3, 1824; Minutes of the Board of Directors, September 23, 1933, vol. IV, p. 248; *Mrs. W. E Neely, et al. v. The Board of Directors of the Agricultural and Mechanical College of Texas et al.*, no. 12,302, District Court of Brazos County, October 6, 1933, seen in Women at A&M: Todd Brief and Charles C. Todd Papers, Cushing Library. Note: In the response from the Texas AG James V. Allred, "The statutes are absolutely silent in so far as A. & M. College is concerned as to whether it shall be co-educational institution or not."

30. "An Industrial School for Girls," *Texas Farm and Ranch*, June 13, 1896; H. and T. C. Railroad: The A. and M. College," *Galveston Daily News*, March 22, 1896; "North Texas Female College," *Galveston Daily News*, November 16, 1896. Note: President Ross had increased the total valuation of the college by more than 400 percent in five years. The largest asset was Old Main, at $100,000; the 2,416-acre campus was valued at $16,912—or $7.00 per acre.

31. "Woman's Council," *Dallas Morning News*, October 17, 1896; "To Help the Girls," *Dallas Morning News*, January 19, 1897; "A Matter of Justice," *Fort Worth Morning Register*, January 22, 1897; "Dr. Ellen Lawson Dabbs," *Fort Worth Morning Register*, February 4, 1897; "Could Admit Girls," *Fort Worth Morning Register*, February 7, 1897; "Work for Girls," *Fort Worth Morning Register*, February 6, 1897;

"Girls' Industrial Education," *Bryan Eagle*, June 6, 1899; "Reasons for Locating the Girls' Industrial School at the A. &. M. College," ca. 1899, Women at A&M Papers, Cushing Library; "Ellen L. Dabbs," *Handbook of Texas*, vol. 2, p. 467.

32. "Governor Hogg's Portrait," *Galveston Daily News*, April 13, 1895; Cotner, *James S. Hogg*, pp. 408–60.

33. "State Agricultural and Mechanical College of Texas," promotion notice, College Station, ca. fall 1894, Cushing Library; "The Agricultural and Mechanical College," *Galveston Daily News*, October 24, 1897.

34. "Second Lieut. B. C. Morse," *San Antonio Daily Light*, September 30, 1890; "Army Orders," *Dallas Morning News*, August 7, 1894; "The A. and M. College," *Dallas Morning News*, December 5, 1894; "From General Ross," *The Daily Hesperian* (Gainesville), June 27, 1895; *A&M College Catalogue*, 1894–95; Minutes of the Board of Directors, June 2, 1894, vol. I, p. 164.

35. "The State A. & M. College," *Fort Worth Gazette*, March 20, 1895; "The A. & M. College," *Galveston Morning News*, June 9, 1895; "Commencement Days," *Dallas Morning News*, June 14 and 15, 1895; "College at Bryan," *Dallas Morning News*, December 16, 1894; "Camels Used to Roam Texas—Science's Storehouse," *Dallas Morning News*, June 4, 1939; "History of Vanished Life Told in College Museum," *TAMC System News*, April 1950; "Fossils Found under Museum after 30 Years," *Battalion*, April 16, 1975; *Texas A&M Catalogue*, 1895–86, p. 74; Dethloff, *The Pictorial History of Texas A&M*, p. 77. Note: The name assigned to the mummy was ANH HR H3CJP, and the hieroglyphic inscription accompanying the mummy asked the gods to provide the deceased with food, drink, and clothing "forever and ever." The mummy was later transferred to the Houston Museum of Natural History for safekeeping.

Chapter 6

1. "Bryan: Gov. L. S. Ross," *Dallas Morning News*, January 4, 1897; "A&M College Notes," *Galveston Daily News*, June 18, 1897. See also Bill Page, ed., "L. S. Ross and Hunting," Cushing Archives, February 9, 2019. Note: The outdoors and "a camp hunt," with good-natured comradery with family and friends, seem to be Ross's only recreation and pastime. As soon as commencement was concluded in June 1897, he departed to hunt and fish. And lest we underestimate the value of a hunter's dogs, note that the following appeared in the *Bryan Eagle* on August 29, 1895: "Ex-Gov. Sul Ross was in the western part of the county [Brazos] last week on a camp hunt when four of his fine dogs were poisoned, and of course died. We learned that the 'Little Cavalryman' is very indignant and will exert himself to bring the guilty parties to justice. The dogs were worth $100 each.—Liberty Vindicator." (Note that $100 in 1895 is valued at more than $2,500 today.)

2. "For Co-Education," *Bryan Daily Eagle*, March 28, 1897; "Obey the Plat-

form," *Fort Worth Morning Register*, January 31, 1897; "Could Admit Girls," *Fort Worth Morning Register*, February 7, 1897. See also "Girls' Industrial Education," *Bryan Daily Eagle*, June 8, 1899.

3. "Reasons for Locating the Girls' Industrial School at the A. & M. College," Women at Texas A&M Papers, Cushing.

4. "H. and T. C. Railroad: Bonnie Bryan of Brazos," *Galveston Daily News*, March 16, 1896; "The A. and M. College," *Galveston Daily News*, March 22, 1896.

5. *Journal of the House of the Texas 25th Legislature*, March 23, 1897, p. 691; "The Agricultural and Mechanical College," *Galveston Daily News*, February 24, 1897; reprinted into "We Need More Men," *Southern Mercury*, March 4, 1897.

6. Merle M. Duncan, "The Death of Senator Coke," *SWHQ*, January 1962, pp. 385–403.

7. Minutes of the Board of Directors, June 6 and 30, 1896; "The Texas Vote," *Galveston Daily News*, November 17, 1896; "The Maintenance of the University of Texas," *Austin Daily Statesman*, January 9, 1897. Note: The good relationships between Ross and Governor Culberson continued in spite of the fact that in the election, Brazos County voted 1,974 for Culberson and 1,924 for his opponent J. C. Kearly.

8. Minutes of the Texas A&M Board of Directors, July 1, 1897; "Recognition at Last," *Battalion*, January 1897.

9. "The 25th Legislature," *Austin Daily Statesmen*, January 15, 1897; "For Co-Education," *Bryan Daily Eagle*, March 28, 1897.

10. Texas Legislative Visit and Report, June 1897.

11. "State Schools Methods," *Dallas Morning News*, June 27, 1897; "Visit to Prairie View," *Houston Post*, March 16, 1987; "Ross Resolution," *Houston Daily Post*, January 8, 1898.

12. "A. And M. Directors," *Austin Daily Statesman*, July 4, 1897: US Census, 1900, Vol. 1 and Supplement for Texas, p. 667.

13. Minutes of the Texas A&M Board, July 1, 1897.

14. "The Agricultural and Mechanical College," *Galveston Daily News*, October 24, 1897.

15. "The Fever Situation," *Galveston Daily News*, October 26, 1897, and "The Fever Ravages," *Galveston Daily News*, October 27, 1897, and "Yellow Fever and Catarrh," *Galveston Daily News*, October 31, 1897.

16. "Yellow Fever and Dengue," *Galveston Daily News*, October 28, 1897; "Yellow Fever and Quarantine" *Galveston Daily News*, October 26, 1897; "The Agricultural and Mechanical College," *Galveston Daily News*, October 24, 1897; "Death of a Cadet at Bryan," *Galveston Daily News*, October 27, 1897; "No Trains Stop" and "Card from the Mayor," *Bryan Daily Eagle*, October 2, 1897. See also John Adams, *Over There in the Air*, College Station: Texas A&M University Press, 2019, pp. 49–53.

17. "Academy of Science," *Bryan Daily Eagle*, December 24, 1897.

18. Clarke, "Life of Sul Ross," Ross Family Papers, Baylor, 130–32; *Bryan Daily Eagle*, December 26, 1897; "Memorial Services in Honor of President Lawrence Sullivan Ross, January 15 and 16, 1898, A. & M. College of Texas," seen in Cushing Archives. Note: Some accounts incorrectly indicate the hunt was on the Trinity River, "Governor Ross Dead," *Abilene Reporter*, January 7, 1898.

19. "Gov. Ross Dead," *Bryan Daily Eagle*, January 4, 1898; Benner, *Sul Ross*, pp. 231–32; "Governor Ross' Last Words," *Dallas Morning News*, January 5, 1898; Adams, *Keepers of the Spirit*, p. 53; "The Funeral Cortege," *Caldwell News-Chronicle*, January 7, 1898; "A Famous Texas Indian Fighter," *San Francisco Chronicle*, January 30, 1898. Note: There was no probate of the L. S. Ross estate and no recorded death certificate; none was required by Texas law until 1903; confirmed by J. A. Harwell, County Clerk, McLennan County, to author, "Probate Record Search," August 21, 2014. The Caldwell, Texas, newspaper reported, "The hounds, spaniels, and bird dogs hung around the house all during the illness of their master and just after he died they gathered in a group in the yard and uttered a mournful howl."

20. J. E. Abrahams to Brooks Cofer, April 30, 1952, seen in *Second Five Administrations*, pp. 73–74; "Conveyed to Waco," *Bryan Daily Eagle*, January 5, 1898; "Grief for Ross: The Funeral Train," *Dallas Morning News*, January 5, 1898. Note: The committee on funeral arrangements was composed of Professors Puryear, Soule, Philpott, Colonel Harrison, and Hooper. Honorary escorts were Professors Philpott, Giesecke, and Pittuck. The committee for the campus memorial service for Sunday, January 16, was composed of Dr. Bittle and Professors Banks, Price, Hutson, Connell, and Pittuck; "Funeral Expenses of Pres. L. S. Ross," Minutes of the A&M Board of Directors, January 17, 1898.

21. "The Ross Funeral," *Bryan Daily Eagle*, January 6, 7, 1898; "Memorial Number," *Battalion*, January 1898; Adams, *We Are the Aggies*, pp. 44–45; "Memorial Service," *Galveston Daily News*, January 15, 1898; "A Tribute to Gen. Ross," *Dallas Morning News*, January 17, 1898; "Sul Ross Monument," *Dallas Morning News*, May 22, 1898.

22. Bill Minutaglio, *A Single Star and Bloody Knuckles: A History of Politics and Race in Texas*, Austin: University of Texas Press, 2021, p. 42.

23. Charles L. Ponce de Leon, *Self Exposure: Human Interest Journalism and the Emergence of Celebrity in America, 1890–1940*, Chapel Hill: University of North Carolina Press, 2002, pp. 18–64; John A. Corry, *1898: Prelude to a Century*, New York: John A. Corry, 1998, pp. 13–31; Candice Millard, *Hero of the Empire: The Boer War, a Daring Escape and the Making of Winston Churchill*, New York: Doubleday, 2016, pp. 313–18; Stephen Kinser, *The True Flag: Theodore Roosevelt, Mark Twain, and the Birth of American Empire*, New York: Henry Holt and Company, 2017, pp. 2–3, 55–60; "Pompeo Coppini to Make Sul Ross Statue for

A. & M." Dallas Morning News, December 22, 1917; "Unveiling Seen by Large Crowd," *The Reveille*, May 6, 1919. Note: The stories and media coverage of Sul Ross from his days on the frontier to the interviewing of incoming cadets remained popular with Texans, and the newspapers were eager to publish stories, such as the item that first appeared in the *Austin Record* and was reprinted in the Jasper *Weekly News* on October 26, 1887, "Sully's First Pair of Boots":

> Captain Shapley Ross, the aged and venerable father of our distinguished governor, has been in the city for several days past, visiting "his boy." He told us a good story about Sul. He says when the aforesaid Sul was a boy of early age the youngster happened to spy a pair of red-top books—the first his eyes had ever behold. He prevailed on his father to buy him a pair. How he did strut with them new boots. That night Sul and his brother Pete slept together. Away in the night Captain Ross heard a fuss going on between Sul and Pete. On inquiring the cause Pete Hallowed out: "Papa, Sul has gone to bed with them boots on, and is just kicking my shins all to pieces." The old gentlemen, thus aroused from his slumbers, commanded the young man to pull off those boots, which he did, and quiet was again restored. He little thought then that the boy who went to bed with his first pair of boots on would ever be governor of this great state!

24. "The Death of Ex-Governor L. S. Ross," *Austin Daily Statesman*, January 5, 1898; "Bryan," *Texas Posten* (Austin), January 7, 1898; "Tribute," *Houston Daily Post*, January 25, 1898; *Battalion*, April 1, 1899. p. 5; Dethloff, *Texas Aggies Go to War*, pp. 26–27.

25. Adams, *We Are the Aggies*, pp. 44–45; "In Memory of Sul Ross," *San Antonio Express News*, May 15, 1915; "In Memory of Ex-Gov Ross," *Galveston Daily News*, January 10, 1898.

26. "In Memory of Ex-Gov. Ross," *Galveston Daily News*, January 10, 1898; "Memory of Late Gov. L. S. Ross," *Houston Daily Post*, February 8, 1898; "The College Monument," *The Little Cavalryman*, April 1, 1898; "Belated Recognition," *Houston Post*, January 6, 1918; "Soon Ready for Erection of Ross A. & M. Monument," *Bryan Daily Eagle*, October 23, 1918; "Lawrence Sullivan Ross Statue Unveiled," *Texas A&M Alumni Quarterly*, May 1919, pp. 11–12; Lester T. Potter, *Lawrence Sullivan Ross*, College Station: Association of Former Students, 1993, pp. xi–xxv, 71–74. Note: After a conflict between Hogg and the legislature over funding for the then governor's official portrait, it was noted that Ross was the only former governor of Texas who personally paid for his own portrait in the capital; "Governor Hogg's Portrait," *Galveston Daily News*, April 13, 1895.

27. Ross Papers, Baylor Archives.

Bibliography

Primary

Baylor University Texas Collection, Waco, Texas
    Elizabeth Ross Clarke Collection
    Ross Family Papers
    George Bernard Papers, with an L. S. Ross picture circa 1859
    W. M. Sleeper Memoirs of the Life of Richard Coke
Briscoe Center for American History, Austin, Texas
    A. J. Rose Papers
    Joseph Taulman Papers
    L. S. Ross Vertical File
    Lawrence Sullivan Ross Papers
    Richard Coke Scrapbook
    Robert T. Milner Papers
    Victor M. Rose Papers
    Walter Prescott Webb Papers
DRT Library at the Alamo, San Antonio, Texas
    Letters of Lawrence S. Ross Jr. to Maj. H. M. Holmes
    Mary Alice O'Dowd, "If This Table Could Talk," n.d., Ross Papers
    "Memorial to Lawrence Sullivan Ross on the Campus of the A&M
        College of Texas," A. and M. College News Service, Curtis Vinson,
        Director, June 28, 1927
    Papers of Henry M. Holmes, 1882–95
    Ross Picture File: President's House at Texas A&M and Mrs. L. S. Ross
State of Texas
    Biennial Report of the Adjutant General of Texas, 1888–1900.
    Biennial Report of the Secretary of State of the State of Texas, 1890–
        1900.
    Bill Allcorn, ed. *History of Texas Land*. Austin: n.p., 1958.
    Constitution of the State of Texas, 1876.
    John Salmon Ford, "Memoirs."

Journal of the House of Representatives on the Twentieth Legislature, Extra Session, Austin, January 18, 1886, and April 16, 1888.

Journal of the Senate of Texas on the Twenty-First Legislature, Regular Session, Austin, January 8, 1889.

Journal of the Constitutional Convention of the State of Texas: Begun and Held at the City of Austin, September 6th, 1875, n.p., Galveston, 1875.

L. L. Foster, Commissioner. "Forgotten Texas Census, 1887–88." Austin: TSHA, n.d.

L. S. Ross. *Governor's Message.* Austin: 1889.

Messages of the Governor, Coke to Ross. Education. January 1889.

Office of the Governor. *Executive Record Book.* December 21, 1859, to December 1861.

Raines, C. W. "Speeches and State Papers of James Stephen Hogg," Austin: The State Printing Company, 1905.

Report of the Commissioner of the General Land Office of Texas, 1930. Austin: A. C. Baldwin and Sons, 1930, p. 5.

Report of the Secretary of State for the State of Texas, 1886–1900.

Texas General Land Office. Commissioner Charles Rogan. *Special Report of the General Land Office, 1899.* Austin: 1899.

Texas A&M University, Cushing Archives and Evans Library

 A&M Catalogue, College Station, 1885–98.

 Alumni Quarterly, A&M College, February 1918, May 1919.

 Battalion, 1893–1902.

 Bernard Sbisa Papers.

 Bessie Ross Clarke. Unpublished recollections of Shapley Prince Ross and Lawrence Sullivan Ross, transcript, n.p., n.d.; original at Baylor University.

 C. B. Campbell. "My Recollections of the College." n.d.

 College Journal, 1889–95, College Station.

 "The College Monument." *The Little Cavalryman.* College Station, April 1, 1898.

 Edward B. Cushing Papers.

 Ernest Langford. "Here We'll Build the College." College Station, n.d.

 Ernest Langford. "Getting the College Under Way." College Station: Texas A&M University Library, 1970.

 Farmers Improvement Society: Constitution and Bi-laws.

 Frederick E. Giesecke Papers.

 George Pfeuffer Papers.

 Governor L. S. Ross. "An Address to the Texas Academy of Science," *Transactions of the Texas Academy of Science for 1898*, vol. II, no. 2. Austin: Publication Society, 1899.

Henry Hill Harrington Papers.

James Reid Cole Papers.

John A. Craig, Secretary. "Campus Map." n.p., ca. 1904.

L. S. Ross. *Education of the Colored Race*. n.p., ca. 1889.

Lawrence Sullivan Ross Papers.

Louis L. McInnis Papers and Scrapbook.

Lucius Holmon Papers.

"Memorial Services in Honor of President Lawrence Sullivan Ross."
    College Station: A and M College of Texas, January 15 and 16, 1898.

Minutes of the Association of Former Students of Texas A&M University, 1885–1902.

Minutes of the Board of Directors of the A&M College of Texas, 1876–1902.

Norman G. Kittrell. Address Delivered at the Unveiling of the Monument of General Lawrence Sullivan Ross, College Station, May 4, 1919.

The Olio, College Station, 1895.

Presidential Papers of Grover Cleveland, 1887, microfilm.

Proceedings of the Annual Session of the Texas State Grange, 1877, 1885, 1886, 1893.

Robert Smith Correspondence Copy Book, Box 1, 1894–1900.

Scrapbook of Florine Ross, daughter of Gov. L. S. Ross.

Texas A&M Football Papers, Unknown–1914, Box 1a.

Texas Agricultural Experiment Station. *Bulletin*. College Station: A&M College, 1890–1893.

Thomas S. Gathright Papers.

W. P. Ratchford Collection.

William R. Cavitt Family Papers.

Texas Ranger Museum, Waco, Texas.

L. S. Ross Biography.

Texas Ranger Picture File.

Texas State Archives, Austin

Governor's Papers: Sam Houston, Edward Clark, Lawrence S. Ross, Stephen Hogg.

Texas Indian Affairs Papers, 1854–60.

Washington D. Miller Papers.

United Confederate Veterans

Confederate Veteran, 1893–1912.

Minutes of the Annual Meetings and Reunions of the United Confederate Veterans, 1891–1915.

"Proceedings of the Convention for the Organization and Adoption of the Constitution of the United Confederate Veterans, June 10, 1889." New Orleans: Hopkins Printing, 1891.

University of North Carolina: Round Special Collections Library, Chapel
  Hill, NC
    Charles Hutson Papers, 1888–1900.
US Bureau of Education. *Circular of Info No.2.* Washington, DC, 1903, pp.
  260–312, 317.
US Congress, House. *House Executive Documents*, 35 Congress, 2nd session.
  Washington, DC, 1859.
US Department of Agriculture. *Yearbook of Agriculture, 1901 thru 1910.*
  Washington, DC: US Government Printing Office.
———. *Report of the Secretary of Agriculture, 1893.* Washington, DC: US
  Government Printing Office, 1894.
———. *Farmers' Bulletin.* Washington, DC, 1898.
US Senate. Secretary of Agriculture. "The Western Range." 74 Congress, 2nd
  session, Senate Doc. no. 199. Washington, DC: US Government Printing
  Office, 1936, pp. 230–34.
US War Department. *The War of the Rebellion: A Compilation of the Official
  Records of the Union and Confederate Armies.* 128 vols. Washington,
  DC, 1880–1901.

Interviews

A. J. Smith '08
E. E. McQuillen '22
Ernest Langford '13
James V. "Pinky" Wilson '20
Joe Utay '08
Lawrence Sullivan Ross Clarke '21
Mary and Sophie Hutson '03

Newspapers and Periodicals

Austin Capitaltion, 1892–93
Austin Statesman, 1885–1900
Austin Weekly Democratic Statesman, 1875
Brazos Pilot (Bryan), 1893–94
Bryan Daily and Weekly Eagle, 1875–1900
Caldwell (Texas) *News-Chronicle*, 1898
College Station *Battalion*, 1894–1922
Columbus (Georgia) *Daily Enquirer-Sun*, 1878
Confederate Veterans, 1893–1915
Daily Hesperian (Gainesville), 1895

Dallas Herald, 1861–62
Dallas Morning News, 1886–1900
Dallas Southern Mercury, 1890–1900
Fort Worth Gazette, 1895
Fort Worth Morning Register, 1897–98
Galveston Daily News, 1875–1900
Galveston Tribune, 1894–95
Houston Post, 1885–1900
New York Times, 1886–1900
San Antonio Daily Light, 1890
San Antonio Express, 1885–1900
San Francisco Chronicle, 1898
Texas A&M System News, 1950
Texas Posten (Austin), 1898
Waco Examiner, 1878, 1885–1900
Waco Herald, 1880–1900
Waco Weekly Examiner and Patron, 1875

Books

Adams, John A., Jr. *We Are the Aggies.* College Station: Texas A&M University Press, 1979.
———. *Softly Call the Muster.* College Station: Texas A&M University Press, 1994.
———. *Keepers of the Spirit.* College Station: Texas A&M University Press, 2001.
Arnold, James R. *Jeff Davis's Own: Cavalry, Comanches, and the Battle for the Texas Frontier.* Edison, NJ: Castle Books, 2007.
Ashcroft, Allan. *Texas in the Civil War: A Resume History.* Austin: Texas Civil War Centennial Commission, 1967.
Barker, Eugene. *A School History of Texas 1874–1965.* Chicago: Row, Peterson, 1918.
Barnes, Donna A *Farmers in Rebellion: The Rise and Fall of the Southern Farmers Alliance and People's Party of Texas.* Austin: University of Texas Press, 1984.
Barnes, Lavonia J. *Early Homes of Waco and the People Who Lived in Them.* Waco: Texian Press, 1970.
Barr, Alwyn. *Reconstruction to Reform: Texas Politics, 1876–1906.* Austin: University of Texas Press, 1971.
Barron, Samuel. *The Lone Star Defenders: A Chronicle of the Third Texas Cavalry, Ross' Brigade.* New York, n.p., 1908; reprint, Waco, 1964.

Bella Starr: The Bandit Queen or the Female Jesse James. New York: Richard K. Fox Publishers, 1889; reprint Steck Company, Austin, 1960.

Bender, James M. *History of the Original Texas Grange.* n.p., ca. 1960.

Benner, Judith Ann. *Sul Ross: Soldier, Statesman, Educator.* College Station: Texas A&M University Press, 1983.

Brands, H. W. *American Colossus: The Triumph of Capitalism 1865–1900.* New York: Doubleday, 2010.

Brown, John Henry. *Indian Wars and Pioneers of Texas.* Austin: L. E. Daniel, 1880.

Brundidge, Glenna F. *The Sesquicentennial Edition Brazos County History: Rich Past—Bright Future.* Bryan, TX: Family History Foundation, 1986.

Buenger, Walter L. *The Path to a Modern South.* Austin: University of Texas Press, 2001.

Buenger, Walter L., and Walter D. Kamphoefner, eds. *Preserving German Texan Identity: Reminiscences of William A. Trenckmann, 1859–1935.* College Station: Texas A&M University Press, 2019.

Burgess, Austin F. *A Local History of the Agricultural and Mechanical College.* College Station: A&M College of Texas Press, 1915.

Buck, Solon J. *The Granger Movement.* Cambridge: n.p., 1913.

Campbell, Randolph B. *Gone to Texas: A History of the Lone Star State.* New York: Oxford University Press, 2003.

———. *Grass-Roots Reconstruction in Texas, 1865–1880.* Baton Rouge: Louisiana University Press, 1997.

Carlson, Paul. *Myth, Memory and Massacre: The Pease River Capture of Cynthia Ann Parker.* Lubbock: Texas Tech University Press, 2010.

Carter, Kathryn T. *Stagecoach Inns of Texas.* Waco: Texian Press, 1972.

Childs, William R. *The Texas Railroad Commission.* College Station: Texas A&M University Press, 2005.

Clark, George. *A Glance Backward; Or, Some Events in the Past History of My Life.* Houston: Rein & Sons, 1914.

Clayton, Bruce. *The Savage Ideal: Intolerance and Intellectual Leadership in the South, 1890–1914.* Baltimore: John Hopkins University Press, 1972.

Clement, Richard. *Books on the Frontier: Print Culture in the American West, 1763–1875.* Washington, DC: Library of Congress, 2003.

Cofer, David B. *Early History of Texas A. and M. College through Letters and Papers.* College Station: Association of Former Students, 1952.

———. *First Five Administrators of Texas A. & M. College.* College Station: Association of Former Students, 1952.

———, ed. *Fragments of Early History of the Texas A. and M. College.* College Station: Association of Former Students, 1953.

———. *Second Five Administrations of Texas A. & M. College, 1890–1905.* College Station: Association of Former Students, 1954.

Coombes, Zachariah E. *The Diary of a Frontiersman.* Newcastle, TX: 1962.

Cooper, Lewis B. *The Permanent School Fund of Texas.* Fort Worth: Texas State Teachers Association, 1934.

Coppini, Pompeo. *From Dawn to Sunset.* San Antonio: Naylor Company, 1949.

Cotner, Robert C., ed. *Addresses and State Papers of James Stephen Hogg.* Austin: University of Texas Press, 1991.

———. *James Stephen Hogg.* Austin: University of Texas Press, 1959.

Cox, Mike. *The Texas Rangers.* New York: Forge Books, 2008.

Crawford, Charles W. *One Hundred Years of Engineering at Texas A&M, 1876–1976.* College Station: privately published, 1976.

Crouch, Carrie J. *A History of Young County.* Austin: n.p., 1956.

Daniell, Lewis E. *Personnel of the Texas State Government, with Sketches of Distinguished Texans.* Austin: Press of City Printing Company, 1887.

De la Teja, ed. *Lone Star Unionism, Dissent and Resistance: Other Side of Civil War Texas,* Norman: University of Oklahoma Press, 2016.

DeShields, James T. *Cynthia Ann Parker.* St. Louis: Charles B. Woodward Co., 1888.

———. *They Sat in High Places.* San Antonio: Naylor Company, 1940.

Dethloff, Henry C. *A Centennial History of Texas A&M University 1876–1976.* College Station: Texas A&M University Press, 2 vols., 1975.

Dobie, J. Frank, ed. *Straight Texas,* vol. XIII. Dallas: Southern Methodist University Press, 1966.

———. *Cow People.* Austin: University of Texas Press, 1964.

Donalson, Barbara. *Kyle Tough: The Saga of Texas A&M's Rise to Power.* Bryan, TX: The Oaks Press, 2003.

Edy, F. *The Development of Education in Texas.* New York: MacMillan, 1925.

Elkins, John M. *Indian Fighting on the Texas Frontier.* Amarillo: Russel and Cockrell, 1935.

Evans, C. E. *The Story of Texas Schools.* Austin: The Steck Company, 1955.

Evans, Wilbur, and H. B. McElroy. *The Twelfth Man: A Story of Texas A&M Football.* Huntsville: Strode, 1974.

Exley, J. E. Powell. *Frontier Blood: The Saga of the Parker Family.* College Station: Texas A&M University Press, 2001.

———, ed. *Texas Tears and Texas Sunshine.* College Station: Texas A&M University Press, 1985.

Ezell, John S. *The South Since 1865.* New York: Macmillan, 1975.

Fehrenbach, T. R. *Lone Star: A History of Texas and Texans.* New York: Wings Books, 1968.

Ford, John S. *Rip Ford's Texas.* Austin: University of Texas Press, 1963.

Foster, Gaines M. *Ghost of the Confederacy: Defeat, the Lost Cause, and the Emergence of the New South, 1865–1913.* New York: Oxford University Press, 1987.

Gammel, H. P. N., ed. *The Laws of the State of Texas.* Austin. The Gammel Book Company, 1898.

Gantt, Fred. *The Chief Executive in Texas.* Austin: University of Texas Press, 1964.

Geiger, Roger L., ed. *The American College in the Nineteenth Century.* Nashville: Vanderbilt University Press, 2000.

George, Alexander L., and Juliette L. George. *Woodrow Wilson and Colonel House.* New York: Doner Publications, 1956, pp. 83–86.

Gould, Lewis L. *Alexander Watkins Terrell: Civil War Soldier, Texas Lawmaker, American Diplomat.* Austin: University of Texas Press, 2004.

Gwynne, S. C. *Empire of the Summer Moon.* New York: Scribner, 2010.

Hagen, William T. *Charles Goodnight: Father of the Texas Panhandle.* Norman: University of Oklahoma Press, 2011.

Haley, J. Evetts. *XIT Ranch of Texas.* Norman: University of Oklahoma Press, 1967.

Henderson, Henry M. *Texas in the Confederacy.* San Antonio: Naylor Company, 1955.

Hendrickson, Kenneth E. *The Chief Executives of Texas: From Stephen F. Austin to John B. Connally, Jr.* College Station: Texas A&M University Press, 1995.

Hodgen, Godfrey. *Woodrow Wilson's Right Hand: The Life of Colonel Edward M. House.* New Haven: Yale University Press, 2006.

Houston, David. *Eight Years with Wilson's Cabinet.* New York: Doubleday, Page & Company, 1926.

Hunt, Robert Lee. *A History of Farmer Movements in the Southwest, 1973–1925.* College Station: A. &. M. College Press, 1925.

Hunter, J. Marvin. *The Trail Drivers of Texas* [1924]. Austin: University of Texas Press, 1985.

Ivey, Darren L. *The Ranger Ideal,* vol. 1. Denton: University of North Texas Press, 2017.

Jackson, Pearl C. *Texas Governors' Wives.* Austin: E. L. Steck, 1915.

Johnson, David. *The Mason County "Hoo Doo" War, 1874–1902.* Denton: University of Texas Press, 2006.

Johnson, Pamela J. *The Corps: The Core of A&M,* 2 vols. College Station: n.p., 2005.

Johnson, Sid S. *Texans Who Wore the Gray.* Waco: Eakin Press, n.d.

Jordon, Terry G. *German Seed in Texas Soil.* Austin: University of Texas Press, 1966.

Kelly, Dayton, ed. *The Handbook of Waco and McLennan County*. Waco: Texan Press, 1972.

Kerr, Homer L., ed. *Fighting with Ross' Texas Cavalry Brigade, C. S. A.* Hillsboro: Hill Junior College Press, 1976.

Kerr, Jeffery S. *Seat of Empire: The Embattled Birth of Austin, Texas*. Lubbock: Texas Tech University Press, 2013.

King, Edward, and J. Wells Champney. *Texas: 1874*. Houston: Cordovan Press, 1974.

Kittrell, Norman G. *Governors Who Have Been, and Other Public Men of Texas*. Houston: Dealy-Abey-Elgin, 1921.

Klein, Maury. *The Life and Legend of Jay Gould*. Baltimore: John Hopkins University Press, 1986.

Lane, John J. *History of Education in Texas*. Washington, DC: US Government Printing Office, 1903.

———. *History of the University of Texas*. Austin: Henry Hutchings State Printers, 1891.

Langford, Ernest. *Remembrance of Things Past*. College Station: n.p., 1975.

Leftwich, Bill J. *The Corps at Aggieland*. Lubbock: Smoke Signal Publishing, 1976.

Lindley, Vick. *The Battalion: Seventy Years of Student Publications at the A&M College of Texas*. College Station: Student Activities Office, 1948.

McCoy, Joseph G. *Historic Sketches of the Cattle Trade of the West and Southwest*. Kansas City: Ramsey, Millett & Hudson, 1874.

McKay, Seth S., ed. *Debates in the Texas Constitutional Convention of 1875*. Austin: University of Texas Press, 1930.

———. *Making the Texas Constitution of 1876*. Philadelphia: University of Pennsylvania Press, 1924.

———. *Seven Decades of the Texas Constitution of 1876*. Lubbock: Texas Tech College Press, 1942.

Miller, E. T. *Financial History of Texas*. Austin: University of Texas Press, 1916.

Miller, Thomas L. *The Public Lands of Texas, 1519–1970*. Norman: University of Oklahoma Press, 1972.

Minutaglio, Bill. *A Single Star and Bloody Knuckles: A History of Politics and Race in Texas*. Austin: University of Texas Press, 2021.

Moneyhon, Carl. *Texas after the Civil War: The Struggle of Reconstruction*. College Station: Texas A&M University Press, 2005.

Murray, Lois S. *Baylor at Independence*. Waco: Baylor University Press, 1972, p. 230.

Neighbours, Kenneth F. *Indian Exodus Texas Affairs 1835–59*. Quanah, TX: Nortex, 1973.

Nunn, W. C. *Ten More Texans in Gray*. Hillsboro: Hillsboro Junior College Press, 1980.

Nunn, William E. *Texas under the Carpetbaggers*. Austin: University of Texas Press, 1962.

Opie, John. *The Law of the Land: Two Hundred Years of American Farm Policy*. Lincoln: University of Nebraska Press, 1994.

Ousley, Clarence. *History of the Agricultural and Mechanical College of Texas*. College Station: A&M College of Texas Press, 1935.

Perry, George S. *The Story of Texas A&M*. New York: McGraw-Hill, 1951.

Phares, Ross. *The Governors of Texas*. Gretna: Pelican Publishing, 1976.

Pickering, David, and Judy Falls. *Brush Men and Vigilantes: Civil War Dissent in Texas*. College Station: Texas A&M University Press, 2000.

Pitre, Merline. *Through Many Dangers, Tools and Snares: Black Leadership in Texas 1868–1898*. College Station: Texas A&M University Press, 2016.

Poage, W. R. *Politics—Texas Style*. Waco: Texian Press, 1974.

Potter, Lester T. *A Centennial Commemoration of Lawrence Sullivan Ross*. College Station: Association of Former Students, 1993.

Reed, S. G. *A History of the Texas Railroads*. Houston: St. Clair Publishing, 1941.

Revsine, Dave. *The Opening Kickoff: The Tumultuous Birth of a Football Nation*. New York: Lyons, 2014.

Rice, Lawrence D. *The Negro in Texas, 1874–1900*. Baton Rouge: Louisiana State University Press, 1971.

Richardson, Rupert N. *Colonel Edward M. House: The Texas Years, 1858–1912*. Abilene: Hardin-Simmons University, 1964.

Robinson, Charles M. *Men Who Wear the Star*. New York: The Modern Library, 2001.

Ross, Lawrence Sullivan. *Personal Civil War Letters of General Lawrence Sullivan Ross: With Other Letters*. Austin: Shelly and Richard Morrison, 1994.

Rozak, Barbara J. *Come to Texas: Enticing Immigrants, 1865–1915*. College Station: Texas A&M University Press, 2003.

Rogan, Octavia F. *Land Commissioner Charles Rogan*. Austin: San Felipe Press, 1968.

Rose, Victor M. *Ross' Texas Brigade*. Louisville: Courier-Journal Book and Job Rooms, 1881.

Savage, William W. *The Cherokee Strip Live Stock Association*. Columbia: University of Missouri Press, 1973.

Schmidt, Hubert. *Eighty Years of Veterinary Medicine at the Agricultural and Mechanical College of Texas*. College Station: College Archives, 1958.

Schultz, Charles. *Making Something Happen: Texas A&M University Libraries 1876–1976*. College Station: Texas A&M University Libraries, 1979.

Shannon, Fred. *The Farmer's Last Frontier: Agriculture, 1860–1897.* New York: Farrer & Rinehart, 1945.

Shelton, Perry W. *Personal Civil War Letters of General Lawrence Sullivan Ross: With Other Letters.* Austin: n.p., 1994.

Shirley, Glenn. *Temple Houston: Lawyer with a Gun.* Norman: University of Oklahoma Press, 1980.

Shuffler, R. Henderson. *Son, Remember. . . .* College Station: The A. & M. [College] Press, 1951.

Sibley, Marilyn M. *George W. Brackenridge: Maverick Philanthropist.* Austin: University of Texas Press, 1973.

Simpson, Harold B. *Hood's Texas Brigade: Lee's Grenadier Guard.* Waco: Texian Press, 1970.

Singer, Jonathan W. *Broken Trust: The Texas Attorney General versus the Oil Industry, 1889–1909.* College Station: Texas A&M University Press, 2002.

Sleeper, W. M., and A. D. Sanford. *Waco Bar and Incidents of Waco History.* Waco: n.p., 1941.

Smith, Arthur D. *Mr. House of Texas.* New York: Funk & Wagnalls Co., 1940.

———. *The Real Colonel House.* New York: George H. Doran Company, 1918.

Spratt, John S. *The Road to Spindletop.* Austin: University of Texas Press, 1970.

Sterling, William W. *Trails and Trials of a Texas Ranger.* Norman: University of Oklahoma Press, 1959.

Thompson, Jerry. *Tejano Tiger: Jose de los Santos Benavides and the Texas-Mexico Borderlands, 1823–1891.* Fort Worth: Texas Christian University Press, 2017.

Tise, Sammy. *Texas County Sheriffs.* Hallettsville, TX: Oakwood Printing, 1989.

Traxel, David. *1898: The Birth of the American Century.* New York: Vintage Books, 1998.

True Alfred C. *A History of Agricultural Education in the United States, 1785–1925.* Washington, DC: US Government Printing Office, 1929.

Twelve Southerns. *I'll Take My Stand.* New York: Harper & Brothers Publishers, 1930.

Utley, Robert M. *Frontiersmen in Blue: The United States Army and the Indian, 1848–1865.* Norman: University of Nebraska Press, 1967.

———. *Lone Star Lawmen: The Second Century of the Texas Rangers.* Oxford: Oxford University Press, 2007.

Waller County Historical Survey Committee. *A History of Waller County, Texas.* Waco: Texan Press, 1973.

Warner, Erza J. *General in Gray: Lives of the Confederate Commander.* Baton Rouge: Louisiana State University Press, 1992.

Webb, Walter P. *The Texas Rangers. A Century of Frontier Defense.* Austin: University of Texas Press, 2003.

Welch, June R. *The Colleges of Texas.* Waco: Texian Press, 1981.

———. *The Texas Governor.* Dallas: G. L. A. Press, 1977.

Welsh, Jack D. *Medical Histories of Confederate Generals.* Kent, OH: Kent State University Press, 1995.

Wilbarger, J. W. *Indian Depredations in Texas.* Austin: Hutchings Printing House, 1889.

Williams, Amelia W., and Eugene C. Barker, eds. *The Writings of Sam Houston.* 8 vols. Austin: University of Texas Press, 1938–43.

Williams, Patrick G. *Beyond Redemption: Texas Democrats after Reconstruction.* College Station: Texas A&M University Press, 2007.

Wisehart, M. K. *Sam Houston: American Giant.* Washington: Robert B. Luce, 1962.

Woodward, C. Vann. *The Burden of Southern History.* New York: Vintage, 1960.

———. *Origins of the New South, 1877–1913.* Baton Rouge: Louisiana State University Press, 1951.

Woolfolk, George R. *Prairie View: A Study in Public Consciences.* New York: Pageant Press, 1962.

Wooster, Ralph A. *Lone Star General in Gray.* Austin: Eakin Press, 2000.

Wooten, Dudley G., ed. *A Comprehensive History of Texas 1685 to 1897.* Dallas: William G. Scarff, 1898.

Wooten, Dudley G., and Robert Wooster, eds. *Lone Star Blue and Gray,* Denton: Texas State Historical Association, 2015.

Wortham, Louis J. *A History of Texas.* 5 vols. Fort Worth: Wortham-Moltneaux Company, 1924.

Wyatt-Brown, Bertran. *Honor and Violence in the Old South.* New York: Oxford University Press, 1986.

Zesch, Scott. *The Captured: Abduction by Indians on the Texas Frontier.* New York: Martin Press, 2004.

Articles

Adams, John A., Jr. "Lawrence Sullivan Ross." *The Texas Aggie,* July 1979, pp. 8–10.

———. "Softly Call the Muster." *The Texas Aggie,* April 1992, pp. 2–9.

———."Sul Ross Defined a Young Texas A&M." *The Eagle,* January 11, 1998.

———."Sul Ross Promoted Education and Rights for African Americans." *Bryan Eagle,* June 14, 2020.

Anderson, Adrian. "President Wilson's Politician: Albert Sidney Burleson." *SWHQ*, January 1974, pp. 339–54.

Anthony, Augusta H. "Lawrence Sullivan Ross Soldier and Statesman." *Texas Magazine*, September 1912, pp. 429–31.

"Appealing for Aid [Veteran's Home]." *Austin Weekly Statesman*, July 25, 1889.

"Arrivals at the Principal Hotels." *New Orleans Times-Picayune*, October 9, 1866, p. 8.

Berthoff, Rowland T. "Southern Attitudes toward Immigration, 1865–1914." *Journal of Southern History*, August 1951, pp. 328–60.

Buenger, Walter L. "Texas and the South." *Southwestern Historical Review*, January 2000, pp. 306–24.

"Called to A College: Gov. Ross Offered Presidency of Agricultural College." *Galveston Daily News*, July 6, 1890.

Calvert, Robert A. "A. J. Rose and the Granger Concept of Reform." *Agricultural History*, January 1977, pp. 181–96.

Campbell, Randolph B. "Reconstruction in McLennan County, Texas 1865–1876." *Prologue*, spring 1995, pp. 17–35.

Carlson, Paul, and Tom Crum, "The 'Battle' at Pease River and the Question of Reliable Sources in the Recapture of Cynthia Ann Parker." *SWHQ*, July 2009, pp. 33–52.

Caulfield, Tom. "Sul Ross Letters Tell Sidelights on War between States." *Waco Tribune-Herald*, July 10, 1960.

"Complementary German Tendered Miss Florene Ross Last Evening." *Austin Weekly Statesman*, January 15, 1891.

Crane, M. M. "Recollections of the Establishment of the Texas Railroad Commission." *SWHQ*, April 1947, pp. 478–86.

Davis, William C. "The Right Way to Remember the Confederacy." *Wall Street Journal*, July 11, 2015.

"Death of Ex-Governor Ross." *San Francisco Call*, January 4, 1898.

Dethloff, Henry C. "Mark Francis and Veterinary Medicine in Texas, 1880–1936." *Journal of the West*, January 1988, pp. 40–46.

Duncan, Merle M., and Richard Coke. "An 1890 Richard Coke Letter." *SWHQ*, July 1862, pp. 68–72.

"Ex-Governor Ross." *Galveston Daily News*, February 26, 1894, p. 2.

Genovese, Eugene D. "The Chivalric Tradition in the South." *The Sewanee Review*, spring 2000, pp. 188–205.

Gougler, Doyle. "Sul Ross." *Cattlemen*, August 1963, pp. 39, 64.

"Governor Ross' Sudden Death." *Dallas Morning News*, January 4, 1898.

Hart, James P. "What James Stephen Hogg Means to Texas." *SWHQ*, April 1952, pp. 439–47.

Holden, W. C. "Law and Lawlessness on the Texas Frontier, 1875–1890." *SWHQ*, October 1940, pp. 188–203.

Hunter, Marvin J., ed. "Captain Shapley P Ross." *Frontier Times*, August 1928, 417–19.

——. "Remarkable Life Story of Quanah Parker." *Frontier Times*, October 1923, pp. 28–30.

"Inviting Mr. Cleveland." *New York Times*, May 22, 1890.

Jones, Lawrence T. "Cynthia Ann Parker and Pease Ross: The Forgotten Photographs." *SWHQ*, January 1991, pp. 379–84.

Jordon, Terry G. "The Forgotten Texas State Census of 1887." *SWHQ*, April 1982.

Koch, Clara Lena. "The Federal Indian Policy in Texas, 1845–1860." *SHQ*, October 1925, pp. 98–127.

Langston, Rosalind. "The Life of Colonel R. T. Milner." *SWHQ*, April 1941, pp. 407–52.

Link, Arthur S. "The Progressive Movement in the South, 1870–1914." *North Carolina Historical Review*, April 1946, pp. 172–95.

Martin, Roscoe C. "The Grange as a Political Factor in Texas." *Southwestern Political and Social Science Quarterly*, March 1926, pp. 363–83.

McKitrick, Reuben. "The Public Land System of Texas, 1823–1910." *Bulletin of the University of Wisconsin*, 1918.

Miller, Thomas L. "Texas Land Grants to Confederate Veterans and Widows." *SWHQ*, July 1965, pp. 59–65.

Miller, Worth R., and Stacy G. Ulbig. "Building a Populist Coalition in Texas, 1892–1896." *Journal of Southern History*, May 2008, pp. 255–96.

Neu, Charles E. "In Search of Colonel Edward M. House: The Texas Years, 1858–1912." *SWHQ*, July 1989, pp. 25–29.

Norvell, James R. "The Railroad Commission of Texas: Its Origin and History." *SWHQ*, April 1965, pp. 465–80.

Peterson, Robert L. "Jay Gould and the Railroad Commission of Texas." *TSHQ*, January 1955, pp. 422–32.

Polley, J. B. "Historical Reminiscences." *San Antonio Daily Express*, November 22, 1908, p. 35.

Richardson, Rupert N. "Edward M. House and the Governors." *SWHA*, July 1957, pp. 51–65.

"Ross' Letter Donated to TAMU." *The Battalion*, July 23, 1975, p. 1.

Runnion, James B. "The Negro Exodus." *Atlantic Monthly*, August 1879, pp. 222–30.

Schilz, Thomas F. "Plight of Tonkawas 1875 to 1898." *Chronicle of Oklahoma*, 1986, pp. 68–87.

"The Slick Clarkies." *Texas Farmer*, May 13, 1893.

Smith, Charles F. "Southern Colleges and Schools." *Atlantic Monthly,* October 1884, pp. 542–557.

Smith, Ralph A. "The Grange in Texas, 1873–1900." *SWHQ,* April 1939, pp. 297–315.

———. "Farmers' Alliance in Texas, 1875–1900." *SWHQ,* January 1945, pp. 346–69.

Sooner, Acie. "'Macuneism,' or the Farmers of Texas in Business." *Journal of Southern History,* May 1947, pp. 220–44.

———. "Texas after the Civil War." *Frontier Times,* April 1927, pp. 36–40.

Spindler, Frank. "Concerning Hempstead and Waller County Texas." *SWHQ,* April 1959, pp. 455–72.

Splawn, W. M. W. "Valuation and Rate Regulation by the Railroad Commission of Texas." *Journal of Political Economy,* October 1923, pp. 675–707.

"Sul Ross Career Full of Thrills from Time He Was Born in a Frontier Cabin." *Waco Tribune-Herald,* October 30, 1949.

"The A. and M. College." *Houston Daily Post,* January 24, 1899.

Tolbert, Frank X. "Sully Saved A&M from 'Lunatic Role.'" *Dallas Morning News,* October 26, 1965.

Trent, William P. "Tendencies of Higher Life in the South." *Atlantic Monthly,* June 1897, pp. 766–78.

"Turn Texas Loose." *Austin Daily Statesman,* March 10, 1892.

Turner, Thomas E. "A Career That Bred Legends: Sul Ross." *Baylor Magazine,* April 1986, pp. 18–21.

"Under A Cloud." *Galveston Daily News,* March 5, 1893.

"Unveiling Seen by Large Crowd." *The Reveille,* May 6, 1919.

Van Dorn, Earl. "Official Report of the battle of Wichita." *Texas State Gazette,* October 23, 1858.

Walker, B. M. "Henry Hill Harrington." *Journal of Mississippi History.* July 1940, pp. 156–58.

Wynne, Mamie F. "History Centers about Cynthia Ann Parker's Home." *Frontier Times,* April 1929, pp. 258–60.

Dissertations, Theses, and Unpublished Manuscripts

Adams, John A. "History of the Association of Former Students 1876–1976." MA thesis, Texas A&M University, 1976.

———. "The Texas Railroad Commission and Progressive Reforms of Intrastate Commerce in Texas, 1891–1915." College Station: unpublished manuscript, December 1982.

Barr, Alwyn. "Texas Politics, 1876–1906." PhD diss., University of Texas, 1966.

Bonner, Michael E. "The Confederate Military Career of L. S. Ross." MA thesis, Texas Christian University, 1969.

Bradley, Cody J. "Lawrence Sullivan 'Sul' Ross: Frontier Survivor, Celebrated Politician, Patient Educator, and Beloved Citizen." MA thesis, Midwestern State University, April 2012.

Casad, Dede Weldon. "The Lives and Legacies of Two Texas Governors, Richard Coke and Lawrence Sullivan Ross: A Comparative Study." PhD diss., University of Texas at Dallas, 2001.

Chamberlain, Charles. "Alexander W. Terrell." PhD diss., University of Texas, 1957.

Dillard, Raymond L. "A History of the Ross Family, Including Its Most Distinguished Member, Lawrence Sullivan Ross." MA thesis, Baylor University, Waco, 1931.

Eddy, Edward D. "The Development of the Land-Grant College." PhD diss., Cornell University, 1956.

Evans, Samuel L. "Texas Agriculture, 1880–1930." PhD diss., University of Texas, 1960.

Kirchenbauer, Amy S. "The Texas Confederate Home for Men, 1884–1970." MA thesis, University of North Texas, August 2011.

Kittrell, Norman G. "Address Delivered at the Unveiling of the Monument of General Lawrence Sullivan Ross." n.p., 1919.

Langston, Rosalind. "The Life of Colonel R. T. Milner." MA thesis, University of Texas, 1940.

Marshall, Elmer Grady. "The History of Brazos County, Texas." MA thesis, n.p., August 1937.

Shelton, Perry Wayne. "Personal Letters Written by Lawrence Sullivan Ross." MA thesis, Baylor University, 1938.

St. Clair, Grady S. "The Hogg-Clark Campaign." MA thesis, University of Texas, 1929.

Street, Katherine. "Philosophy of and Plans for Education Found in the Legislative Messages." MA thesis, Baylor University, 1940.

Stuart, Ben C. "The Texas Indian Fighters and Frontier Rangers." MA thesis, University of Texas, 1916.

True, Clyde A. "Development of the Cattle Industry in the Southwest." MA thesis, Texas Christian University, August 1928.

Turner, Oreta. "Border Troubles along the Rio Grande from 1848–1878." MA thesis, East Texas State Teachers College, August 1940.

Walker, John. "The Poll Tax, Suffrage, and the Making of the Texas Constitution of 1876." MA thesis, Texas Tech University, 1973

Webb, John M. "The Public Lands of Texas and Their Use for the Benefit of Education." MS thesis, North Texas State College, August 1949.

Webb, Juanita Oliver. "The Administration of Governor L. S. Ross." MA thesis, n.p., August 1935.

Whiteside, Myrtle Flossie. "The Life of Lawrence Sullivan Ross." MA thesis, University of Texas, August 1938.

Items under Review and Other Nonpublished Sources

Brazos County Historical Timeline, 1875–1899, http://www.brazos genealogy.org/data/time4.htm.

Davis, James S. "The Occupations of Some Southern Soldiers after the War." n.p., 2011.

Mayfield, Henry D., "Address: Lawrence Sullivan Ross Chapter United Daughters of the Confederacy." October 21, 1960.

"A Memorial and Biographical History of McLennan, Falls, Bell, and Coryell Counties, Texas." Chicago, 1893.

Index